ESSAYS IN HISTORY

HIS HOLINESS POPE PIUS XI

ESSAYS IN HISTORY
WRITTEN BETWEEN THE YEARS 1896-1912

by

THE RT. REV. MGR. ACHILLE RATTI
Doctor of the Ambrosian Library, Milan
NOW
HIS HOLINESS POPE PIUS XI

NEW YORK
P. J. KENEDY & SONS
12 BARCLAY STREET

MADE AND PRINTED IN GREAT BRITAIN

1934

CONTENTS

LIST OF ILLUSTRATIONS

TRANSLATOR'S PREFACE

THE purpose of the following paragraphs is to indicate very briefly the special points of interest presented by these Essays, not by reason of their authorship—which would be little short of impertinence—but by reason of the information they contain, and to help English readers to bring them into the right focus.

To the student of history the first of these Essays, dealing with the history of the Church in Milan will be specially interesting. So will be some of the shorter Essays dealing with St. Charles Borromeo, with his contemporaries and some of the repercussions which that great man and Saint has caused even down to our day and in our country as well as in America.

Milan, towards the end of the Roman Empire the most important city of Italy after Rome herself, ' the first great stage on the roads from Rome to Gaul, the Illyrian provinces and Constantinople ' (p. 3), has always played a prominent part in Italian history. Its Archbishops ruled at one time over an immense diocesan area, stretching west as far as Nice, on the east bounded by the patriarchate of Aquileia, southwards reaching into Tuscany, extending to the north over the Alps even to Ratisbon. Its topographical position as the natural objective of the roads leading to Italy over the Brenner and St. Gotthard passes, placed it on the line of Germanic invasions and of the journeys of prospective Emperors to Rome for their coronation. It became the centre of the Leagues of free Lombard cities in their resistance to Frederic Barbarossa

and Frederic II, and in the eleventh century won
its communal freedom, represented by that curious
symbol, the ' carroccio,' that stroke of genius of
the remarkable personality of Archbishop Aribert
of Entimiano, a thrilling story told on pp. 64 ff.
During the fourteenth and the following centuries,
under the rule of the gifted, if unscrupulous dynasty
of the Visconti, it became during the greatest
expansion of its territorial power the storm-centre of
Italian political history in the north. The French
invasion at the end of the fifteenth century, provoked and indeed invited by Lodovico Sforza,
broke the power of the Duchy. It became the seat
of the Spanish administration, succeeded by that
of Austria with the interlude of the French occupation during the Napoleonic régime. ' It might be
said with justice,' the author notes (p. 2), ' that the
history of the Church in Milan is the golden thread
of the history of Milan itself ' : the history of that
Church which, thanks to St. Ambrose, assumed the
name of ' Ambrosian ' Church, and became identified with the city from the fourth century onwards.

This history is traced by the author with more
detail in its earlier parts than in the later, with great
advantage to the reader, for these earlier centuries
are much less well known, but illustrate in striking
manner the transitions from the late Roman times,
through feudalism, down to the ' Comune ' and
the rule of the Visconti. It is a story which has its
parellels in so many other Italian cities and might
almost be taken as a paradigm of the historical
developments in many other parts of northern and
central Italy.

The Essays on St. Charles Borromeo (1538–1584)
introduce us to that period of Italian, and indeed
European, history which has been called—though
by no means disposed of by being called—the
' Counter-Reformation.' It is to this time that Italy

owes even now the greater part of her external
appearance in the architectural picture presented
by so many of her towns. To Italians generally it is
probably best known from the Italian classic, the
Promessi Sposi of Alessandro Manzoni, himself a
Milanese, with its minutely accurate historical
setting of Milan during the seventeenth century.
Its earlier phases in the second half of the sixteenth
century, in which St. Charles towers as the most
perfect embodiment of the ideals of the reform-
movement, initiated by the Council of Trent,
form part—and an often misunderstood part—of
the ' Renaissance.' One aspect of the ' Renaissance '
is precisely the prodigious activity put forth by the
reform, headed by men like St. Charles, in the arts,
in administration, in science, in social work, above
all in education, promoted by the many new orders
which spring up during this time. This activity
must be brought into account to redress the weight
of abuses, sloth, greed and ignorance which the
' Counter-Reformation ' is so often taken to represent, but which precisely it set out to reform. The
part played by St. Charles and those in contact
with him, described in these pages (pp. 112 ff.), will
be found enlightening by the student of history,
however unpretentious these short essays are,
designed as articles of a periodical with the title
San Carlo Borromeo which Mgr. Ratti founded on the
occasion of the Tercentenary of the Canonisation
of the Saint for the benefit of Milanese readers.

The student of antiquities and of art will be most
attracted by the Essays dealing with Leonardo's
Codex Atlanticus, one of the greatest treasures of the
Ambrosian Library, and by the curious connexion
of its appurtenances with the Far East and the
travels of Marco Polo. This chapter forms an
interesting contribution to the history of that taste
for ' chinoiseries ' which became so pronounced in

Europe in the seventeenth and early eighteenth
centuries.

The account of the 'Settala Museum,' and of its
reconstitution due to Mgr. Ratti's enthusiasm
and enterprise, throws light on another passion of
the seventeenth century, not only in Italy but in
Europe generally, the passion for collecting : books,
pictures, antiquities, art-objects and curios of all
kinds. These collections 'may well be considered
as typical of their time, so important in the history
of Italian thought in all its expressions, so characteristic in the mixture of tradition and novelty, of
scientific and empirical methods, of childishness
and seriousness, destined to give rise to the specifically scientific achievements of the seventeenth
century ' (p. 274). Settala's was a collection
world-famous in its day, and eagerly visited by
students and men of learning from all over Europe,
among them also by our own traveller and diarist,
John Evelyn, who was duly impressed by its wealth
and interest.

The Essay on Luini's famous painting of the
' Holy Family,' one of the great art treasures of
the Ambrosian galleries, gives combined expression
to the author's intimate knowledge of the founder
of the Ambrosian Library, Cardinal Federico
Borromeo, who first acquired this picture 'satis
magno pondere auri,' as the Cardinal notes himself (p. 289), and of the thrilling experience of seeing
it restored by the hand of Prof. Cavenaghi to whom
we owe also the preservation of Leonardo's ' Last
Supper.' The connexion of Luini's painting with
Leonardo's cartoon of the same subject at Burlington House adds a special interest for English readers.

For the Catholic these Essays have an appeal
beyond their historical, antiquarian or artistic
interests, by reason of the specifically Catholic and
spiritual aspects they present. Even if he be not

perhaps a professed historian, he will appreciate the continuity of the Catholic tradition embodied in the ' Ambrosian Church,' the part played by the Archbishops of Milan in the civic life of their city and in the vicissitudes which befell both Church and city in the course of their joint history. He will be grateful for the living portraits of the great Saints, of St. Charles Borromeo, especially in that peculiarly intimate vision of him by his younger cousin, Cardinal Federico (pp. 174 ff.), of St. Philip Neri, of St. Andrea Avellino, of men like Castellino da Castello, the founder of Sunday schools for poor children in 1536, or for the account of St. Charles' personal relations with some of the great figures of the Renaissance like Cardinal Baronius or Cardinal Sirleto, or for that glimpse of St. Charles' own spiritual life granted to us in the essay on St. Charles and the Spiritual Exercises of St. Ignatius ' (p. 163 ff.).

Again the essay devoted to the history of the Guilds of the Blessed Sacrament (pp. 210 ff.), will impress the Catholic reader not only by the sense of continuity, but also by the often vivid picture of the internal functionings of these Guilds from the end of the fifteenth century onwards.

But behind all these appeals, whether to the historian or the antiquarian or the artist or the Catholic, there is unmistakably felt the appeal of the ' Ambrosian Library ' itself, of its founder, and of the author's devotion to that remarkable institution.

The appeal of the Ambrosian Library is that indefinable fascination which belongs to any institution, founded centuries ago for the disinterested pursuit of learning and research, faithfully served by a succession of devoted men, and still permeated by the spirit of its founder; such as of many a college, for instance, in our ancient Universities.

The 'Ambrosiana' was founded in 1603 by Cardinal Federico Borromeo (1564–1631). Libraries open to all students had even then a long tradition behind them in Italy, beginning with the Vatican Library opened by Pope Nicholas V (1447–1455) 'pro communi doctorum commodo.' The 'Laurenziana' in Florence, the 'Marciana' in Venice, whose nucleus had been the private collection of codices of Cardinal Bessarion, had also been foundations of the fifteenth century. More or less contemporary with the Ambrosiana, if slightly later, were the University Library of Padova created in 1629 by the Venetian patrician Domenico Molino, and the Library of the Seminary there, founded in 1671 by the Bishop of Padova, Gregorio Barbarigo, and endowed by him with a private printing press which continues down to the present time. The 'Magliabecchiana,' in Florence, the 'Casanatense' founded by Cardinal Casanate in Naples, the 'Angelica' in Rome are creations of that same century.

The far-sighted genius of Cardinal Federico projected much more than merely a Library. While his own love of books and his passionate search for manuscripts formed the first nucleus, his love of art and antiquities suggested the idea of an Academy of Fine Arts, devoted to the improvement of art among his generation. This idea was realised in 1625, though his Academy was eventually suppressed during the Austrian régime in Lombardy in favour of the Academy of the Brera. Another project had been that of a college for the education of youths, who were to devote themselves to the service of the Library, a grandiose plan, including studentships, which unfortunately did not survive the political and other troubles of that time. By the constitution of the Ambrosiana, he formed two

bodies of men or ' Colleges ' : the ' College of the
Conservators ' whose task was (and is) to superintend the whole material maintenance of the Library,
and a ' College of Doctors,' charged with the care
of the books and manuscripts, with assistance to be
given to students and men of learning who might
visit Milan, and with the pursuit of research in
various branches of knowledge. It was to them that
he gave as their motto ' Singuli singula ' with the
special significance explained on page 270 of these
Essays. He placed at the disposal of the Doctors a
printing press, attached to the Library, for the
publications of works not only in Latin or Italian,
but in Greek, Syriac, Arabic, Persian and Armenian.

The enthusiastic devotion to education and
research which inspired the foundation of the
Library, equalled that to his native city over which
he had been called to rule as Archbishop—with
how heavy a heart, but with how much determina-
tion, can be judged from his own notes jotted down
at the time (pp. 198 ff.) : ' Ambrosiana' was the
name he gave to the realisation of his dream. How
deeply he, no less than his great cousin St. Charles,
has penetrated into the memory and mind of
Milan can be judged no less from the famous pages
(Chapter XXII) of Alessandro Manzoni's *Promessi
Sposi* which contain a classical portrait of the
Cardinal, than from the tribute paid to him more
than once in the pages of these Essays. For the
author, born at Desio, near Milan, writes indeed as
a Milanese with devoted loyalty to his native city,
the city of St. Ambrose, of St. Charles and of
Cardinal Federico. Returning there in 1884 he was
himself elected one of the Doctors of the Ambrosian
Library, succeeding as its Prefect in 1907. The
work which occupied him chiefly during these
years, apart from his administrative duties and the
fundamental re-arrangement of the whole (cf. for
instance the ' Settala Museum ' in these Essays),

B

had been his researches into the history of the
Church in Milan : *Acta Ecclesiæ Mediolanensis ab
eius initiis usque ad nostram aetatem*, three volumes
of which appeared between 1890 and 1897. The
first of the Essays in this volume is based on
these researches, and constantly reveals the erudition which lies behind the summary sketch of a
history, compressed into the compass of a single
lecture. His most ambitious work, similarly based
on years of research in the Library, the *Missale
Ambrosianum Duplex*, appeared in 1913. By then
he had been called to Rome as Librarian of the
Vatican Library, where he succeeded as Prefect soon
after the outbreak of the War. Events moved very
rapidly. Mgr. Ratti was suddenly, in 1918, called
away from his books and manuscripts and sent first
as Apostolic Visitor, then as Nuncio, to Poland,
where he remained during the last stages of the
War amidst indescribable chaos and difficulties
until 1921. In February of that year, Cardinal
Ferrari, Archbishop of Milan, died and Mgr.
Ratti was appointed to succeed him, at a time
difficult above all others, especially in an industrial
city like Milan with a long-standing tradition of
social troubles and labour-agitation, and exposed
to the Communist menace, of which Mgr. Ratti had
had such fierce experience during his Nunciature.
His nomination was announced in March of that
year, while he was still in Warsaw ; at a Consistory
in June he was raised to the dignity of Cardinal
and made his official entry into Milan early in
September. But he was destined to rule the Archdiocese of Milan for but a few months : in January
1922 the choice of the Cardinals' College fell upon
him and he ascended the throne of St. Peter, as the
successor of Benedict XV.

So he, who had worked as a ' Doctor of the
Ambrosian,' came to succeed in the long line of the
Prefects of whom the first had been appointed by

Cardinal Federico ; devoting years of study and research to the history of the Church at Milan, especially under her great ruler, St. Charles, he was called to become one of St. Charles' successors, to leave his native city for that seat which had been the centre of gravity of his own 'Ambrosian' Church all through its long history. Indeed, as Cardinal Federico said in reference to St. Charles : 'Benedictus Dominus Deus Israel, qui facit mirabilia solus.'

The present translation is made from an Italian edition, published in 1932, by the *Libreria Editrice Fiorentina*. Six short essays contained in the Italian edition have been omitted from this English version as bearing perhaps too exclusively on Italian interests, in order to compress the whole into a manageable volume. The Italian edition contains a reproduction of a small picture of Settala which has been replaced in this edition by that of a woodcut, showing the interior of the Museum in its original form ; a reproduction of a portrait of Cardinal Federico Borromeo has been added ; for both these the publishers are indebted to the courtesy of the Prefect of the Ambrosiana for his permission to reproduce them from the guide-book to its collections. A photograph of the portrait of St. Charles by Crespi has been inserted, as well as a reproduction of Leonardo's cartoon for comparison with Luini's picture of the 'Holy Family.'

EDWARD BULLOUGH.

CAMBRIDGE, 8 *December*, 1933.

ESSAYS IN HISTORY

I

THE AMBROSIAN CHURCH OF MILAN

A paper read in the spring of 1896 before the 'Circolo
Filologico Milanese,' as part of a series of lectures contributed
by various authorities on the History of Milan.

The paper was published with seven others in 1897 in a
volume entitled : 'Conferenze di Storia Milanese,' by Fratelli
Bocca, Milano.

The captions here used to indicate the subdivisions are
not part of the original publication.

THE AMBROSIAN CHURCH

THE subject requires at the outset some explanation
in order to determine its real meaning, the extent
and the manner of its treatment. Other lectures
on subjects, related to this, deal with that stretch
of time which runs from the fall of the old Roman
'Municipium' to the formation of the Milanese
Commune, and invite us to consider the manner in
which civil government came to change from the
one to the other of these two forms. But it is evidently impossible to confine ourselves strictly to
this period. I should have to speak of the Ambrosian
Church without mentioning, even with one word,
St. Ambrose who gave to the Milanese Church,
although full-grown by then, the name which she
boasts still to-day. The very name, 'Ambrosian
Church,' has been for centuries and will never cease
to be synonymous with the Milanese Church, without any distinction of periods, so that, as it were,
centred in the time of St. Ambrose and extending its

meaning both backwards to past ages and forwards towards the new, the ' Ambrosian Church ' means the whole ecclesiastical life and functioning of Milan from the earliest Christian times onwards. It would not seem unfair to present the whole subject in this way ; for the very purpose of these lectures is to present, and spread a knowledge of the history of Milan, at least in its general outlines and within the chronological limits of the programme.

The Roman ' Municipium,' the Commune, the Duchy of Milan, then the French and Austrian rules correspond each with a given period of time, after which each in turn disappears as a living fact and merges into the domain of memories. But this is not true of the Church. The Church, established in our city while the ' Municipium ' was still flourishing, was destined never to abandon the city, but to be its companion, and to play often a great part in the vicissitudes through which the city passed, down to our own days. It might be said with justice that the history of the Church in Milan is the golden thread of the history of Milan itself. We shall follow this thread, and our road will quite naturally fall into three distinct stages : the first, the beginnings of the Church in Milan down to the time of St. Ambrose ; the second stage, from St. Ambrose to the constitution of the Commune ; the third, from the constitution of the Commune to the time of the Italian Kingdom.

It is, as you see, a long road to travel ; we shall follow it rapidly and, I hope, with not too much difficulty, certainly not without advantage. Many matters can be touched on only in passing ; we shall tarry only over such men or events as represent the great phases of the institutions which are the object of our study. There was a time when the memories of sacred things in Milan, the names and deeds of our Archbishops, the customs and prerogatives of the Ambrosian Church were the object of widespread study and held in affectionate esteem. Perhaps, witnessing the spoliation of all our rights and the predominance of foreign rule, our forefathers felt that these memories represented something profoundly patriotic, a precious and homely heritage, still surviving, still capable of bearing fruit. I shall be happy, if I shall perhaps have been able to offer new facts to some, or to recall to others, not indeed without pleasure, the memory of things which they knew.

THE BEGINNINGS OF CHRISTIANITY IN MILAN

When and by whom was Christianity brought to Milan? How did the life of the Christian community and the organisation of the Church develop from their beginnings down to the time of St. Ambrose? This is the first stage of our journey.

The *terminus ad quem* is clear and certain ; it is far otherwise with the *terminus a quo*. That Christianity was bound to be transplanted to Milan, is obvious from what has been said of the Roman ' Munici- pium.'[1] The city of Milan, having grown to such importance under the Roman Empire as the first great stage on the roads from Rome to Gaul, the Illyrian provinces, and Constantinople, became the natural objective of those who first spread the Gospel in Italy. The best, not to say the only reliable documents concerning almost all the oldest Churches, also for that of Milan, are the ' diptychs ' or folding tables whereon the names of the Bishops were inscribed and carefully preserved, with a plain indication of the years of their episco- pate ; from these in turn the manuscript ' cata- logues ' are derived. Milan too has its catalogue, or rather catalogues. A MS. copy of the eleventh century exists in our Ambrosian Library. The

[1] i.e. in another set of lectures included in the programme. (*Translator's note.*)

writing displays different hands ; the oldest carries
the list of our first Bishops down as far as Guido
(1071) ; other hands continue it down to Philip
(1206), with a note concerning Archbishop Giovanni
Visconti (1355). It may confidently be asserted
with due consideration of all critical exigencies,
that the oldest part of our catalogue is a combination of several very ancient catalogues, the first of
which is not later than of the sixth century. It is
obviously a document of primary importance,
especially for the earliest of our Archbishops, at
least as far as their existence and their names are
concerned ; indications of their burial-places were
added only later and the years of their episcopates
are often doubtful, in view of the ease and frequency
of errors in transcribing figures. There are also
other catalogues : but they are of more recent date
and their authority in regard to more remote
times is more doubtful. We have also other
writings which recount the lives and acts of our
Archbishops, even of the earliest ; but possibly none
of these documents is earlier than of the eleventh
century, and, although we may hold that they
preserve something of the old memories and traditions, we have not sufficient information on the
sources on which they are based, nor can we tell
how large a part legend or invention plays in
them.

The first important piece of information in our
catalogue is negative : there is no mention of the
name of the Apostle, St. Barnabas ; or rather there
is mention of him, but manifestly as a later addition,
which is even more significant. You cannot live
for any length of time in Milan without hearing of
the tradition which attributes the introduction of
Christianity in the city to this Apostle, formerly
St. Paul's companion. The tradition took material
form in a monument, namely in the little Church
called ' St. Barnabas by the Font ' (S. Barnabà al

Fonte), the font in which the Apostle is said to have baptised the first converts. The little Church stood not far from that of S. Eustorgio ; it was rebuilt by Cardinal Federico Borromeo in 1623 and pulled down about the middle of last century. An inscription of quite recent date (1881) marks the house which was said to contain that ancient font, the first baptismal font of Milan and the first milestone of Christianity amongst us. As you see, I am very cautious in the choice of my words ; for this tradition is open to many and very grave objections. Recent (and not only recent) studies suggest that we are dealing here with a legend which cannot be scientifically supported, though it was widespread even in Liguria and in Gaul. It took root here much later in circumstances presently to be noted.

The first name inscribed in our catalogue is that of Anatalon, with thirteen years of tenure of the episcopate. A Greek, as the name indicates, the disciple and companion of Barnabas, he is said to have been left by him in charge of the government of the budding churches both of Milan and of Brescia, in which latter city he is supposed to have died. So the writings to which I referred above, inform us. What may give rise to doubt is the close conjunction in these texts of St. Barnabas and Anatalon and some chronological difficulty concerning him, so much so that the information is suspected of being a later addition. But strictly speaking, the old catalogue seems to offer no evidence either for or against it : it merely registers Anatalon with thirteen years of episcopal tenure. He is followed by Gaius. Who was he? Where did he come from and when ? What did he do here ? Summarising what the above-mentioned texts tell us about him, I should have to record that he was born in Rome ; that he was a disciple of St. Barnabas ; that he ruled the Church in Milan from

61 to 85 ; that he converted the later saints and
martyrs Vitalis and Valeria, Gervase and Protase,
and the rich and generous Philippus with his
children Portius and Fausta ; that he consecrated
the house of Philippus as a Christian basilica, with
the name, precisely, ' of Philip ' (subsequently
called ' Naboriana,' dedicated to the Saints
Nabor and Felix, and standing where later, in
1256, the Church of St. Francis stood, or near by,
where to-day the barracks of the same name stand) ;
that he converted the garden belonging to the house
of Philippus into a Christian burial-ground ; that
he went to Rome to venerate the Apostles Peter and
Paul ; and, as these had already fallen victims to
the persecution of Nero, he found there their
successors, Linus and Clemens, and having returned
to Milan, where also a persecution was raging, he
received there the palm of martyrdom. But again,
the catalogue says nothing of all these things, and
only mentions the years (XXIV) of his episcopate
and the place of his tomb or his burial ; even, in
its primitive form, it gave, as I said, merely the
years, as was the custom.

Even in regard to the number of years, we have
in the absence of corroboration to walk very warily
for the reasons I have mentioned. Fortunately such
corroborative evidence, abundant for the episcopate
of St. Ambrose, is not wholly lacking for some of his
predecessors, as for instance, in the case of Mirocles,
the fourth after Anatalon. Taking the figures in
the catalogue as they stand—for the moment we
can do nothing else—we find 210 years between the
beginning of the episcopate of Gaius and the last
year of Mirocles, 314. Thus, the foundation of the
episcopal See of Milan would, even on the strictest
reckoning, go back to the year 104, during the
reign of Trajan. I say, on the strictest reckoning,
because we have to go a little farther back, if we
take into account the probability of some years o₁

vacancy which the catalogue disregards. However the matter stands, the fact itself is so important and indeed of such capital significance that it is worth while stopping for a moment to consider it.

It may be asked whether the foundation of the episcopal See does not presuppose the previous existence of a Christian community in Milan. But this does not necessarily follow : St. Irenæus, Bishop of Lyons, wrote in 202 that the first founders, the Apostles, appointed Bishops for those who should later be converted to the Faith. In this way the Bishops themselves were the real originators of Christian communities, like fathers of families ; for that very reason they were called ' fathers,' or ' papae,' a title which they widely retained for a long time. Thus, wherever there was a Bishop, provided with the apostolic mandate, there was also, in germ, a whole ecclesiastical organism.

We are not able to give a definite answer to some other questions. The name ' Caius ' or ' Gaius ' is certainly Roman ; his being sent direct from Rome is certainly most probable at a time when everything came from Rome and Rome was everywhere imitated. Both traditions and documents of the greatest reliability assert that Italy and Spain received, together with the Faith, the Christian rites from Rome ; for this, the ' Ambrosian Rite ' itself, when studied scientifically, is one of the strongest arguments.

Gaius was succeeded by Castritianus, who was buried in the Roman cemetery ; then came Calimerus, buried in the so-called cemetery of Gaius ; then Monas, buried in the same cemetery, finally Mirocles, buried in the Basilica of Portius. The extraordinary longevity and the length of the episcopates, attributed to these ancient Bishops by our catalogue, are less incredible than some other details with which they are credited, as, for instance, Monas is with the erection of parishes within and without the city : as for the rural parishes—that might pass ; but to suggest that 115 city parishes existed at the end of the third and even the beginning of the fourth centuries, exceeds all bounds of probability.

I have mentioned Monas last, because here we must stop for a moment to gather up such general information as the scattered indications supply.

THE LIFE OF THE OLD CHRISTIAN COMMUNITY IN MILAN

How did the Christian community develop in Milan ? It is a question I raised just before.

One answer is given by the conversion of the garden of Philippus into a cemetery : it was near Sta Maria ' alla Porta,' outside the Roman wall ; it is the same cemetery which was also called the ' Poliandrum ' of Philippus and Gaius. Another answer is given by the Roman cemetery, outside the ' Porta romana ' near the actual Basilica of S. Nazaro. A third answer, though less precise, is furnished by another cemetery which must have lain outside ' Porta Ticinese.' A ' cemetery ' means a ' dormitory ' : it was a new name suggestive of new ideas : to die is to go to sleep, to sleep in peace, in the peace of Christ, as the language of the ancient burial traditions significantly expressed it. A ' poliandrum ' means the gathering-place of men, as if those who were buried together in these early cemeteries, continued their assemblies and their practices as they had done during their lifetime. In those cemeteries, or near by in the secret oratories, the first Christians of Milan assembled ; there they hid the sacred rites from the insults of the pagan mob and from the violence of their persecutors ; gathered together there in the new charity, they celebrated the holy ' agape ' which St. Ambrose later forbade when he observed that the practice had degenerated into abuse ; there they deposited in peace the harvest of persecutions and came to venerate the victims. For here in Milan too persecutions were raging, especially in the time of Maximianus Herculeus who set up his residence here, and the memories and the ancient cult of our martyrs bear witness to them.

Meanwhile we notice that persons also of the wealthier classes were among the Christians and that the faithful were soon very numerous and even perhaps formed into distinct groups sufficiently important to have separate cemeteries. We know moreover that as early as in the second century, private houses were used as oratories, still, however, in secret ; in the next century, in the time of the Emperors Philip I and II, who were so favourably disposed to the Christians as to suggest that they were Christians themselves, these secret oratories were changed into churches and basilicas and new ones were erected on ground either given to or purchased by the Christian community.

This is the history of our most ancient basilicas : of those of Philippus, later called ' Naboriana ' ; of Fausta, perhaps still represented by the ' Cappella di S. Satiro e S. Vittore,' incorporated later in the Basilica of S. Ambrogio ; of the Basilica of Portius or ' Porziana,' which was built where now ' S. Vittore al Corpo ' stands, but somewhat farther back, its altar much farther to the east ; and the Basilica—perhaps the oldest of all—of S. Babila, formerly called ' Ad concilium sanctorum,' as it were, at the ' Gathering of the Saints.'

We can observe with fair clearness from the famous Edict promulgated in Milan by Constantine in 313, that the Christian community had by then found means to acquire a legal existence and personality, so as to be able to hold property either by gift or purchase, in the shape of an association, or, as it was then called, a ' Collegium.' For the

Edict ordered among other things, the restitution of the ground and the buildings owned, not by individual Christians, but by the Church as a whole.

AFTER THE EDICT OF CONSTANTINE

It was, of course, not this provision that has rendered that Edict so famous, even glorious and important : it is rather that it marked the explicit recognition of the full and public liberty of cult granted to the Christian religion and the Church. More than a revolution itself, it was the sign and recognition of the completion of a revolution, achieved by the divine irresistible power of truth and justice, won by faith, by love and heroism : to believe, to love, to die and thus to win the victory : that was the whole programme, henceforth completed.

Its results were bound to be incalculable : the conversion of the Emperor ; the mass conversions with their advantages and drawbacks followed ; the prestige and authority of the Bishops grew ; Christian conceptions began to predominate in law, in institutions and in the conduct of life.

Our Bishop Mirocles being buried in the Basilica Porziana, three years after the Edict, is a sign of the changed times. He deserved certainly to have witnessed those days of triumph. Optatus of Milevis in Africa, in the fourth century, gives him first place among the champions of the unity of faith and of discipline, threatened by dissensions ; he appeared also as one of the most prominent men in the two councils of Rome and of Arles. In a famous discourse St. Ambrose mentions him later as among his most worthy predecessors, whose example gives him encouragement in moments of extreme difficulty.

But before we reach St. Ambrose, there are, apart from Maternus, of whom nothing is known except perhaps that he was buried in the Basilica Naboriana, three Bishops who need mention :

Protase, Eustorgius, and Dionysius. It is in this order that the old catalogue gives their names.

During the pontificate of Protase, Milan became the scene of two great ecclesiastical events. Two Councils were held to continue the defence of orthodox faith against the Eastern attacks of Arius, who denied the Divinity of the Logos. This was the first great heresy, which, tolerated as it had been, and often supported by the Emperors, promoted by the intrigues and violence of some, by the ingenuousness and ineptitude and occasionally by the ambitions of others, had at a certain moment led to Christendom ' feeling almost completely Arian ' : such is the expression used by St. Jerome, certainly emphatic, which throws a dismal light upon those times. Even then the general Council of Nicæa and the Council of Sardica had been held in 325 and 343, at which our Bishop signed himself ' Protasius ab Italia de Mediolano.'

Eustorgius I is mentioned by St. Athanasius, the champion of orthodoxy in the East, and Ambrose honours him with the title of Confessor.

Under Dionysius another great gathering of three hundred bishops took place in Milan in 355. Its purpose was to subscribe to the faith as defined at Nicæa and to support the rights of Athanasius. The Arians and the Emperor Constans who favoured them, wished otherwise. The Emperor finally replied to the remonstrances of the Bishops : ' My will shall have the force of the canons,' and threatened the opponents with death and exile. It is the glory of Dionysius not to have given way on a point of orthodox faith and not to have yielded to what in effect was an abuse of might against right. He went into exile with many of his brethren and died in 365 in Cappadocia. Ambrose later requested the return of his body from the great St. Basil who sent it back together with a letter which we still possess.

ST. AMBROSE

The predominance of the Arian governmental party lasted from 365 to 374, and for that reason Aussentius was hated both by the clergy and the people. At his death the Catholic party rose in reaction ; clergy and people assembled in the church for the election of the new Bishop ; fierce and threatening riots occurred ; Ambrose hastened to re-establish order and to prevent worse excesses : he was himself acclaimed as Bishop. Who was he ? How did he happen to appear here ?

Constantine had divided the Empire into four prefectures : the East, Italy, Gaul and Illyria. Each prefecture was subdivided into dioceses, each diocese into provinces. Italy herself was divided into seventeen such provinces, of which ten were dependent on Rome, and seven on Milan. Prefects of inferior rank were at the head of each, and Petronius Probus, the Prefect of Italy, had appointed Ambrose Sub-Prefect of the provinces of Insubria, Emilia and Liguria. On his election as Bishop, his own protests and refusals and all his efforts to change the popular decision proved of no avail ; of no avail even the fact that he had not yet received baptism, but was still aspiring to it as a catechumen : the consent of the Emperor was sought and obtained, since Ambrose was a magistrate and his representative ; within a few days he received baptism and the various Orders, and on December 7, 374, he was consecrated Bishop of Milan by the Bishops of the Province.

The son of a great Roman family, highly educated, experienced in the handling of large issues, richly endowed with the gifts both of intelligence and of heart, spotless in conduct, a character both forceful and kindly, frank and loyal, an elegant writer and pleasing speaker, he possessed in a rare measure and balance all the qualities which destine a man to occupy an outstanding position and enable him to exercise the greatest and most beneficent influence ; and indeed few men exercised anything like as great or as beneficent an influence as Ambrose.

It is impossible to record here or even to summarise, how he became almost at once the father of his people, the councillor and friend of Emperors and princes, the undefeated opponent of tyranny, the fearless defender of the rights both of his Church and of the poor and oppressed, the perfect pattern of a citizen, magistrate and Bishop. It was his merit and his work, that the last remnants of official paganism disappeared ; that a Christian spirit permeated the laws more and more ; that the Empire as such became finally Christian. The name of St. Ambrose is identified both with the city and the Church of Milan ; many centuries later, to fight for St. Ambrose meant fighting for Milan ; to make a gift to St. Ambrose meant making it to the Church at Milan ; the ' Ambrosian Church ' meant the Milanese Church, and the original rite of our Church came to be called the ' Ambrosian Rite.'

Our information on St. Ambrose and his work, supplied by our records and the writings of his contemporaries, among them of his deacon and biographer Paulinus, is as abundant as our information on his predecessors is scanty. We are unable to form a precise picture of the condition of the Church at Milan as he found it ; but we can easily form an idea of what it was when he left it at his death on April 4, 397. The Church buildings had grown both in number and importance ; basilicas which had so far been built outside the walls, began now to be erected within the city ; after the time of Constantine the Church of Sta Tecla had been built in front of the present Duomo ; now Ambrose speaks of the ' new, great, inner ' basilica which was then called ' Maggiore ' and ' Sta Maria,' and must have stood in the same place that was

c

taken later by our Duomo. He also mentions
the baptismal Basilica near there, and that of the
Apostles or the ' Basilica Nazariana,' and the
' Ambrosiana,' built by himself and still called by
his name.

The faithful gathered in the churches, men and
women in separate ranks, for Mass at dawn, for the
frequent sermons which expounded the doctrines
of faith and the Holy Scriptures. The virgins who
had dedicated themselves to God were given a
place of honour and the ladies of Milan eagerly
sought their company. The eloquence of St.
Ambrose preaching chastity, and the example of his
sister Marcellina came to form such an attraction
that girls came from distant countries to receive
the veil at the hands of Ambrose and the mothers in
Milan became alarmed : wherefore he, with subtle
irony, said that he had better go abroad to preach.
The alternate singing of psalms, hymns and melodies,
a fair number written by St. Ambrose himself, was
introduced for the education of the people and in
the days of the intrigues and violence of Justina,
when they shut themselves up together with their
Bishop in the Basilica, rejoiced and edified these
gatherings. The processions of sacred relics were
carried out with great pomp. Public penance in
its various degrees was in full use and Theodosius
himself had to submit to it. The House of the
Bishop was also the home of his priests and deacons
who assisted him within and without the city and
shared with him their common life of prayer and
meditation, as St. Ambrose tells us he had been
taught to do in the school of other Bishops. Forestalling the decisions of the Council of Chalcedon
(451), Ambrose entrusted the administration of the
temporalities to his saintly brother Satyrus who filled
the post of steward or procurator.

But on two matters especially the rule of St.
Ambrose throws light : on the election of our

Bishops and on the constitution and exercise of metropolitan jurisdiction.

The clergy and the people gather in Church and designate the person ; the neighbouring Bishops assist, examine the nomination, and according to the case, give their approval and confirm the election ; then, if required, they confer the consecration. These are the factors to which Ambrose himself repeatedly attributed his own election. The consent of the Emperor had in his case a special and wholly adventitious reason in the fact that here the person elected happened to be one of his superior magistrates. It is only very much later that documentary evidence can be found which proves the intervention of the Emperor in episcopal elections to be normal. It is clear on the other hand from the Council of Chalcedon, already mentioned, that the consecration of Metropolitans was conferred by the Roman Pontiff or by his delegate in a place designated by him. All this is moreover in full accord with what is to be observed elsewhere at the same time and is in conformity with the teaching of St. Paul.

The second point is no less important. It is common knowledge that the hierarchical and administrative units which we call dioceses, are subordinate to a higher unit called a province. At the head of the diocese stands the Bishop, at the head of a province the Metropolitan or Archbishop. This latter title is not used in reference to our Bishops before the time of Charlemagne ; more ancient is that of Metropolitan which incidentally indicates the reason of the title before ecclesiastical provinces had been formed by making the smaller sees dependent on the larger. This formation of smaller sees in Upper Italy does not for the majority go back farther than the fourth century, as in the case of Vercelli, Pavia, Como, founded by St. Ambrose himself, and Novara, founded by his

immediate successor. Aquileia, Ravenna, Verona
and Brescia are of older date.

We possess a certain amount of information
concerning the metropolitan authority exercised
by Ambrose over Verona, Vercelli and Aquileia :
for instance, appeals against episcopal decisions are
referred to him ; he intervenes in the elections ;
he signs first at Councils, and he himself summons
Councils of the Bishops of the province.

But how far did the province extend ? Everything
goes to show that the province comprises what was
covered by the ' Province of Italy,' according to the
division of Constantine, and thus included Liguria,
Venetia, Emilia, the two Rhætias, the Cottian Alps,
part at least of Tuscia ; it extended from Ravenna
to Chur, Augsburg, Ratisbon ; from Aquileia to
Turin, Nizza and Genoa : an immense area which
was gradually reduced by the later formation of the
Metropolitan Sees of Aquileia, Ravenna, Genoa,
Turin and Vercelli.

THE AMBROSIAN RITE

What is meant by the ' Ambrosian Rite ' ? What
are its special features ? Is St. Ambrose actually
its author ?

The Ambrosian Rite means the whole of the
sacred functions in and by which the Divine service
is publicly carried on, and the rules which regulate
these functions, in so far as they are peculiar to the
Church in Milan in distinction to other rites and
especially the Roman Rite. These peculiarities and
differences are of various kinds : some can easily
be observed, as that the celebrant does not turn
round during Mass ; baptism is by immersion
instead of by infusion ; there is a greater variety
of hymns and chants with their own modes ; Advent
has six instead of four weeks ; Lent is shortened by
four days (with the result that the Carnival is
correspondingly longer and forms the so-called

Ambrosian ' carnevalone,' (or great carnival) : I mention these as only some of the main differences.

But there are others less easily grasped or less noticed by ordinary folk, but not for that reason any less important : rather the contrary. The biblical text of the Psalms is that used before the revision by St. Jerome ; there is a somewhat different arrangement of the parts of the Mass and of the Office, and differences of readings in these parts. I must add, however, that in any case it is a matter of purely accidental differences.

But nothing of all this, with the exception of what we said earlier concerning hymns and chants, can reasonably be attributed to St. Ambrose, however easy and intelligible it is to give him the credit of having revived the ecclesiastical institutions of Milan and of having added to their renown and reputation by the prestige of his name. Hence not only the Rite itself has been attributed to him as author, but also many of our Church institutions which are really of much later date. The Church in Milan certainly possessed a Rite before St. Ambrose, and we have no proof, barring the exceptions stated before, that he introduced any innovations. Neither can it be proved that the Ambrosian Rite is of Oriental origin or character.

What then is the significance of all this ? It comes to this that our Rite is simply nothing but the Roman Rite as it was practised in ancient times. The older the documentary evidence that can be found, the more the differences disappear : no proof of the historical and theological value of our Rite could be more convincing or more effective. As early as the fourth century the Ambrosian Rite is fixed in the form which it retains at the present day, except for some unimportant details.

Various explanations can be given of this fact, but it certainly is not due to any systematic opposition to Rome. This is out of the question in view of what has been said and also of the times, not to mention other reasons. It is equally certain, more so than may be thought, that the veneration for St. Ambrose himself was a special factor.

Another point that emerges from the episcopate of Ambrose and anticipates the future of the Archbishops of Milan, is that Ambrose held and exercised complete power in the civil and political sphere.

This consideration prepares us for the second stage of our journey which runs from the pontificate of Ambrose to the establishment of the Commune.

THE RULE OF THE BARBARIANS

The last sound pillars of the Roman Empire had fallen with the deaths of Theodosius, Ambrose and Stilicho, and it became the object of the threats and attacks of the barbarians. After Alaric came Odoacer, king of the Heruli ; after Odoacer, Theodoric, king of the Goths, and his successors down to Teja ; then followed the brief revival of the Greeks and the government of Narses on behalf of the Emperors Justinian I and II ; in 569 Alboin, king of the Longobards, conquered the dominion of Italy, including Milan, which had been fiercely assailed and almost destroyed by Uraia in 539.

Meanwhile eighteen Bishops, from Simplicianus to Honoratus, had followed each other in the See of St. Ambrose. I mention but in passing the most notable men and events. The old but kindly Simplicianus, as St. Ambrose who had been almost a father to him, called him, when on his deathbed he designated him as his successor, maintained the honour of his See to such effect that the African Bishops, gathered at the third Council of Carthage in 397, turned to him for advice.

The same honour was shown by the fifth Council of Carthage in 401 to Simplicianus' successor,

Venerius, who was highly esteemed and employed in various important matters by the Popes Anastasius and Innocent I ; it was to him that the great Chrysostom addressed a letter of thanks for his good offices in setting him free from exile, and there are references to a Council in Milan called together by him. The building of new churches (without mentioning which they are) is attributed by Ennodius to Martinianus (423–about 435). St. Lazarus (438–449) is credited with the institution, certainly very ancient, of a rite peculiar to the Church in Milan, viz. the Triduum Litanies or Rogations which are still celebrated after the Feast of the Ascension. Of Eusebius (449–465) we still possess a noble document in the form of a synodial letter to Pope Leo I, signed by him and the Bishops united in the Provincial Council of 451 ; quite twenty Bishops are represented there, among whom we find those of Pavia, Aosta, Chur, Turin, Como and Genoa. Much has been written about St. Benignus, but nothing based on reliable evidence. On the other hand, we know that Senator, then still a simple priest, was sent as Legate by Leo I to the Council of Chalcedon.

The memory of St. Laurence I (490–512) is still living and honoured, thanks to information about him left in writing by Ennodius, the Bishop of Pavia, his devoted contemporary. He says that he deserved well of Pope Symmachus for the assistance which he gave him in several delicate affairs ; of Italy for having conciliated Theodoric ; and of Milan for having restored several old, and built new churches. Eustorgius II (512–518), his worthy successor, not only built a second baptismal font in Sta Radegunda, but also raised an immense sum of money for the ransom of a large number of our people who had been taken prisoners by Gundobald of Burgundy. For this he received a letter of high praise, which we can still read, from Avitus, the

famous Bishop of Vienne in France. St. Dacius
(530–552), not a fugitive but an exile, is credited
with the authorship of a Milanese Chronicle
which would undoubtedly be of great value, if
we could prove with certainty that it was his
work.

Meanwhile, at the time when Leo the Great had
ordered with ever greater insistence that Metropolitans, with due regard to ancient practice, should
be elected from among the priests and deacons of
the Metropolitan Churches, a new feature appears
in Milan in connexion with the consecration of her
Bishops. From a letter of Pelagius I (555–560) to
Narses, it can beg athered that as early as towards
the middle of the sixth century it was regarded as
an ancient practice that the Metropolitans of Milan
and Aquileia should consecrate each other. It is
impossible to say when this usage began ; we
mentioned earlier that the law provided that the
Metropolitans should be consecrated by the Bishop
of Rome or his delegate, and perhaps repeated
delegation and the difficulties of communications
with Rome owing to the barbarian invasions, helped
to fix the above ancient practice permanently. It
ended in 566, when the Metropolitan of Aquileia
fell into schism over the famous question known
by the name of the ' Three Chapters.'

Another novelty had made its appearance which
was wholly in favour of the Church in Milan : even
as early as the reign of Theodoric she found herself
(as also Ravenna) in possession of large properties
in Sicily. How and when she became possessed of
them, cannot be said with certainty. They were
lost to her probably in the ninth century through the
Saracenic conquest of Sicily. They must certainly
have been of great help on the invasion of the Longobards ; for even before their hordes, preceded by the
terrifying repute of massacres and the burning of
cities, reached Milan, Bishop Honoratus (568–570)

with a part of the clergy and the people took refuge at Genoa. He was generously received there and the Milanese Church was, so to say, transferred to Genoa until the middle of the seventh century. We know that his successor Laurence II took no little trouble over these Sicilian possessions. At Genoa, perhaps thanks to its easier communications, we find the old rule concerning the consecration of our Archbishops re-established. The election is made by a vote of the clergy and the citizens, but a Legate is sent from Rome for the examination of the Bishop-Elect, the scrutiny of the election and the consecration itself.

So it happened at the election of Constant to whom the Legate also brought the Pallium. Many in Milan, I have no doubt, must have noticed with some curiosity a special sacred vestment which is worn by our Archbishops for solemn functions. It is a strip of white wool which falls from the shoulders over the back and the chest, decorated with black crosses. It is a very ancient emblem and has more significance than appears at first sight : for instance, an Archbishop cannot exercise any jurisdiction over the Bishops of his province until he has obtained the Pallium. To obtain it application must be made for it *instanter, instantius, instantissime*, and it is only bestowed after a special oath of allegiance to the unity of the Roman Church has been taken, which at the time of which I am speaking, and for many centuries, was called the ' caution.'

It is not known which Archbishop of Milan was the first to receive the Pallium. The first documentary evidence is that of the aforesaid Constant to whom the Pope, however, writes : ' we are transmitting to you the Pallium according to custom.' Although it does not appear clearly whether it refers to a general custom of sending it or to a custom peculiar to our Archbishops, the former is the more probable, for the expression soon became stereotyped. This observation may be useful later.

As regards the ' caution ' or oath of allegiance, it arose from the schism of Aquileia, which had been followed by several Bishops. Our Archbishops who, with the exception of Vitalis and Fronto, had kept clear of it, cannot have found any difficulty over this oath. Some doubt about it arose in the mind of Queen Theodolinda, when Constant was elected Archbishop (593–600), but was speedily dispelled by a declaration of Pope St. Gregory the Great. Except for this episode and a feeble attempt of Agilulf (explained also by the fact that Agilulf resided much at Milan) to interfere in the election of Constant's successor, the rulers of the Longobards, although Arians up to Theodolinda, do not seem otherwise to have interfered with the elections ; the Edict of Rotharis hardly touches questions of religion or ecclesiastical discipline at all. Rather, after Theodolinda and following her example, those kings were often munificent founders and benefactors of churches. To give only a few instances, S. Giovanni at Monza, S. Pietro in Civate, S. Pietro in Ciel d'oro in Pavia, the Monastery of Sta Giulia in Brescia are a standing proof of it. It is true that somewhat later elsewhere, for example in Lucca, the priest appointed by the Bishop to a church is elected with the consent of the people and of the ' centenarii ' ; but a document of 746 referring to this matter, mentions no other interferences, and here in Milan there is no sign of them. The most notable innovation, in which perhaps the Longobard kings had a hand, was that the Bishop of Pavia dropped out of the number of the suffragans subject to the authority of the Metropolitan. He thereby acquired the right to be consecrated by the Supreme Pontiff, instead of as previously by the Archbishop, although Archbishop Benedict, about 710, went to Rome to submit a protest. The change occurred

at the beginning of the eighth century : possibly
Pope John VII (705–707) intended thereby to thank
King Aripert for having returned the Patrimony of
the Church which Rotharis had confiscated. It is
well known, moreover, that the Longobard Kings
resided by preference in Pavia or in Monza.
Among many other monuments of this predilection,
we find at Monza the Iron Crown, which was later
used for the coronation of the Kings of Italy at the
hands of the Archbishop of Milan. With Johannes
Bonus (645–655) the Bishops of Milan returned to
their See from Genoa after an absence of more
than seventy years. This absence can hardly have
been advantageous to the ecclesiastical institutions
of Milan, and it is intelligible that the credit of
having restored the splendour of the Ambrosian
Rite and of having composed a treatise in explanation of it, should have been attributed to Archbishop Theodorus (725–739). But neither of these
points can be adequately proved. It is to the sister
of this Archbishop that we must give the credit of
having founded in the neighbourhood of Porta
Nuova a convent of Benedictine nuns which remained famous for a long time under her name,
Aurona or Orona. It was built near the Via Monte
di Pietà, formerly called ' Via dei Tre Monasteri,'
when a second convent of Augustinian nuns was
founded near that of Aurona, and then a third, a
Franciscan convent. It was in the Church of the
Convent of Orona that Archbishop Theodorus
desired to be buried, and in the garden attached to
it Guido della Torre later took refuge. Among the
immediate successors of Theodorus, besides Benedict, Mansuetus (672–681) must be mentioned, who
wrote a notable doctrinal letter to the Emperor
Constantine IV against the heresy of the Mono-
thelites, called an important Provincial Council by
direction of Pope Agathon and took part in the
Council summoned to Rome by the Pope himself.

We know little or nothing about Natalis, Arifred and Stabilis, successors of Theodorus ; and I should not be able to add anything concerning Lætus (745–759), if we did not possess a fragment of a Council held by him in a MS. of the Chapter Library at Verona and another in the Ambrosiana.

With Archbishop Thomas (759–783) we reach the overthrow of the Longobards by the Franks under Charlemagne.

THE RULE OF ODOACER, THEODORIC AND NARSES

But what had happened meanwhile at Milan as regards civil and political government ? The first barbarian invasions had passed like a destructive meteor of fire, blood and iron, and had dealt the last blows to the decrepit Western Empire. Odoacer had given it its *coup de grâce*, and by his hand, 1229 years after the foundation of Rome, the crown was wrested for good and all from the brow of Romulus Augustulus, who was banished with a modest pension to the Castle of Pizzofalcone. His very name seemed chosen and predestined as an epigraph, I was going to say ' epigram,' on the fallen greatness of the Rome of Romulus and of Augustus. Odoacer, acclaimed by his people on the ruins of Pavia (August 23, 476), after its conquest and destruction, seemed to recognise the supremacy of Byzantium by sending to the Emperor Zeno the imperial insignia and receiving from him in exchange the government of Italy and the title of Patrician. In reality he acted as supreme ruler and, having established his residence at Ravenna, governed Italy with full powers ; it was under him that the barbarians definitely established themselves on Italian soil. He preserved the old municipal government intact, and in 480 restored even the Western Consulate which for seven years had fallen into disuse ; he left the civil posts in the hands of the original inhabitants, but excluded them from

the army except as auxiliaries, and divided a third
of the conquered land among his own people. The
proof that he struck money, is furnished by the
finds, as elsewhere, in the urn at S. Ambrogio, when
it was last opened in 1871. It is very noteworthy
that Odoacer was not stinting in his deference to
the Bishops and the Church : on the intercession
of St. Epiphanius, Bishop of Pavia, he freed that
city for five years from fiscal taxes ; and the Church
of Milan is perhaps indebted to him for the properties which, as mentioned before, belonged to her in
Sicily.

Odoacer, after an heroic defence, had in March of
493 to open the gates of Ravenna to Theodoric,
King of the Ostrogoths, who, after the barbarous
murder of his rival and a massacre of his troops,
remained sole and undisputed master of Italy.
And he behaved indeed as true Emperor, *verus
imperator*, as Procopius says, although he hastened
to declare the peninsula a part of the Empire and
himself as nothing more than the lieutenant of the
Emperor, to whom, as well as to the Roman Senate,
he protested his devotion. But neither Emperor
nor Senate were more than vain shadows of those
great names.

The least barbarous of the barbarians, Theodoric
left behind him the fame of magnificence as ruler
and of a capacity for noble ideals. By an example
which might be followed even to-day, he obtained
through the good offices of Epiphanius, Bishop of
Pavia, the liberation of more than 6000 Italians,
carried off as slaves by the Burgundians of King
Gundobald who had invaded the country over the
Alps and had come to the very gates of our city,
our Bishop Eustorgius II lending his aid, as we saw,
for their ransom.

All Romans, enjoying a reputation for virtue
and learning, were called to his court : the philosopher Boëthius, the historian Cassiodorus, the

doctor Rusticus Elpidius, the poet Cornelius Maximi-
nianus, Flavius Mavortius, who emended the text
of Horace, Rufus Austerius who corrected the text
of Virgil, Symmachus, Albinus, Paulinus, Liberius,
Faustus and others responded to the call of the
king. Theodoric not only saw to the preservation
of ancient monuments in Rome itself, by deputing
an urban cohort for this purpose, but also ordered
the erection of new buildings. Not only in his
favourite residences, Ravenna and Verona, but also
in Pavia, Milan, Monza, Spoleto, Terracina and
Naples, works of public utility arose which are not
lacking a certain grandeur, almost as a record and
promise of better things, even if they fall short in
gracefulness and finish of workmanship. If he
forebade his Goths, lest they should become soft
by the study of letters, to attend the schools of the
Romans, he urged them to discard their barbarism
and to follow the examples of the Romans in dress
and customs. The famous *Edict*, issued by Theodoric (whether actually in 500 is not certain) and
subsequently amplified by Alaric, clearly shows the
intention to establish a law common to both Goths
and Romans and to secure, if not a fusion of the two
peoples, at least a mutual toleration based on law.
Many provisions in it are taken over from the
Codex Theodosianus ; several barbarous customs,
like the guerdon, judiciary duel, the ordeal are no
longer admitted ; lawsuits of the Goths are submitted to a Gothic judge or Gothic count, those of
the Romans to a Roman judge, mixed cases to a
Roman and a Gothic judge sitting together. Again,
the main lines of the division of Italy into provinces,
and of the old imperial and municipal administration were preserved by Theodoric as they had been
by Odoacer. But for all that, the hand of the conqueror weighed heavily on the land. From the beginning a harsh law—perhaps a reprisal for the
conspiracy and rebellion of Tufa—took away the

' Roman liberty,' i.e. the faculty of testamentary
disposition of property to whom the testator wished
to bequeath it. This iron law, it is true, was soon
afterwards abrogated by Theodoric himself at the
instance of the two Bishops, Epiphanius of Pavia
and Laurence of Milan. It is true that the cities
had a ' defender ' who was to protect them against
excessive charges and was elected by the citizens ;
but he had to be confirmed by the Emperor. The
civil posts were left in the hands of the Romans,
but the officials had to be nominated by him, as he
also nominated the ' Curator ' who presided over
the Curia. Exemption from the exceedingly heavy
imposts, the use of arms, the commands in the army
were reserved to the Goths, and the highest honours
were always and everywhere bestowed for military
service ; and again a third of the landed property
of the vanquished was granted to the victors. The
Gothic king, although an Arian, displayed a very
yielding attitude towards the Holy See, the Bishops,
the Catholics and their affairs ; but later he took
vengeance upon them, with reprisals as unjust as
they were ferocious, for the severity of Justin against
the Arians in Constantinople, and caused the
saintly Pope John I to die in harsh imprisonment,
guilty of nothing more than of failing to carry out
orders both unjust and unreasonable. Later on,
seized by a sinister greed of tyranny and suspecting
treason and rebellion everywhere, he sent the most
worthy and distinguished men to their death, like
Symmachus, or Boëthius who was cruelly murdered
in prison at Calvenzano, not far from our city.

Though Milan had remained in the background
during the reigns of Theodoric, Amalasuinta and
Theodatus, she had been able to make good the
damage she had suffered, thanks to her considerable
resources, and resumed under Witigis her former
first place among the cities of the West after Rome.
Belisar, after landing in Sicily under the pretext of

avenging the death of Amalasuinta, but in reality with the intention of reconquering Italy for the Empire and already in possession of lower Italy and of Rome, was visited by a deputation from Milan headed by our Bishop, Dacius, begging for aid against the barbarians. A small detachment of troops, which had come viâ Genoa, was welcomed with enthusiasm within the walls of our city. But the vengeance of the barbarian king was not long in coming and was tremendous.

Uraia, grandson of Witigis, assisted by numerous hordes of Franks who had descended from the Alps to devastate the country, laid siege to the city in 539, and having taken it after an heroic defence, gave it over to massacre and destruction, a destruction if not complete, at any rate sufficient to continue as a lasting and fearful memory in the local traditions and legends. The victories of Narses put an end in 553 to the rule of the Goths in Italy and re-established that of the Byzantine Emperors.

Narses governed Italy for sixteen years which were for Milan a period of slow and painful recovery. The great Basilica of Sta Maria, head and heart of the city, rose again with new life, as it had done from the ruins left by Attila ; the walls and, much less imposing, the houses, were rebuilt to protect it. The municipal administration was revived, though with a change in the titles of the offices, and the population was divided into corporations or guilds or ' schools.' Especially important for the future of our country, and not only of ours, is the high degree of authority and power to which we find the Bishops have risen. They take part in the election of the higher magistrates ; the control of municipal revenues and expenditure is placed in their hands ; they are sometimes entrusted with the office and authority of ' Defender,' so that, as has been well said, they seem almost the transition-point from the Roman municipal constitution to that of the Middle Ages. It was not only an un-witting preparation for a future which no one could foretell ; it was also a wise provision for the present, for the Dukes, the leaders of the army and the other ministers were so iniquitous and rapacious that they seemed worse than the barbarians ; yet they were merely following the example of Narses himself.

THE RULE OF THE LONGOBARDS

In 568 the Longobards set out for the conquest of Italy—whether called in by Narses who thus is said to have retaliated on the Empress when she recalled the old eunuch to spin with the maids of her palace, or whether rather urged and determined by their own greed, by the ambition of their king Alboin, by the internal distribution of their popula-tion or by their political position, allured perhaps also by the beauty and wealth of our country-side which many had come to know while they were fighting as auxiliaries of the Greeks against the Goths. They were destined to link for ever their barbarous name with our beautiful and rich region. They broke in over the Julian Alps, and advancing with fire and sword, soon came to Milan. Pavia resisted longer, but in 572 she also fell, and was chosen by the invaders as their capital after having been threatened with total destruction.

We possess no document to prove that Milan suffered yet another massacre at the hands of Alboin ; yet it is incredible that the city, as the seat of one of the principal Duchies into which Italy and more especially Neustria or the western region was divided, could have escaped the spolia-tions and other afflictions which raged during the ten years' interregnum (574–584), following on the death of Clefis, the immediate successor of Alboin.

It is not our intention here to review the exten-sion and consolidation, also in the matter of Law, of the Longobard rule in Italy under its successive

D

kings, notably Autaris and Agilulf with his kindly
and pious Queen Theodolinda, Rotharis, Grimuald
and Liutprand ; nor its rapid decay from Hilde-
prand and Ratchis down to Astolf ; nor the disastrous wars against the Franks down to the final
victory of Charlemagne against Desiderius, and
down to Adelchis ; that same Adelchis who furnished
Manzoni with the subject of one of his beautiful,
nowadays so little known, tragedies, giving him
the opportunity of throwing upon the obscure topic
of the Longobard rule, as far as the state of knowledge then permitted, that light of genius which the
acuteness of his great mind and the limpid depth
of his judgment invariably enable him to cast upon
anything he touches.

To confine ourselves to Milan alone, we would
only add that in addition to being the seat of the
Duke, whose residence or court or curia may perhaps be recalled by the still surviving name ' Cor-
dusio,' the city now became also a royal residence
under Agilulf and Pertarit. But it was only to see
once more the horrors of war. Exploiting the fraternal discord between Pertarit and Godibert, Duke
Grimuald set out to secure the throne and seized it
by capturing Milan and driving Pertarit into exile,
after having slain Godibert.

There is no doubt that our city, as far as civil and
political government is concerned, did not share
the common fate of the vanquished, nor even the
distinction and privileges, often so onerous, of
being a capital ; for the victors had preferred
to confer on Monza and Pavia that humiliating
honour. But what precisely the fate was that
the Longobard conquest brought to the Italian
population, we are not yet able to define with
accuracy, despite the constantly growing light
which scientific research, working on the events and
the Law of that time, has been able to cast upon
that difficult problem. Some of its features are as

surely established as they are well known, like
the following : under the supreme authority of the
King, elected by him and often at war with him, the
Dukes were invested with full military and judicial
powers within their duchies, composed of families
(or ' fara '), powers which in course of time became
hereditary and were shared with the ' centenarii,'
or ' sculdasci,' and the ' decani '—the nucleus of the
later feudal nobility of the Middle Ages ; military
service was confined to all freemen, therefore called
' heermanni,' or ' arimanni,' military service, not
territorial ownership being the basis of all prerogatives and rights, instead of property, although later
' arimannia ' was the name given to the stable
property of freemen ; public affairs were discussed
and decided in the assemblies, called ' malli,'
presided over by the King, or if provincial, by the
Duke, held annually or on special occasions ; the
civil and judicial administrations were conducted
on the lines of the Edict of the Rotharis, gradually
amplified and improved by his successors, notably
by Grimuald and by Luitprand, perhaps the best
of the Longobard kings ; subjection (' nundius ')
affected everyone in varying degree except the head
of a family ; blood-feud (' faida ') was hereditarily
transmissible down to the seventh generation in
certain grave cases ; in others, replaced by com-
promise or a monetary fine (' guiderigildum ')
which in the degree of the fine bears witness to the
legal inequality of the classes ; the ' good ' or
' sincere ' men, supplementary judges of the act,
were called in by the ' sculdascius ' or the ' decanus,'
for the administration of justice to attest on oath
the existence of the crime ; the ' judgment of God '
by ordeal or by duel, was admitted, even in cases
where the accused denied his guilt on oath. But
whether, after two hundred years and more, victors
and vanquished ever fused into a single people, or
whether the Longobards maintained always to

the full extent the fierce attitude of conquerors
and barbarians and never mixed with the Italians,
who were kept in a state of oppression and ostracism;
whether the latter were ever invited to take part in
the government or were strictly excluded from it,
only a few of them being admitted to Longobard
citizenship, later to be violently suppressed and
reduced like the others to serfdom in conditions
ever more abject than those of the barbarian slaves ;
whether the conquered Italians retained the use of
their ancient laws and of their municipal administration, or whether they had their curias and their own
magistrates taken from them and the whole public
and obligatory use of Roman Law abolished—these
are all questions which, as mentioned, have not yet
received a definite answer. Certain positive indications suggest, indeed, that the survival of some
remnants of the old and indigenous institutions is
much more probable, as a germ which was destined
to develop and mature in better times. And this
is likely to have occurred not only in Venetia, in
Rome, in Amalfi, in Naples, where the Longobards
never were able to establish themselves, but also
in the rest of Italy, even if only in ecclesiastical
administration and in the private associations of
merchants and craftsmen. Famous among the
latter is the Guild of the Comacine Masters, so
noteworthy as to receive consideration even in the
Longobard law itself. In course of time the works
of this Guild covered many countries of Europe and
to it perhaps we owe originally the monuments of
Lombard Architecture which still survive in our
city and its territory in Brescia, Pavia and Verona.

THE RULE OF THE FRANKS

Seeds of a brighter future were cast among the
ruins of the Longobard domination as the result of
the Frankish conquest of our land which, if indeed it
may be said ' fatta per servir sempre o vincitrice o

vinta,'[1] seemed destined always to rise again. We shall have to follow for about two centuries the rapid succession of events in political history and the formation and growth of new social conditions ; it is these that throw light upon the history of the Ambrosian Church during this same period (later the opposite happens), and it is by reason of these developments that our Archbishops rose ever more rapidly to the highest political and civic power which they were later to hand over to the resuscitated Commune.

The immense dominions which numberless wars had united in the strong hands of Charlemagne, were first divided by himself, when in 781 he gave to his sons Louis and Pepin respectively the kingdoms of Aquitaine and of Italy, the latter consisting for the main part of the regions formerly in possession of the Longobards. When Pepin died in 810 here in Milan, his place was taken by his son Bernhard.

Meanwhile Pope Leo III had in a sense placed the coping-stone upon the work of Charlemagne by crowning him Emperor in the Basilica of St. Peter with the golden crown, taken from the altar, on Christmas Day of the year 800. This was not, as is well known, a transfer of the Empire from the East to the West, nor did the Pontiff claim the right to give or to take the crown ; nor did he mean to establish a Universal Monarchy, nor even less to subordinate the Church to the feudal power of the Empire or the Empire to the Church. It was a new creation, wholly papal : an elective and not simply hereditary Empire, requiring the sanction of the Pontiff to render the election valid, destined in the intention and by the explicit declarations of its

---

[1] This is the famous ending of an equally famous sonnet by Vincenzo da Filicaia (1642–1707), beginning :

> ' Italia, Italia, o tu, cui feo la sorte
> Dono infelice di bellezza. . . .'

(*Translator's note.*)

creator for the defence and advantage of the Universal Church, to which the ruler-elect bound himself under oath. It is true that, not long afterwards, partly through the fault of persons, partly by the very nature of things, the Holy Roman Empire, having become German, became, I know not, whether less Sacred or less Roman, at any rate an inexhaustible source of trouble both for Italy and for the Church.

Like the other parts of the Empire, so also Italy was divided into ' counties,' governed by ' counts ' with political, judicial and military powers according to the laws or ' capitulars,' assisted by ' scabini,' judges of the law and not merely of fact. The frontier counties were formed into ' Marches,' governed by Dukes, later called ' Marquesses,' and the county of Milan together with Genoa became such a ' March ' after the time of Charles the Fat. ' Imperial Messengers ' (*missi dominici*), ancient officers in the Frankish kingdom, travelled four times a year all over the Empire, checking the government and administration of the counties, dispensing justice (' placita '), securing concord between the counts and the Bishops. This by itself is proof of the high esteem in which the Bishops were held by the pious and beneficent sovereign. But there was more than that : the Bishops were exempt from the lower jurisdictions and depended directly from the Emperor ; one of the ' Messengers ' had to be a Bishop or Prelate, and Bishops and Prelates were summoned, together with the lay magnates and freemen, for the national assemblies, or ' campi di maggio,' which dealt with matters of general interest and of high concern at which presents were offered to the sovereign and laws were made. While religion and the Christian cult received every care and honour, education and culture were not neglected ; old schools which had fallen into decay were restored and many others founded, especially in the episcopal sees and monasteries, and the ecclesiastics and monks who lent their aid, were handsomely rewarded.

These practices, thus briefly sketched, were destined to last for a long time, although they were modified and developed into the feudal system. But the heritage of Charlemagne was soon to be broken up and to fall to pieces. The causes of disruption were the discords over questions of succession ; the invasions and conquests of the Saracens, the Hungarians, the Slavs, and the Normans ; the feudal system itself, as fully developed ; the racial antipathies and national tendencies of the various peoples ; perhaps also the premature introduction of some of these institutions among the barbarians ; and, without a doubt, the disappearance of the great mind and the strong hand of Charles himself

More effective, if only because more violent, were the civil or rather domestic wars of his successors : of Bernhard against Louis the Pious and his son Lothair, of Lothair and his brother Pepin against their father, and more than once, of Louis the German, the third son of Lothair, against his father and his brother Lothair ; of Louis the German and Charles the Bald against Lothair, not to mention minor tragedies. The crowns of the Empire and of Italy passed from one to the other, or were united and then again separated, to be brought together upon the head of Charles the Bald, the favourite of Pope John VIII. The two crowns were again united in the person of Charles the Fat ; but in 887 he was solemnly deposed by the magnates exasperated by his incapacity. The magnates then proceeded to divide up definitely the Carlovingian heritage. Italy fell to Berengar, Count of Friuli, Germany to Arnolf of Carinthia. Hence new wars and new vicissitudes and fresh changes of the crowns which passed from Berengar I to Lambert, and from him back to the former, who once again was both King of Italy and Emperor ; from Berengar to Louis the Blind, and back again to Berengar ; from him to Rudolf II, King of Burgundy. From Rudolf it passed to Hugh who, crowned King of Italy in Milan (926), covered himself with shame in Rome, with the result that the Italian princes replaced him by Berengar II, from whom Otto I of Saxony, called in by the beautiful and unhappy Adelaide, by the Italians and by his own ambition, took it and made it his own. Crowned with the Iron Crown in Milan in 961 and with the golden Crown in Rome in 962, he restored the Empire of Charlemagne, but it was an Empire which had become and was to remain German.

FEUDALISM AFTER OTTO I

This was not the only new development or even from our point of view the most noteworthy : by new institutions, Otto curtailed much of the author- ity and importance of the counts and correspond- ingly increased that of the Bishops. The Bishops having been invested by an instrument called ' chart of immunity,' or count's diploma, with full jurisdic- tion to be exercised by them through viscounts, all that was left to the counts was the country districts, and even these, it would seem, not always. This change meant a great step in the direction of the freedom of the Communes.

Other changes had meanwhile been brought about by the development of the feudal system. It is essential here to recall at least the main outlines of this system and the principal phases of its evolution, lest the very terms used in what follows, should cause confusion. At Milan, no less than elsewhere, the social and ecclesiastical conditions were almost wholly dependent on this system. It contained the various factors which in their recurrence, their combinations and collisions in civil and religious struggles gave birth victoriously to the communal liberties.

Feudalism, arising from the distribution of land which had been carried out by the victorious barbarians among their fellow-conquerors, had its centre in the Emperor ; round him developed and from him depended a whole hierarchy arranged in various orders. *Fiefs* were the lands granted by the sovereign to his subject or feudatory who thus remained bound to him as a *vassal* by a new link of fealty and public service (vassalage), first and principally in the form of military service, whence the term ' miles ', describes the title and position of the vassal. There were, moreover, major and minor vassals or ' milites ' accordingly as the fief was granted direct by the Emperor or by a vassal : hence the distinction between ' vassal ' (in Germany ' principes,' in Italy ' Barons ' or ' Magnates '), and ' valvassours.' Later on came the distinction between greater valvassours, still later called ' capitani ' (a title first reserved to dukes, marquesses and counts) as those who had been invested by the sovereign or by a baron with a lordship or a parish or part of a parish (which at one time was both an ecclesiastical and civil district) ; and ' valvassini,' or simply ' valvassori,' as those who held ancient fiefs or sub-fiefs from barons or ' capitani.' Thus in the tenth century we find within the feudal hierarchy three orders of ' milites ' : the barons, the ' capitani ' and the valvassours ; the first two forming the higher nobility, the lords, and the third the lower nobility. Among the lords the bishops occupied the first place and in Italy there were no princes properly speaking outside the ecclesiastical ranks.

A natural extension and a direct and unintentional offshoot of the feudal militia was, as has been well said, that ingenious institution so characteristic of the Middle Ages, namely Chivalry. It is greatly to the credit of the Church and of the clergy to have absorbed it at the time, and, through the ceremonies of investiture, the taking of an oath and the directions given to the knight, to have inspired it with an ideal purpose, high as well as sacred. This was after all a notable and beneficent achievement, however rarely its intention may have been realised in actual practice.

But there was a fourth order, destined to prevail over all the others, viz., the people, divided into a hierarchy of their own ; the citizens, the merchants, and the common people. By these names were designated and distinguished all those who held no fief of any kind.

The diversity of names was reflected in the diversity of prerogatives and rights, whence sprang usurpations and discontent, oppressions and struggles and a new order of things. While the lord enjoyed the right of hereditarily transmitting his fief from father to son, if not actually by law, certainly by tacit consent of the sovereign and usage sanctioned by time, the valvassours remained down to the eleventh century exposed to an arbitrary revocation of their fiefs, or rather ' benefices ' as they were more properly called. In the most favourable circumstances the ' benefices ' were limited to the lifetime of both the grantor and the holder of the ' benefice ' ; yet they had no resemblance to or connexion with ecclesiastic or canonical ' benefices,' which were of much older origin and, though not hereditary, were not limited to the life of the grantor.

The lords alone possessed feudal or so-called legitimate jurisdiction ; a term which comprised an enormous mass of prerogatives, rights, of absolute and despotic, often strange and barbaric powers, which fear and violence imposed from dark strongholds upon everything around : on houses and roads, pastures and cattle, fields and harvests, money and measures, things and persons, life and death. It was a harsh yoke under which the groaning people suffered ; against it, first in the cities, later in the country, first by recourse to law and judges, later taking up arms, they eventually rebelled.

FROM THE CARLOVINGIANS TO THE COMMUNE

The splendour of the Ambrosian Church developed within the social environment, created in course of time by these institutions and interwoven with the events which we have indicated.

When Charlemagne came to Milan in 781, Archbishop Thomas was ruling. He is the first of the Milanese Bishops to be designated by this title. He is called Archbishop as early as 777 in a most interesting document which provided, among other things, for the foundation of a hospital for the poor at Campione, placing it wholly and for ever under the authority of the Archbishop and of the Church of Milan.

It was the privilege of Archbishop Thomas to baptise Ghisela, the daughter of the great conqueror. The people at the time liked to see in this, as it were, an act of reparation of the Frankish king for the attempt he had made, on his return from Rome in 774, to abolish the Ambrosian Rite and to replace it by the Roman. It had been an attempt which they believed to have been frustrated by a miraculous intervention of Heaven as the result of the prayers of Eugenius, a Bishop from beyond the Alps who had died in Milan in the odour of sanctity and was buried in the Church of S. Eustorgio, and has always remained, as all old Ambrosians know, an object of veneration. But although the cult of the Saint among us is a matter of certainty, the reason for it is much less certain, for the first notice of this alleged attempt occurs only three hundred years later. An attempt of this kind was actually made by Cardinal Branda

Castiglione, the Legate of Eugen IV in 1440, but he had to abandon it and to flee from the menacing indignation of the people.

THE BENEDICTINES. CHARITABLE INSTITUTIONS

Archbishop Thomas died, it seems, on September 27, 783, and was buried in the Basilica of S. Lorenzo. He must have been very wealthy, if, as is alleged, he presented a golden frontal to the High Altar of the Church of S. Calimero, where indeed his name appears to have been held in special honour. He is the first whom we find in documents referred to as 'Archbishop'; his immediate successor, Pietro, was the first to sign himself as such. Under him and thanks to him, the Benedictines established themselves in 789 near the Basilica of S. Ambrogio and were a real godsend to that venerable old building. It is largely due to them that, often rebuilt and ceaselessly restored, the Basilica still stands, as the first monument of a clearly defined Lombard Architecture, with its tombs of Saints and Emperors, Archbishops and Kings, its treasures, its ancient remains and restorations : real pages of history, gathered and superimposed on each other to recall the glorious days of St. Ambrose, the massacres of the barbarians, the coronations of the Kings of Italy and the royal weddings, the investiture of knights, the truces, the judgments of God, the Councils and Diets, the solemn processions and incessant pilgrimages to that sacred tomb from which, a quarter of a century ago, the great Bishop of Milan seemed again to smile down upon and bless his Church, still Ambrosian after 1500 years.

The Benedictines themselves had to become Ambrosians and were subject to the Archbishop, especially in the election of their Abbot. Their disputes with the secular clergy soon began and became interminable, for the clergy, ever since they were constituted in the ninth century as a canonical Chapter down to the present day, have had, together with the cure of souls, also the use of the Basilica. The two towers or campanili can be said to be the monument of such disputes, and, if these achieved nothing else, they produced at least a great number of documents of the greatest value to all students of the history of our city.

Another important event which occurred two years earlier thanks to the Archpriest of the Church of St. Datius, requires to be recorded, namely the foundation of an orphanage for abandoned children. It was an act of charity which, like the foundation of the hospital for the poor at Campione, throws a kindly light on what we are accustomed to call, and what in some ways indeed was, the darkness of the Middle Ages. They were fine examples which one would like to see more widely followed, compensating to some extent for the miseries which they reveal. The home for the abandoned children was also to belong to the Archbishop and the Church of Milan, and the Archpriest of the great Basilica was to be its head and director ; to enable him more easily to fill this office without detriment to the duties attached to his position, the home was erected in close proximity to the Cathedral. The ' Coperto dei Figini,' at one time well known to the Milanese, stood at that spot and before it a little Church, called ' S. Salvatore all' Ospedale *in Xenodochio* '.

BETWEEN EMPEROR AND ARCHBISHOPS

In 794, at the great Council of Frankfurt called together against the Spanish heretic Elipandus, a late offshoot of Arius, our Archbishop Pietro figured prominently, but did not occupy the first place, though he came second after the Patriarch of Aquileia who mentions him honourably. His opinion is confirmed by two letters addressed to

Pietro by the most famous writer of that time, Alcuin. It is hardly worth while to record a spurious diploma by which Charlemagne was said to have granted the city of Milan, its walls, the surrounding country and all the royal revenues to Archbishop Pietro who had gone with Pope Leo III to visit him in France.

In 805 Pietro was succeeded by Odelpertus or Oldepertus, written so variously that out of the one Archbishop two have been made. But the one who really existed, deserves special mention ; while he was Archbishop, Charlemagne in 811 in view of his possible death made large grants to the Cathedrals of his kingdoms—Milan was considered and mentioned before Aquileia and after Ravenna, but never was able to obtain the share assigned to her. There is also a curious exchange of letters between him and Charlemagne. Charlemagne, not from any wish to dogmatise or from any despotic caprice, but because he had observed that many among the faithful were ignorant of the most elementary and essential notions of Christian teaching, especially concerning baptism, sent a circular to the Bishops of his Empire, asking them to report to him what they taught or caused to be taught concerning this sacrament. It was a sort of examination of their theological knowledge. We possess the reply of our Archbishop as of other prelates. Considering the times, his answer reflects no discredit on his manner of writing and his erudition, and certainly bears witness to his skill. Odelpertus begins with a mellifluous effusion ; but when he comes to the explanation of the various parts and ceremonies of Baptism according to the Ambrosian Rite, he merely reproduces bodily some well-known passages from ecclesiastical writers. This is unfortunate for us, as he might have left us a more interesting document on the Ambrosian liturgy. But there is another matter which he is said to have to his credit concerning the liturgy, if, as some of our historians assert not without show of reason, he reformed the institution of the Rogations. Certainly this institution was the object of many changes and additions, especially in the matter of the churches to be visited by the customary processions, and as we still possess documents on the itinerary followed by them, we can find in these records most valuable indications on the antiquity of many of our churches and on the topography of the town.

The zeal of Charlemagne, the honours which he heaped upon the clergy and the churches, his munificent example had greatly increased the wealth of the Church and of the Archbishop, as can easily be observed ; correspondingly the import-ance of the Metropolitan among the nobility also increased.

This importance became more evident, especially in the political sphere, when, in 813, Anselm, who succeeded Odelpertus, appeared among the prin-cipal supporters of the King of Italy, Bernhard, in his revolt against Louis the Pious. It could be little to Bernhard's taste to find himself a King merely in name and almost a simple vassal, as he was in fact considered ; the Italian lords were far from satisfied with this situation, since the abasement of their own sovereign necessarily reflected upon themselves who were in closest contact with him. This consideration may avail, if not to justify, at least to explain the conduct of Anselm. The wretched King died, blinded, in 818 ; Anselm, imprisoned and brought before a tribunal, was deposed from his See, and it does not seem likely that he was reinstated before his death in 822.

There is nothing to report on the short reigns of Bonus and Angilbert I (823), except that the latter, on the evidence of his successor, had bestowed ecclesiastical property on certain laymen, after having unjustly deprived the monks of S. Ambrogio of it, and had thereby given proof of what threatened the Church and her discipline and goods, when abuses and spoliation on the part of lay feudatories were to be followed by similar conduct on the part of ecclesiastics.

ANGILBERT II

The fierce and imposing personality of Angilbert II (824–860) must now engage our attention.

Some historians, each one according to his fancy, reproach him, and others praise him, for having taken up an attitude of opposition to the Roman Pontiff, starting thereby a cleavage or even a regular schism between the See of St. Ambrose and that of St. Peter, between the Church in Milan and that in Rome, which is said to have lasted quite two centuries. There is no truth in all this and no reliable documents to support any such view. On the other hand, it cannot be denied that Angilbert was among the Italian lords who advised Lothair to rise against his father, Louis the Pious, probably for the same reasons which had led Anselm to adopt a similar course. When the rebellious son had to submit, he saddled his evil councillors with his guilt and made them pay for it; but he did not dare to do so in the case of Angilbert. He limited himself to mere reproach, and, having invited him to come and see him, he entrusted him with the task of bringing about a full reconciliation with his father. Angilbert accepted the mission, but was unable to reply to the reproach except by silence. Yet, when the king, surprised and angered by Angilbert's proud bearing, exclaimed : ' You behave as if you were St. Ambrose himself,' he replied : ' I am not St. Ambrose, but neither are you God.' Again, having accomplished his mission, he told Louis plainly : ' Love your enemies and do good to those who hate you,' and when the latter

asked him : ' And if I don't ? ' he answered :
' If you don't, and if you persist in your hate until
death, you will lose Paradise '—thus keenly did he
feel his own position and his dignity as Metropolitan
and Milanese lord. He never abandoned this high
position : he acted repeatedly as ' Imperial Messenger ' ; assisted at the Council of Mantua to fix
the jurisdictions of the Patriarchs of Aquileia and
Grado (827) ; confirmed at another gathering of
his suffragans the foundation of the Monastery
of SS. Faustinus and Jovitas, made by the Bishop of
Brescia (842), took part and presided at a Council
of Cisalpine Bishops in Pavia (855) and promulgated
there certain canons concerning discipline, as
beneficent at the time as they are instructive for us.
Full of zeal and energy for the promotion of the
spiritual welfare of his diocese, he was founding
new monasteries and reformed the old (they needed
it, especially that of S. Ambrogio, where the
increased wealth was already beginning to produce
its obvious effects). A munificent benefactor of
S. Ambrogio, he restored the Basilica and presented
it with a magnificent golden altar frontal, the work
of Volvinio, while his charity added to the Basilica
and cloister an hospital for the poor and the pilgrims ; kindly and charitable, lamented as a father
of the poor, he died on December 13, 859, and
was buried at S. Nazaro.

TADO, ANSPERT AND THEIR SUCCESSORS

After a vacancy of eleven months Tado succeeded
him. The splendid title ' the Wise ' that was given
him was not undeserved ; it is proved among other
things by the Latin verses addressed to him by
someone—perhaps Sedulius—among the Irish (or,
as they were then called, Scottish) monks to whom
he offered hospitality and protection, to promote
studies as well as the spiritual life in his diocese, since
these monks whom the poet calls ' sophoi,' must

E

have been learned men and came to continue
the work of Columbanus and of his disciples,
established by favour of King Agilulf at Bobbio.
They collected there those treasures of manuscripts
of sacred and profane learning which went later to
add to the wealth of so many libraries, notably of
that of Turin, the Vatican as also of our own
Ambrosian Library. Having mentioned Columbanus, I must add that he also laboured here in
Milan for the conversion of the Longobards and
possibly of King Agilulf himself from Arianism to
Catholicism.

It is by a misunderstanding that some historians
attribute to Tado the institution of the Feast of
the Exaltation of the Cross, which was introduced
only in 1053, in the time of Archbishop Guido da
Velate, a solemn Feast until the present day in the
Universal Church. On the other hand, it is true that
Tado held a Council with his suffragans in 863,
renewing and amplifying the canons of Angilbert
and adopting the title of ' Primate of Milan.' It is
also true and does great credit to Tado, and
positively disproves any notion of a schism between
his predecessor and Rome, that Pope Nicholas
delegated to him a matter as grave as it was delicate
and dangerous, namely to give judgment on the
scandalous behaviour of Engeltrude, the faithless
wife of Count Bosone, safe, as she thought herself
to be, and therefore defiant, under the protection of
Lothair, King of Lorraine. In 860 Tado, according
to orders received from the Pope, held a large Council of his suffragans and excommunicated her for
adultery ; the sentence was confirmed by the Pope
at a Council in Rome, in the acts of which our
Metropolitan is most honourably mentioned. There
is also a story of another important mission which
Tado accomplished, when in 863, together with the
Primate of Belgium, he addressed a letter to
the Bishops of France to secure peace between the

Archbishops of Rheims and of Sens : this is perhaps
that peace to which allusion is made in the previously mentioned verses which also refer to a journey
of Tado to Rome. Two rescripts from the Pope to
Tado, one of which was later incorporated, with
the name of Tado, in the ' Decretum ' of Gratian,
give evidence on various matters during Tado's
rule, as on the later, perfectly regular, relations of
Tado with the Roman Pontiff, the subjection of
Augsburg to the metropolitan jurisdiction of Milan,
violence done to the clergy and the neglect of
justice, the piety of our Archbishop and the wisdom
of the Pope in respect of the veneration of relics.

Tado died on May 26, 868 and was succeeded in
the same year by Anspert of Biassono, another
interesting figure among our Archbishops. He was,
it seems, Archdeacon of the metropolitan Church.
The political predominance of the Milanese Metropolitan had no more firmly convinced and courage-
ously tenacious a champion than Anspert with the
exception of Aribert ; and Anspert prepared the
way for Aribert. The failure to allow for this
aspect of the situation and of the public behaviour
of Anspert, is the cause why so many writers regard
him as a hierarchical rebel against the supreme
ecclesiastical authority of the Roman Pontiff. They
insist on seeing the first spark of discord, if not in the
autocephalous traditions and tendencies of the
Milanese Church—traditions and tendencies that
never existed,—at least in a Bull of 874 in which
John VIII gave judgment in favour of the Bishop
of Pavia against certain claims of jurisdiction of
Anspert over two monasteries. It is quite likely that
Anspert remained dissatisfied : the two monasteries
had been built in territory subject to his jurisdiction,
but one of them had been founded by the Bishop of
Pavia. Absolutely speaking, the right was on the
side of the Pope, and it is probable that, as on later
occasions, he seized the opportunity to enhance the

See of Pavia in order to set a limit on that side to the predominance of the Milanese Metropolitan who was unfavourable—and perhaps could not help being so—to the Pope's political schemes concerning the Kingdom of Italy and the Empire. But the mention of political considerations exhausts what would appear to be the true aspect of the question. There is not the slightest trace of any opposition, strictly speaking hierarchical and in matters purely religious and ecclesiastical. And if Anspert—by no means the Church of Milan—stood in opposition to John VIII, with such fierce obstinacy that he was finally deposed from his archiepiscopal See, this opposition finds its explanation, and up to a certain point its *raison d'être*, in motives of high policy, motives certainly not lacking in the conduct of John VIII himself.

As early as 874 the Emperor had delegated to Anspert the authority of ' Imperial Messenger ' in the delicate and still unsettled affair of Engeltrude. It was another proof of the high position of the Archbishop and of the recognition of its importance. It was at the same time a factor in adding still further to its importance. Its importance grew still more, when, two years later, Charles the Bald attached the office of ' Messenger ' permanently to the episcopal position, for he had always been at pains to preserve that office, so essential in the combination of public powers then, whereas in Germany, under the rule of Louis the German, it had almost disappeared, not without great harm to both the sovereign and his subjects.

The importance of the measure taken by Charles the Bald and its influence on the formation of the episcopal political power may seem somewhat lessened by the fact that the Bishop acted as ' Imperial Messenger ' only within the confines of his diocese. But it is sufficient to note that the confines of the territories and of the counties which belonged politically to the episcopal cities, coincided at least as a rule and more or less precisely with the confines of the respective dioceses.

When the Emperor Ludovic II died in 875 in the diocese of Brescia, and was buried by the Bishop there in the Church of Sta Maria, Anspert showed energetically how much he valued his prerogatives both as Metropolitan and as noble. Having made request for the body and not having at once obtained it, he proceeded himself to Brescia, with orders to the Bishops of Bergamo and Cremona to meet him there with their clergy, and taking possession of the body, brought it to Milan and gave it burial there in the Basilica of S. Ambrogio.

On the death of Ludovic, the political issue presented itself in its full force. The crown of the Holy Roman Empire required the approbation of the Roman Pontiff, the crown of the Kingdom of Italy needed the votes of the Italian nobles who for this purpose assembled in a diet at Pavia. A conflict was, humanly speaking, inevitable. The Italians could not elect a king of their own without imposing an emperor upon the Empire ; Pavia could not commit itself without at the same time committing Rome. But it must be recognised in fairness that the Pope represented not only his own interests and those of his people, but also the superior interests of his high office, and therefore could and indeed had to take the view that the decision rested with him by right. Such, to judge by his words and deeds, was the opinion of Pope John VIII, who entertained ideas of his own concerning the Holy Roman Empire, and undertook subsequently certain engagements, which, together with their motives, have recently been the subject of learned research. Notwithstanding, John VIII proceeded over the election of Charles the Bald with both moderation and regard for the electoral rights of the Italian magnates, confining himself to acting rapidly, while they wasted time in dissensions at Pavia. After Charles had come to Italy and had been crowned at Rome, he went to Pavia, and the diet under the presidency of Anspert at once recognised him as King of Italy and crowned him with the Iron Crown, probably at the hands of our Archbishop himself. The right of the Archbishop of Milan to occupy the first place among the nobles of Italy, especially in the matter of royal elections, was in a way confirmed on that particular occasion when Anspert took more explicitly the oath of obedience to the new King and Emperor, and the Emperor in his turn swore to maintain and protect the prelate. The Emperor gave this undertaking to no one else among those present, and immediately displayed his gratitude by the grant of rich lands and properties which the already wealthy Archbishop used for the erection of a hospital near the Basilica of S. Satiro, also built by him.

Things did not pass off as smoothly, when John VIII pressed his intention of appointing a French successor to the still living but infirm Carloman, whom the diet of Pavia had recognised, when Charles the Bald died (October 13th, 877), even before the Pope had elected and crowned him as Emperor.

In vain did the Pope, who had gone to France to settle this grave matter with King Ludovic the Stammerer, invite Anspert to the Council of Troyes. Anspert sent his excuses and refused to move. In vain did the Pope, when he came to Italy with Bosone whom he had designated for the crown, invite him to come to the pass of the Mont Cenis to meet him. The silent immobility of the Archbishop was too eloquent, and the Pope wrote from Turin to the Bishop of Pavia to be on his guard and to remember that he was dependent not on the Archbishop, but directly on the Roman Pontiff. From Turin the Pope proceeded to Pavia and invited the Archbishop with his suffragans and with the nobility to come there ; but suspecting that it was his intention to depose Carloman, nobody stirred.

The dissatisfaction of the Pope with the Milanese Metropolitan reached such a pitch that he ordered him and his successors to take part in any Council summoned by the Bishop of Pavia. Up to then the Pope had indeed allowed his mind to be known, but had never given explicit expression to it ; when he did so, matters naturally did not improve. However many letters and Legates the Pope dispatched, however much he launched sentences of excommunication, he was unable to induce the Archbishop to come, or to send any one in his place, to two Councils which the Pope assembled in Rome. Matters went further, and contrary to the express order of the Pontiff not to elect any one as King without his consent, the Archbishop with his suffragans and the whole diet of the Kingdom of Italy elected Charles the Fat as King, towards the month of October 879. The Pontiff declared Anspert deposed from the Archbishopric for disobedience and contempt of excommunication. He wrote to Charles with whom he had made his peace, to the suffragans, the clergy and the people of Milan that they should proceed to a new election, for which purpose he was sending his Legates. The opposition of Anspert was but too real and notorious, however evidently inspired by political motives, and however much collective rather than individual given the obvious unanimity of the Italian electors, even if exacerbated by the personal attitude of Anspert. Charles the Fat, however, interceded with the Pontiff and Anspert was absolved and restored to grace without a new election (880). A trifling and short-lived incident, the first cause of which is not perfectly certain, arose almost at once ; but it was settled, and the harmony re-established between the

Roman Pontiff and Archbishop of Milan was complete and cordial, to judge from several letters which are still there for us to read. The Archbishop submitted to the Pope what he has done in several grave questions of metropolitan administration ; the Pope approves and commends and writes to the Archdeacon of the Metropolitan Church to act in obedience to his Archbishop ; writing to all the bishops, clergy and people of Milan, he bestows high praise on an Abbot, a certain Adericus, on account of his loyal and faithful co-operation with his Archbishop for the spiritual welfare of the Milanese Church. In this state of complete and perfect reconciliation, Anspert died on December 7, 881, and was buried in S. Ambrogio, recommended to posterity by an inscription which is still preserved there. The fact that the inscription bears the date of 882, is immaterial, since there is no doubt that it is given according to the Pisan calendar-reckoning which began the year with the date of Incarnation properly speaking, i.e. March 25.

Political reasons, the obligations of an alliance with the nobility and his own energetic, impetuous and tenacious character were the causes which led Anspert, as a magnate, to take up for some time an attitude which it is difficult fully to appreciate. On the other hand, we possess many proofs of his zeal as Bishop. If the aforementioned inscription refers to his political attitude, it does so with great tact, by calling him ' effector voti propositique tenax ' ; but it also extols the faith, the moderation, the eloquence, the spotless life of the Bishop and his charity towards the poor, and mentions the churches restored and the building of the hospital and of the Basilica of S. Satiro. Anspert is also credited with the restoration of the Palace of Stilicho and the erection of the atrium which is one of the beauties of the Basilica of S. Ambrogio if we may accept a view which, not fully proved and supported by general consensus, is yet not disproved by contrary evidence.

The inscription also refers to another work, namely the restoration of the city walls of the towns committed to his care. From this point of view he only lacks the official title of political head of Milan.

On the other hand, the letter of John VIII, in praise of the priest Adericus just mentioned, indicates clearly that Anspert was engaged in a real and large work of reform of his Church. It may be sad that it should have been in need of such, but it is only too explicable during this wretched time. It is good and consoling that the reform should have found the right men and should have been effected. The example of the Metropolitan and Bishop was followed both in Milan and outside : a certain Werolf built a Church called even now by the surname of the founder ' Sta Maria Pedone,' or ' Podone,' in a place called since that time ' Cinque Vie,' ' Ad quinque vias ' ; and Garibald, Bishop of Bergamo, founded a hospital at Inzago, and repeated mention is made in documents of several churches and holy places and monasteries which arose in those years in the city and in the country.

But the fact which stands out above all the others is the growth of the political hegemony of our Archbishops. One is tempted to think that this could only have happened at the expense of all the other social forces that might aspire to the acquisition and the exercise of a controlling influence in the commonweal. This did happen and could not but happen as regards the count : his powers and attributes lay precisely in the sphere which the Archbishop increasingly occupied, and they could not but diminish to constantly smaller proportions. The count does not in fact actually disappear ; he remains side by side with the Archbishop, but second to the Archbishop and under his control. The Archbishop's function of ' Messenger,' first recurrent and then permanent, might suffice to explain this phenomenon, even without reference to the other powerful factors, both in law and in fact, which have been mentioned.

The city was governed according to a division into 'gates' and parishes, still now in use in the ecclesiastical government. The heads of the 'gates' were the 'capitani.' It is evident that a part of the spoils of the counts had fallen to the valvassours from whose ranks the 'capitani' were taken, while the counts henceforth take a share in government only by way of exception and in specially grave circumstances. And some share had been acquired even by the people. When the Abbot of S. Ambrogio desired to occupy a street near the cloister to secure greater quiet and safety, he applied for it to the venerable Bishop, Anspert, to Count Alberico, to all the clergy and all the people. When King Adalbert in 959 proposed to enter Milan and reside there, the whole of the citizens rose against this violation of the privilege enjoyed by the city, that no sovereign should reside within its walls. The privilege certainly did not date from the time of St. Ambrose, nor from Theodosius, as was then believed ; but it was a real privilege, indications of which appear as early as the ninth century. Other cities in Italy enjoyed it also. Adalbert concealed his anger and yielded to the popular will, *videns populi voluntatem*, and was satisfied with the so-called Ambrosian Palace, remains of which may possibly even to-day be seen in the column standing near the Basilica of S. Ambrogio. The fact is that the wealth, accruing from business and commerce in our city, together with the effective solidarity of the numerous corporations and 'schools' (guilds), had increased the importance and power of the citizens ; even the serf population of the country districts is beginning, as instances were soon to prove, to shake off the yoke ; the whole people felt the breaking of the dawn of better times in the very extremity of misery, and foresaw in the struggles among the magnates, of which it was as yet only the spectator and the object, other struggles in which it was to be itself one of the champions.

Anspert was succeeded by Anselm II. I mention him because John VIII addressed to him a letter, breathing the most peaceful spirit, almost like that of a friend, confirming the Milanese Church in her privileges and exhorting him to faithfulness towards the Holy See. It offers the most evident proof that the opposition of Anspert, whatever it amounted to, was only the expression of a personal attitude and in no way that of his See and Church.

When Guido, Duke of Spoleto, and Berengar, Duke of Friuli, were crowned as kings of Italy, they received the crown probably at the hands of Anselm. But during the ambitious and fierce struggles between the rivals for the crown, Milan came to be besieged by the troops of Lambert. Even then, as in all great emergencies, Milan felt herself to be the city of St. Ambrose, and attributed to an apparition of the Saint her delivery from this pass with but little damage. It was fortunate that the city found herself with her walls restored and enlarged and her monasteries transformed almost into fortresses.

Two months after the death of Anselm, in September 896, the See was occupied for only three years by Landolf, a peace-loving man, esteemed by Berengar as councillor. He perhaps deserves the credit of having saved Milan from the Hungarians, who just then were beginning their devastating incursions into Italy ; if indeed the inscription which was put up in S. Ambrogio, where Landolf was buried, refers to them, and not to the rapacious soldiery of the rival princes. The allusion to the Hungarians would be the more probable, if it could be proved that a fresh reform of the Litanies and Rogations of Penance, and the Ambrosian Mass against the pagans, go back to this very period.

The people of Limonta contested in the court of Bellano the right of patronage of the Abbot of S. Ambrogio, at least within limits, before Landolf's successor, Andreas. This was a sign of the times and certainly not an isolated case. Other cases, brought by the same people, came up before the tribunal of the same Andreas and that of Aico, or Atto (906–918), his successor. The advantages of a decision, as far as we know, in favour of these poor people amounted to very little ; still, it is pleasing to note that the poor and oppressed still had the strength to rise, that the sense of their own rights was still alive in them and that they had not lost all means of making them felt. It must be reckoned among the greatest merits of the Church that by every means, theoretical and practical, at her disposal, by the continuous inculcation of evangelical principles, by a mitigation of the laws, by favouring in every way manumissions, by the protection of the weak, the care for the poor, the constantly easier admission to Holy Orders, she laboured incessantly to bring the classes together, to tame the higher, to raise up the lowest, to break down more and more the barriers founded on nothing more than birth and origin.

After the short reign of Garibert (918–921) and that of Lambert (921–931), who lived through and largely shared in the vicissitudes of the kingdom of Italy from the time of Berengar to that of Rudolf of Burgundy, from the rule of Rudolf to that of Hugh of Provence, there followed by favour of the latter a Belgian, Hilduin, for whom, when he was still Bishop of Liége, Hugh had procured the See of Verona. On his being made Archbishop (931–936), the famous Raterius, his successor in Verona, brought him the pallium from Rome, a clear indication of the friendly relations continuing between Rome and Milan.

At this point the succession of our Archbishops is interrupted for some time by the ambitions and the avarice of King Hugh, who, having set his heart upon the rich and powerful See for his son Theobald, who was still too young, favoured meanwhile the succession of the old Arderic (936–948). Later, finding him too hale for his project, he attempted to suppress him. The example of Hugh was speedily followed by his disciple Berengar, who brought the greed and avarice of Manasse, Archbishop of Arles, into the service of his own ambition. Manasse governed the Tridentine March and enjoyed the revenues of the bishoprics of Trento, Verona and Mantua. Berengar offered him the See of Milan and assisted him in his intrusion.

It was an evil which had been growing since the beginnings of feudalism and had since then made immense strides. Lay princes should have disposed only of lay benefices, and those elected to episcopal sees should only have been given the investiture of feudal properties with their attached jurisdictions, leaving the Church property and ecclesiastical jurisdictions at the free disposal of the Church authority and of the canons. Instead, out of greed for wealth, as a protection against enemies, to win and reward friends, the princes began to dispose also of ecclesiastical benefices and to claim all authority in episcopal elections, so that nothing could be done without their investiture and everything by it alone. The example of sovereigns and princes was all too easily followed by the minor vassals in dealing with minor benefices. The Church and the party of order did not fail to rise up against such abuses, the fruit of vices and the germ of even worse vices ; the impending great struggles over simony and investitures are already discernible, and precisely from them our Commune, fully formed, was to arise.

Arderic died in 949 ; he perhaps had been the founder of the former Church of S. Andrea ' by the broken Wall,' *Ad murum ruptum*, to mark the breach by which Lambert during the aforementioned siege, had entered Milan ; we certainly owe to him a Chapel of St. Linus in the Basilica S. Nazaro. He may also have lent his authority in a more important matter, if a famous document is genuine which at one time was considered authoritative, but was then rejected by almost all as spurious, though even now it finds defenders : I mean the testament of Atto, the great Bishop of Vercelli. It is said to have been read before Arderic in full Provincial Council held at Milan in 945, in the presence of the Legates of Pope Marinus and of the two Kings Hugh and Lothair.

In and by this testament Atto gave to our Metropolitan Chapter the civil and ecclesiastical overlordship of certain Swiss valleys. It is certain that the Chapter was, at least down to the beginning of the eleventh century, Lord of the three valleys Blenio, Leventina and Riviera which, divided into four counties, were ruled and administered by four ordinary canons, hence called ' Counts of the Three Valleys ' ; but it has been shown that the author of the gift was our Archbishop Arnolf II, not Atto. This title has been preserved down to our own day. The civil government passed from the canons to Gian Galeazzo Sforza and from him to the Canton of Uri in 1487. The ecclesiastical government remained in the hands of the Archbishop of Milan, except, until recent times, the spiritual jurisdiction over benefices which belonged to the Chapter. After many vicissitudes the three valleys were detached from the Diocese of Milan in 1888 and incorporated in that of Lugano which was erected in that year. In memory of and as compensation for the

loss of these ancient rights, abandoned with spon-
taneous and quiet generosity, the Metropolitan
Canons received not very long ago from Pope Leo
XIII the privilege of prelatial dress, as earlier, in
1716, they had received from Clement XI the
privilege of wearing the mitre.

After the death of Arderic, Manasse, by favour of
Berengar and on the order of Lothair, came as
Archbishop to Milan. He was an intruder and the
majority rejected him, canonically electing instead
Adelman. But those in power always find someone
to adjudicate in their favour, and some supported
Manasse, others tolerated him ; yet others, perhaps
genuinely mistaken, considered him as legitimate :
if not the suffragan Bishops, who were almost all
under the protection of the chief supporters of the
intruder and some even tainted with simony, yet
certainly later Pope Alexander III—a fact explicable
perhaps by the distance of time.

Of course—it is an ill wind that blows nobody any
good : the subsequent Archbishops availed themselves of the right of minting which Lothair had
granted to ' St. Ambrose,' or rather to the Archbishop of Milan in the person of Manasse, certainly
not best fitted to represent that great Patron of the
Church.

The disturbances caused by the intrusion which
had despoiled our Church of a great part of her
wealth and treasures, only ended with the advent
of Valpert to the archiepiscopal See, when Adelman
had retired into private life, after having enjoyed
the favour of King Otto I to the extent of becoming
his archchancellor, and when Manasse had disappeared from the scene, we do not quite know
when and how. Having gone over to the party of
Otto, he still appeared as Archbishop of Milan at the
Diet of Augsburg in 952, where among other items,
the celibacy of the clergy came up for discussion, as
it had at some of the recent Councils elsewhere.

THE STRUGGLE AGAINST THREE EVILS

We cannot too often repeat that laws are symptomatic of customs. Incontinence, concubinage and the so-called marriage of priests completed, with simony and the investitures, that fatal triad of evils of the time, linked by a far closer and deeper connexion than might appear at first sight. Simony opened the door of the sanctuary to men fired by ambition and adventure, while the treasury of the prince grew rich despite the continual drains on it by wars. The investitures bringing the Church into subjection to lay caprice, introduced into her ranks courtiers and soldiers both impatient and incapable of those mortifications and virtues which are indispensable in one who ought to be a model of virtue to others in his office as their teacher.

The easy wealth of accumulated benefices fomented passions and vices by increasing the means to gratify them. It is easy to imagine the state of public morals in these conditions ; and it can cause no surprise to find that people tried to pass off as legitimate what proved so convenient, and that they ended by proclaiming concubinage as a regular marriage, since by that means the beneficiaries established a family link among themselves and perpetuated by hereditary succession the possession and enjoyment of ecclesiastical property within their families. What is really astonishing is that in the midst of so much anarchy and confusion, with so complete a disregard and defiance of the most fundamental principles, the Church organisation did not fall to pieces, but, on the contrary, discovered within itself the secret of a perpetual renascence, and constantly improved its constitution ; and that at a time, when the evil assumed really awful proportions, the people should have kept their faith in St. Ambrose and—with all due difference between the one and the others—in his successors.

Adelman died in 956 in retirement. It would

seem that the statue which he intended to set up for himself is that old friend of every Milanese, the ' uomo di pietra,' perhaps a remains of Roman art which had been adapted to the new purpose. Thus does the ridiculous get mixed in human affairs with the most serious things and tragedy ends with an epigram.

Skilfully holding his own between Adelman and Manasse, Valpert had been elected and found himself perhaps as early as 953 the sole occupant of the archiepiscopal see.

It is certain that he played no small part in calling in Otto to put an end to the discords and the destruction spread by Adalbert and Berengar. For this purpose he travelled to Germany to see Otto, and promised him the crown of the kingdom of Italy. He kept his promise and crowned him with the Iron Crown, not at Pavia as was the custom, but at Milan in the Basilica of S. Ambrogio, and received a large reward of lands and favours. Too much a partisan of the sovereign, he took part in 963 in Rome in the illegal Council which deposed the legitimate Pope John XII and replaced him by the anti-pope Leo IX. In its acts Valpert is mentioned before the Archbishop of Ravenna and after the Patriarch of Aquileia. In 967 we find his signature, together with that of the legitimate Pope John XIII, and after that of the two aforementioned prelates, in a diploma which deposed the Bishop of Salzburg. Valpert, following an invitation of the Pope and of the Emperor, and carrying out the instructions of the Roman Synod of the same year, held here, in the Basilica of Santa Tecla, a Provincial Council of his suffragan Bishops in 969, to provide for the distress of the See of Alba, which had been devastated by the Saracens and Hungarians, by decreeing the union of that See with that of Asti. Among the suffragans appears still, perhaps for the last time, the Bishop of Aosta.

F

After him Arnolf I (971) passed by like a shadow,
for although he held the See for four years, we know
nothing of him but his name. For five years it was
held by Godfrey, of whom we possess a small
ivory vessel to hold the holy water at the coronations
of the Kings of Italy : it can still be seen among the
treasures of our Cathedral. The inscription on it
calls Godfrey ' vates ' ; but this does not mean
that we had a poet as Archbishop, for that term
occurs in medieval poetry also in the plain meaning
of Bishop and seems to have no other significance
in this case.

The reign of Landolf II of Carcano was the
occasion of great changes and the herald of even
greater events. The government of Milan under-
went under his rule a very notable change. He had
come to the archiepiscopal See by favour of Otto
II, and perhaps also thanks to the intrigues and the
gold of his father Bonizone, who owed his elevation
to the rank of count or duke (as was said) also to
Otto, and had already caused himself to be hated
by the people, domineering over them much more
than the changed times henceforth allowed. Landolf followed this paternal example and even exceeded it ; occupying the first place, as he did,
among the Lombard princes, in possession of the
highest power in Milan, and of immense wealth,
he began to abuse his position, behaving as the only
and absolute master. Those days of oppression of
the people were so bad as to make them regret the
more orderly and quiet rule of the counts.

The result was a fierce struggle with the citizens.
Bonizone was killed and Landolf driven out.
Landolf, not content with having called in Otto II
to besiege the people of Milan, then turned to
the valvassours or higher knights for help, and in
order to secure their support against the people,
invested them in 983 with all the possessions of the
Ambrosian Church, parishes and lands and dignities,

favouring especially his own family and creating three of his brothers ' capitani.' Yet for all that, he was unable to increase the importance or the powers of the valvassours and ' capitani.' It had been an alliance of the nobles against the people, but the outcome was to be a league of these latter against the former. The people did not allow themselves to be overpowered and the citizens took an oath for the defence of their common rights. Landolf had to agree to treat and peace was re-established.

In 985 our Archbishop took part in subscribing the decree of Pavia which carried out the union of the Sees of Alba and Asti. In 997 we find him at the Council held in Pavia by Pope Gregory V and there he signs after the Archbishop of Ravenna, who still sat, contrary to the ancient rite, on the right of the Pope, in place of our Archbishop.

After having made some sort of restitution for the immense damage done to the property of his Church by founding the monastery of S. Celso (where later the Cistercians were), he died in 998 and was buried in S. Celso.

Arnolf II maintained the high dignity of ruler, with great worthiness, and still more that of Metropolitan and Bishop. Otto III made use of him as the Legate who was to bring his bride from Constantinople. It is from there that legend says he brought, in place of the bride whom he had to leave behind owing to the death of Otto (in 1002), the brazen serpent which can still be seen in S. Ambrogio and was supposed to be that of Moses in the desert. Popular fancies ! The serpent with the cross which recalls its symbolical meaning, is merely another proof of that, even then ancient, use of this symbolism in the Christian basilicas and churches.

It was on his return from Constantinople that, to claim his rights as the first among the Italian nobles, he opposed Harduin of Ivrea who meanwhile had been elected King of Italy. He called in against him Henry, King of Germany, and crowned him as King of Italy in Pavia in 1004.

Aleric, who was an intruder into the see of Asti, found himself opposed by the Metropolitan and in spite of the power of his father, the Marquess, and in spite of the consecration, which he had received from John XVIII as a gift, was not reinstated until after having made humiliating and somewhat strange amends.

Although he had been forced to undertake military expeditions against some of the nobles who had failed in their due obedience, Arnolf left behind him the repute of having governed his Church as a true Bishop, in the interests of the welfare of his clergy and his people and generous in benefactions to the churches. Perhaps following his example and certainly in his time, a certain Fulcuin or Folcorin founded in 1007 a Church of St. Mary which inherited his name, surviving even now, although the church itself has disappeared. Arnolf was certainly the founder of the Monastery of St. Victor, where he was buried (1008). A curious note added to a diploma of the year 998 of Otto III by the chronicler of Farfa has given rise to the idea that Arnolf was deposed from the See of Milan or actually from the Papal See which he was supposed to have illegally occupied after Gregory V. But this chronicler was too far away from the spot and began writing his chronicle only in 1105, so that story is probably due to a confusion, caused by identical names and similar events which happened almost at the same time in France.

THE INVENTOR OF THE 'CARROCCIO.'
DAWN OF THE COMMUNE

The successor of Arnolf bears a name both glorious and dear to the Milanese : it is the name

of the inventor of the ' Carroccio,'[1] Aribert of
Entimiano. With him the powers of the Ambrosian
Metropolitans reach their highest point ; and from
this to the formation of the Commune is now
but a short step. His whole life shows that, as a
man of large and combative mind, he defended
energetically all his prerogatives of prince and
Metropolitan. But the assertion that he was the
embodiment of the ancient rivalries between Milan
and Rome—rivalries which in reality never existed,
except in the sense and within the limits indicated
above—has remained without proof. If at his time
the legend of St. Barnabas took definite shape
among us and a whole tendencious literature grow
up to support it, we shall presently see how and why
this happened. It is a much more probable and
simpler explanation that he was intent purely and
simply on increasing the greatness of his Milan
and of the power he held therein. Later on, in
carrying out this programme, Aribert found himself
obliged to fight against the Emperor, and with him
arose and grew the undying antagonism between
Milan and the Empire ; yet he might, in his beginnings, have been taken for the representative and
champion of the Imperial idea, which had naturally
to rely on the support of the Italian magnates
whose interests were most closely bound up with the
fate of the Empire. It was in alliance with them
that Aribert had invited Conrad to come to Italy,
offering him the crown, and receiving the grant of
the lordship over the Bishopric of Lodi. And
when Conrad had come, he had crowned him ;
he had entertained him magnificently with all his
soldiery on the vast archiepiscopal estates ; he had
accompanied him to Rome for the Imperial
Coronation and had favoured and helped him in
every way.

All this, combined with his despotic and violent

[1] See *Note* on p. 111.

manner, was bound to set the valvassours against him, who were in any case ill-disposed and in continual ferment against the Emperor and the magnates, mainly over the question of hereditary succession which was still denied to their fiefs and benefices. In the days of Landolf II it had been the people who rose against the nobles ; now it was the lower nobility that rose against the higher. It is an evident symptom that we are passing through a period of profound change, when we see none of the elements, composing the feudal organism, retaining its stability.

Unable to prevail alone and shut in within the walls of city, the valvassours of Milan sallied forth into the country districts and launched their counter attack, their numbers swelled by those coming from other parts and parishes, principally from Lodi. There the cession to the Archbishop, arranged by Conrad, and the siege that forced the people of Lodi to come to terms, when they had refused to submit, were a cause of implacable hatred. Aribert called up the Bishops and Counts of Lombardy ; a fierce and murderous battle began on the ' Campo Malo ' near the Motta, but without bringing about a decision. The Archbishop realised that the danger was more serious than he had thought and had recourse to the Emperor. He naturally came without delay ; but whether he saw through the ambitious schemes of Aribert, or whether he yielded to the complaints which were raised in many parts and particularly by Cremona against him on account of his prepotence and usurpations, the result was that, having become suspicious of him, the Emperor's mind was set on reducing the power of the all too powerful Metropolitan.

Events showed what a long road the people had travelled meanwhile, and of what prompt and energetic collective action they proved capable. Whether the rumour spread among the people

that the Emperor meant to take Lodi again away
from the Archbishop, or whether they wished to
incline the Emperor in favour of the valvassours
who, if they did not fight for the same interests
as the people, yet enlisted some sympathy even
among them, since they too were oppressed and on
the point of following the example of popular
action, it is anyway certain that Conrad, no sooner
in Milan, was forced very speedily to leave in face
of a mass rising. A more serious development
occurred soon afterwards, when Aribert, called to
the Diet of Pavia to defend himself against the
accusations pending against him, appeared there
and protested that he would not give up a single
right or property of S. Ambrogio. The Emperor
in full session caused him to be imprisoned and
handed over to the custody of the Patriarch of
Aquileia. The people of Milan then realised that
the safety of each lay in the concord of all. In the
eyes of the people, Aribert, as prisoner, stood for
St. Ambrose and for Milan, herself suffering
violence ; and when Aribert audaciously escaping
from custody, came back to Milan which his
imprisonment had cast into mourning, the kindling
and then the outbursts of general joyous enthusiasm
swallowed up suspicions and hatred and anger.
The different classes, high and low, weak and
powerful, fused into a single force to place themselves under the orders of Aribert, and taking up
arms, vowed with lips and hearts that they would
die rather than yield. Milan was surrounded and
besieged, and for the first time history witnessed
the spectacle of an Emperor who had to retire
before an Italian city defended only by its citizens
and its Bishop. It need hardly be mentioned that
the Emperor had declared Aribert deprived of all
his honours and had easily obtained from the
Pope his excommunication and deposition, and the
recognition in his place of a Canon of the Metro-

politan Church, Ambrose, whose property was immediately destroyed by the populace. Benedict IX stood too much in need of the toleration of everyone and most of all of the Emperor to have missed this opportunity to secure it.

Not all, however, condemned Aribert : even Conrad's son and future successor, Henry III, disapproved of his father's rigour against the Archbishop whose cause had not yet been submitted to the impartial and competent judgment of a Council, as it should have been. But Aribert knew only too well how to defend himself. Continuing the negotiations which the Milanese had opened, while he had been prisoner, he offered the crown of Italy to Odo, Duke of Champagne, whom he himself only shortly before, crossing the Alps with a strong army, had helped to bring into subjection to the Emperor.

Conrad adopted another expedient to break the strong coalition that had formed round the person of Aribert : he made the cause of the valvassours his own and by the Constitution of 1037 assured them of the hereditary possession of their benefices. If, on the one hand, this measure obtained for him a few more men faithful to his service, it is certain, on the other, that it marked but another step towards the levelling-out of the social classes and the destruction of the feudal system.

Finally, before his return to Germany, Conrad took an oath from the Italian nobles that they would every year make war upon the rebellious city and devastate her lands. But just then Aribert reached the peak of his success. He proclaimed the fatherland to be in danger, called to arms everyone capable of bearing them both in Milan and outside, and invented the ' Carroccio.' With its tall mast and its white banner, with its great cross and the image of Christ crucified extending his arms over the surrounding army and blessing the people, the

Carroccio, setting out from the Cathedral near which it was housed, was indeed an emblem for a people that rose up in the name of St. Ambrose with its Bishop at its head. If in its numerous imitations the Carroccio achieved success in other cities, in Milan it accomplished miracles. Meanwhile Conrad died. Even before his death he had bequeathed the crown to his son, Henry, who, favourably inclined to Aribert who came in 1040 to do homage to him at Ingelheim, received him again in his favour and found in him a faithful follower ; there can be no doubt that, thanks to this imperial favour, Aribert was also reconciled with the Pope, since imperial disfavour had been the whole cause of the rupture.

What were Aribert's motives for doing homage to the Emperor ? Perhaps he was weary of the struggle ; perhaps he wished to secure the support of the sovereign against the power of the people whose strength had proved even then so great in the fight against the valvassours, while the latter's importance had also been increased by Conrad's Constitution ; it is still more probable, I believe, that his own political programme was neither as vast nor as radical as some later writers have liked to assume.

However it may have been—the return to the former situation was not complete : in drawing up contracts, our forefathers henceforth refused to mention the year of the Empire, and stated only that of the Incarnation.

THE POWER OF THE ARCHBISHOP AND ITS CAUSES

Having reached with Aribert the apex of the rising curve which represents the conquest of civil and political prerogatives by the Milanese Archbishops, we seize this opportunity to cast a glance back upon the long road covered and to look for the causes of such success.

Without giving way to general and abstract considerations, we may indulge for a moment in the so-called ' philosophy of history.' Such a philosophy replaces only too often the real events and the no less real rights which have sprung from them in particular circumstances, by purely personal notions and theories that have never existed outside the mind of the philosopher and are often in flagrant contradiction with the events and the documents, on which they are supposed to be based.

But we must not indulge in visions of ambitious ideals, of grandiose programmes of political hegemony and ecclesiastical independence, programmes audaciously conceived and religiously handed on or inherited, systematically developed and executed, sometimes with the boldness of a personal consciousness of power, sometimes with the pretence of the peaceable submissiveness of him who ' serves while dreaming of the crown.'[1] The very events which we have sketched, give us warning that we would thus become merely the victims of a mental mirage. They tell us that here happened what happens in almost all things of this world, where nothing is really rarer than a predetermined plan ; they tell us, that here too one thing sprang from another according to the circumstances of the moment and insensibly created conditions, as the result of a fateful development which a will other than our own impresses upon things on this earth. Historians have tried in vain to find the ' Count's Diploma ' which transferred to our Archbishops the political power with which we find them invested ; very likely every search will, for good and all, prove unsuccessful. More and more overshadowed by the predominance of the Archbishop, losing more and more of their authority, reduced

[1] Quotation from Alessandro Manzoni's poem, ' Il Cinque Maggio ' on the death of Napoleon I : ' . . . un cor che indocile *serve pensando al regno.*' (*Translator's note.*)

to little more than passing supernumeraries, the counts continue to exist all the same in Milan ; we find them there still about the middle of the eleventh century. It looks as if the distant Emperors welcomed the dualism which the counts preserved, at least nominally and in principle, as long as they were or might serve in the hands of Cæsar as a weight, which, skilfully used, could be employed to balance somehow the authority of these powerful Archbishops. In smaller and less important cities the same need cannot have been felt, and there the ' Count's Diploma ' could be and was issued with greater readiness. In Milan other factors had operated with more effect than any Diploma could have done, so as to render it in point of fact useless.

Consider the position of Milan in Italy and the great name and immortal memory of St. Ambrose, the personal qualities of many of his successors and the juridical situation created for the Bishops and the clergy by the Roman-Christian Law, a situation variously but constantly maintained also by Odo-acer, by the Goths and the Longobards. Consider in particular the great favours and privileges granted to the Bishops, the clergy and the churches, by the Carlovingian sovereigns and by their legisla-tion, the immense wealth donated to ' St. Ambrose,' as the phrase went, the precedence which our Archbishops enjoyed as a matter of course among the Italian nobility, and the part which they therefore played in the elections and coronations of the Kings of Italy. If we bear all this in mind, there will be little left, I believe, that remains obscure or unexplained in the happenings which reached their full development with Aribert of Entimiano, even though there be no reason for thinking that these happenings had to come inevitably.

Having reached its height with Aribert, the political power of our Archbishops had also reached

the edge of that slope, down which we shall see it
not descend, but precipitate. We see the symptoms
and the beginning even during Aribert's lifetime :
fresh and ever clearer indications of the coming
to power of the people.

During the struggles of the last years, the populace
had displayed and increased both its strength and
a consciousness of it. Yet it must be admitted that
it had reaped but little in the way of practical
results. The increased power of the valvassours
had merely added to the number and the prepotence of the masters whose tyranny oppressed
the people. Its anger gathered rapidly, and soon
their minds were in that sort of tension when any
occasion gives rise to a great explosion. A wound
inflicted by a valvassour on a man of the people
roused the whole populace against the nobles who
in that first outburst of anger were driven out of the
city, but soon, returning for the attack, laid siege
to it. One point is notable : it is not the Archbishop this time who was arbiter in the dispute,
but a nobleman, Lanzone, another glorious name,
who sided with the people, while the Archbishop
took the part of the nobles and left the city with
them.

Extreme necessity, rarely a wise councillor,
prompted Lanzone to call in the Emperor ; but
thinking better of it, he himself, to forestall the
descent of the Emperor, secured peace and concord
between the warring parties. The peace was
sealed by an oath in 1015 : the nobles renounced,
even though more out of fear of the Emperor than
for other reasons, the fruit of their victory and the
vengeance which they believed in their power, and
agreed to return peaceably to the city, while
Royal Messengers proclaimed and confirmed with
oaths the mutual pardon and perpetual truce as
the result of the deliberations and with the
authority of the whole kingdom.

The circumstances here mentioned and others too long to report, seem to exclude the possibility that the Commune was established here as early as in the year 1045, a view which has found and still finds distinguished champions. The three orders, nobility, clergy and people are indeed more clearly distinguished and brought into closer contact in the documents of the time ; it is also noticeable that there is an awareness of important new changes having taken place ; but there is no proof that innovations have gone beyond this and that the people, the real people, have come into possession of the government of the commonweal ; for if it is stated that the successor of Aribert was elected in that same year 1045 by the concourse of all the citizens, it seems that this term still implies merely the nobles, while the people themselves apparently took no active part in it. The fully formed Commune was to be the result of the religious struggles about to break out.

Aribert ended his toilsome life on January 17, 1045 and was buried in S. Dionigi, as is recorded still to-day on a stone tablet near Porta Venezia. Thence, when the Church of S. Dionigi was demolished in 1783, his remains were transferred to the Cathedral, to the granite tomb which stands in the southern aisle. He had been a great benefactor of that Church to which he had added a complete monastery. This was not the only display of his munificent zeal as a pastor. Other churches and monasteries benefited largely by it, both during his lifetime and by his generous will ; so also did the poor of Milan and of the surrounding country during the long time of dearth that lasted for the first eight years of his reign, when he poured out his wealth in relief. While intrigues and political and military factions could not but be fatal to ecclesiastical discipline, it is only fair to note that Aribert has the merit of having introduced canonical order into the life of many of the churches. This should suffice by itself to rebut the accusation made without any basis in fact, that he had favoured concubinage among the clergy, setting even the example himself by having taken a wife, Usseria, who is a sheer invention and legend.

It is the sheer truth, on the other hand, and wholly in accord with the character of Aribert, that he displayed the utmost energy in the defence and exercise of his Metropolitan rights. He exercised it in the diocese of Asti, putting down by force of arms certain sectarians, half-heretical half-socialistic. They were reduced to order, but were against his will—*nolente Ariberto*—forced by the violence of the nobles, who showed little obedience to the Archbishop, to chose between abjuration and the stake. He defended his right against the Bishop of Pavia, of whom Aribert, though he might no longer claim his submission, demanded at least a more modest attitude in his presence (if we may presume that the writer who informs us of this, writing within the same century, is correct, at least in substance). He also defended his right in Rome against Ravenna, as we shall see.

The Metropolitan rights of the See of Milan had by then suffered various restrictions and became the object of attack from various sides, so that in regard to it the opposite may be said to have happened of what occurred in regard to its political powers. The elevation of Aquileia and Ravenna to the position of Metropolitan Sees was old history : the greater part of the churches of Rhætia Secunda, or Vindelicia, of Venetia and Emilia had passed into their jurisdiction and had been withdrawn from that of Milan. In the ninth century Chur of Rhætia Prima, and Augsburg had passed into the Metropolitan jurisdiction of Mayence. But the memory of the ancient relations with Milan and a sympathy for the Ambrosian Rite persisted in the churches beyond the Alps right down to the twelfth century. We have mentioned the independence of the Bishop of Pavia at the beginning of the eighth century ; and the attitude of John VIII is significant :—he tended actually to subordinate Milan to Pavia ; a tendency towards creating a rival to Milan in Aquileia has even been suspected in the fact that about the middle of the ninth century Pavia was placed under the protection of St. Hermagoras who is the Patron-Saint of the Patriarchate of Aquileia. At any rate, by the end of that same century, Como, which had first belonged to Milan, was part of the province of Aquileia and remained such down to the beginning of the nineteenth century.

While thus on the one side the suffragans escaped from the jurisdiction of the Milanese Metropolitan See, its historical claims to being the first see in Italy after Rome had begun to be contested. Indeed Aquileia, soon after the middle of the tenth century, had contested it with success, and had obtained the first place among the Italian sees after Rome. It had claimed, as early as the eighth century, the rights of a Patriarchate mainly on the strength of a tradition which held St. Mark to have been its founder, and it was surely not an accident that Aribert, during his imprisonment, was given in charge of the Patriarch of Aquileia. Then Ravenna also rose to claim precedence. The ancient order : Milan, Aquileia, Ravenna, changed to : Aquileia, Milan, Ravenna and was more than once debated and modified. In 1027 on the occasion of the solemn consecration of Conrad II in Rome, the Archbishop of Ravenna boldly occupied the first place, in the presence of Aribert ; fierce disputes arose ; once more the Metropolitan of Milan won the day, and his claim was recognised and confirmed by the Pope in full Council, a few days afterwards. But the attitude which the Archbishops of Milan and, latterly, Aribert had repeatedly adopted in the political party-strife, was not calculated to predispose Rome to a final solution in favour of their see. Indeed when the decision was taken in 1047 by decree of Clement II in the time of Guido, the immediate successor of Aribert, the third place was assigned to the Archbishop of Milan, the first being given to Ravenna and the second to Aquileia. It would seem that the legend of St. Barnabas took shape here in Milan under the influence of these circumstances. It represents the main issue of these disputes. It was not equality with Rome which was asserted by Milan ; Milan was to be the second see equipped with certain traditional privileges, like that of receiving the Pallium as the unquestionable symbol of its subjection (but without having to go to Rome to fetch it). To claim as the founder of the see an Apostle of second rank, seemed to meet the case. Nor was it a wholesale invention. That St. Barnabas had been the first Bishop of Milan had been falsely asserted in Greek catalogues as early as the seventh century. Produced now—as we can well imagine, in perfect good faith—as a weapon of defence at the right moment, the legend was accepted even officially in the liturgical books and the catalogues of our Archbishops : though this would seem to have happened not before the thirteenth century—too late, as is evident. Very much later still, in the sixteenth century, appeared certain inscriptions explicitly supporting the legend and supplying it with proofs from the eighth and even the fourth centuries—if they were genuine. These inscriptions have been the object of recent research ; but as far as St. Barnabas is concerned, they continue to be, it seems, a spurious work, or, if you prefer to put it in this way, a literary exercise of that famous jurist of ours,

Alciato.[1] The restriction of the Metropolitan authority of our Archbishops was the prelude to the decay of their political power which was as rapid as the formation and constitution of the Commune during the years that followed upon the death of Aribert. Up to this point, as we have seen, the events of our political history are the background and explanation of the events of our religious history ; henceforth the political vicissitudes are carried along by, and as it were, form part of the religious developments. It is from the struggles against concubinage, simony and investitures that the formation of the Commune resulted. It was a half-century of party-strife, contests, disputes and bloodshed, a half-century in which the spirit of the Middle Ages is revealed in all its fullness.

FIGHT AGAINST DISORDERS. THE PATARINES

We have indicated the manner in which these three grave disorders emerged and took root. The Lombard churches, at their head that of Milan, can be said to have been their sadly characteristic scene. Contemporary writers have left us terrifying descriptions of the deplorable conditions into which the ecclesiastical orders and everything that depended on them, had fallen.

It must be noted that in several of these writers the colours of their pictures are sometimes deliberately, sometimes unwittingly exaggerated, according to the party to which the writer belongs. It must also be observed that the wretchedness of the conditions appears perhaps greater than it actually was. We are placed at so great a distance and almost in the impossibility of reconstructing completely the social environment, of picturing to ourselves and of assessing with fairness all the adjustments

[1] See the essay : 'St. Charles and the Alciati Family,' pp. 115 ff. (*Translator's note.*)

G

which, then as always, are bound to temper, according to circumstances, even the most absolute principles when they are applied to concrete human events and are used as standards. The very presence of a party of order, its power and its speedy predominance, might go to prove that corruption was neither general nor far-reaching.

The clergy, tainted with concubinage and simony, found, as we saw, in the circumstances created by feudalism, a natural ally in the nobility of which the higher clergy formed part. A contemporary writer in a few vividly revealing phrases, points to the nobles as the real sellers of churches and the blood-relations of clerical concubines. Still, the party of order did not lack representatives among the higher clergy and the nobility, and it was particularly these that gave it strength by their direction. But it found support and powerful agents also among the people. This term is not meant to indicate only the lower populace, although it was perhaps after them that the clergy charged with concubinage called their opponents ' Patarines' or ' Pataria' (a gang of ragamuffins)— whether in an attempt to use the weapon of ridicule where that of reason failed, or in one of those verbal revenges in which a tottering cause indulges. The ' Patarines' retaliated with the defamatory name of ' Nicholites' which they gave to their enemies. From our point of view, we must not lose sight of the fact that the people had a reason of their own for supporting the ' ragamuffins'; they were merely continuing their fight, begun earlier, against the nobility, and it is from their victory over them, not from their fusion with them, that the communal order, in fact, emerged.

The close connexion between incontinence, simony and investitures on the one side, and, on the other, the ruthless war which the Popes declared against these disorders, naturally ranked the Papacy and the people together against the Empire. The incontinent and simoniacal clergy, on the other hand, proclaimed in defence of their convenient vices and their ill-gotten wealth, the honour of St. Ambrose, the prerogatives of the Milanese Church and the independence from the yoke of Rome— large words which naturally were not without repercussions, then and later. Though it is an exaggeration to see in all the partisans of the disorders examples of deliberate vice and of bad faith, and though inveterate habits, sanctioned by high example and the harsh and rough social *milieu* and ignorance and misinterpretations of the canons might invest the disorders with some appearance of a peaceful legality, all this in no way detracts from the reality of the disorders themselves or from their overt contradiction to the canonical prescriptions which had never fallen into abeyance.

ANSELM, LANDOLF, ARIALD, ERLEMBALD

Two of the principal priests of the Metropolitan Church, Anselm of Baggio, later Bishop of Lucca and finally Pope Alexander II, and Landolf Cotta, a deacon of noble birth, Ariald, and a rich layman Nazario, director of the Mint, stood at the head of the party of order and reform, when the struggle broke out.

The occasion for it was the election of Aribert's successor. In place of four names, including that of Anselm, presented by the clergy and nobles of Milan, the Emperor preferred a country priest, Guido da Velate, belonging neither to the nobility nor to the higher clergy, and granted him investiture with ring and staff. Suspicion credited him with doubtful merits damaging to Aribert, with having procured his elevation by simony, and with having made concessions prejudicial to the State of Milan. But even without all this, after the fierce collision with the Empire, a man elected by the

caprice of the Emperor could not longer be an
Archbishop acceptable to the people, nor could a
plebeian Archbishop be welcome to the nobility.
A connexion existed perhaps between all this and
an attempt of the nobility to recapture and usurp
the whole government of the city, with the conse-
quent exile of Lanzone, and positively unjust
provisions were decreed against the people, exasper-
ating them still further against the nobility and the
clergy, who belonged to or sided with it.

As soon as Anselm set to work on a reform, the
Archbishop endeavoured quietly to cut the ground
underneath his feet, and seemed partly to succeed.
In 1056 Anselm was appointed to the Bishopric of
Lucca. It was a promotion but also a removal ;
for Guido it was a defeat. Ariald and Landolf,
however, remained and began in that year to
rouse the people by frequent addresses directed
against priests guilty of concubinage and simony,
exposing them to the contempt and ostracism of
the people. Guido thought he might tame and
silence them ; but worse befell : angry scenes
occurred ; tumult followed on tumult ; there was no
lack of violence which made the guilty men into
the martyrs of oppression : they appealed to the
Archbishop, to the suffragans, to Rome. Stephen
IX, badly informed, ordered a Provincial Council
which in fact assembled at Fontaneto in the
district of Novara, and there Ariald and Landolf,
summoned to it, but naturally not putting in an
appearance, were excommunicated.

The good cause was for the moment in great
difficulties, but managed soon to master them.
The two champions made their way to Rome.
Landolf was wounded on the road and Ariald
arrived alone ; he was able to throw light on the
real state of things. Henceforth happenings press
on each other ; two Legates were dispatched from
Rome : they were Anselm of Baggio and that

Hildebrand who later became Gregory VII. The Archbishop and his party were condemned ; the city took heart again ; vehement disputes, violent action, fierce reprisals began afresh.

Meanwhile Stephen IX had been succeeded by Victor II (1059). Anselm was again at Milan, in company with Peter Damian, Bishop of Ostia ; their authority, their energy and presence of mind in face of the inconstancy of the populace who had allowed themselves to be persuaded that the honour of St. Ambrose and of his Church was at stake, forced the simoniacal party to a formal surrender : restitution and pardon settled the past and a solemn oath provided for the future, an oath which Guido renewed in full Council in Rome, where the reform movement received fresh encouragement.

But it was on the part of Guido and of the simoniacs mere pretence ; only it secured a respite, though even this was stained with blood by the wars of Ghiara d'Adda and Pavia.

Meanwhile Landolf died in 1062 and was succeeded by a knight, Erlembald, the attractive figure of an ex-crusader, attractive then and later, despite the calumnies of the simoniacs against the integrity of his spotless life. Having gone to Rome with Ariald in 1064, they came back from there with the encouragement and instructions of Anselm who had become Alexander II and had made Erlembald ' Confaloniere ' and Defender of the Church.

The Patarine party awoke to vigorous action on their return, but again vigour degenerated into violence which provoked reaction, all the stronger owing to the lavish use of money. Erlembald and Ariald were forced to flee ; shamefully betrayed, the deacon fell a victim to a horrible murder (June 28, 1066), a true martyr whom only two years later Alexander II added to the list of Saints. The people who in spite of its natural inconstancy had remained Patarine, loyally surrounded at once his tomb with the honours and the veneration given to a Saint.

The triumph of Guido lasted only a short time. Unable to maintain himself, he sold the Archbishopric to Godfrey, the favourite of Henry IV. When he granted him the investiture, the citizens drove him out and the Pope excommunicated him ; Erlembald pursued him and besieged him in Castiglione near Varese, and was only prevented from capturing him by the tremendous fire in Milan which has remained famous under the name of the ' Fire of Castiglione.'

Guido died in 1071. This was the occasion when Erlembald presented the question of Archiepiscopal elections in definite terms : no one shall be received as Archbishop unless he be canonically elected, whatever the Emperor may do. Thereupon Atto was elected in 1072. But fresh discords and violence arose from the election and Atto had to renounce the See, even before he was consecrated or inducted into possession of it. After that the city returned to the allegiance of Erlembald. The exasperation of the anti-reform clergy and nobility broke out afresh, when Erlembald was joined by a priest, Liprand, an eager mind, but inclining to excess, who even went so far as to refuse to recognise the simoniacal Suffragan Bishops and to administer solemn baptisms in their stead. People again took up arms and Erlembald fell, considered and honoured as a martyr to the good cause, as undeniably he was. But the ' raggamuffin ' party had been defeated ; Liprand had been captured and had had his nose and ears cut off, and Henry IV again intervened and in 1075 created Tedaldo Archbishop, while both Atto and Godfrey were still alive. The ' Pataria ' partisans, defeated but still in good order, rose again under another knight, Vifred. True, he was not an Erlembald ; but then, neither was Tedaldo Aribert ; and meanwhile Henry was going to Canossa, and who would receive popular support soon became evident when the Bishops of Ostia and Lucca, the Legates of Gregory VII, having come to Milan to absolve the city from the Interdict provoked by Henry's partisans, were joyfully welcomed despite the impotent anger and vain resistance of Tedaldo.

Silence leaves the last ten years of his life in dark shadow. He was succeeded in 1086 by Anselm III from Rò, who having received the dignity at the hands of Henry IV, renounced it in order to receive it from the Pope who also sent him the Pallium. The example of Anselm found imitators and the ideals of order and discipline made another advance under his successor, Arnold III, who, as he had been consecrated by only one Bishop, withdrew, on the intimation of the Legate, into private life, from which he issued again only in 1095, when Urban II, passing through Milan on the way to the Council of Clermont from that of Piacenza, had him duly consecrated and gave him the Pallium. This was the occasion of the canonisation of Erlembald by Urban.

ANSELM DA BOVISIO AND THE CRUSADES

When Ariald and Erlembald amidst general rejoicing were raised to the dignity of the altars and papal authority decided the elections, it can be said with justice that the struggles against simony, incontinence and investitures had reached their end and that the ideals of order had triumphed. As this triumph had, as will be evident, been accompanied by that of Rome, it is impossible not to recognise the advantage which it brought to the latter. The symptoms and results of this victory were immediately felt under Anselm IV of Bovisio, *De Buis* (1097–1101). He made his whole Metropolitan authority felt against Oberto, who had

been intruded into the See of Brescia by the
Emperor, and in support of Armanno, who had
been legitimately elected. Anselm, in 1098, summoned to Milan an important Council, among the
signatories of which were also some foreign Bishops,
for the full re-establishment of discipline and order
after all the past storms. Under him the cult of St.
Ariald received a further impetus and that great
and characteristic event of those times, the Crusades,
found a profound echo among our forefathers.
Here, on July 15, Anselm celebrated the first
anniversary of the capture of Jerusalem, when he
restored, in the likeness to the Church of the Holy
Sepulchre and dedicating it to the Holy Sepulchre,
the Church which still bears that name and had
been built sixty years before in honour of the Holy
Trinity. The Archbishop, ' having assembled all
the ecclesiastics and the people, by the general
advice of all,' granted the permanence of this feast
together with large indulgences, and further sanctioned *ante magistratum* a truce ' for the whole of
our County,' as he said, of eight days before and
after the Feast, in order to facilitate the concourse
of all for its celebration. Three years earlier,
perhaps the same Anselm IV had issued similar
orders for the Feast of the Saints Gervase and
Protase ' with the common advice of all the city.'
Towards August of the year 1100, our Archbishop
with the Provosts of S. Nazaro and S. Ambrogio,
set out on a crusade to the Holy Land with an
army of about 50,000 Lombards—those Lombards
of the First Crusade who were to have so little success
in the verses of Grossi but became so popular
and dear to all Italy in the music of Verdi.[1]

[1] Tommaso Grossi (1790–1853) made an unsuccessful
attempt to write an Epic (in 15 books) on the subject under
the title : ' I Lombardi alla prima Crociata.' In 1843 Verdi
produced one of his earlier operas under the same title, the
subject being taken from Grossi's poem, and achieved a great
success. (*Translator's note.*)

Anselm died in Constantinople in 1101 and was buried there in the monastery of St. Nicholas.

THE FIGHT AGAINST SIMONY AND INVESTITURES
CONTINUED

The fight against simony flared up again for some time when in 1101 Chrysolas, Bishop of Savona, who had been left behind by Anselm as his Vicar-General, was elected as his successor. He was a native of Greece, not without learning, who had won distinction in the dogmatic disputes with the Greeks, as a surviving work of his proves. Thanks to his manners and his way of dressing, or perhaps rather as a humorous disfigurement of his foreign name, the populace called him ' Grosso-lano ' (' Yokel '). He was accused of simony by the priest Liprand, who was supported by a part of the people. Liprand was willing to sustain his accusation by undergoing the ordeal by fire in the Piazza Sant' Ambrogio, and passed through it unscathed. There is mention of a ' general assembly ' and of persons ' elected to the assembly ' and of ' ministers of the republic ' charged with the affair. But behind Liprand the nobility were hiding and the populace remained divided. New struggles arose from the divisions and Grossolano had to leave the city.

A Council held in Rome in 1105 declared his innocence and restored him to his See. But it was in vain that, supported by his party, he occupied Arona ; he was driven out and had to leave for the Holy Land. Meanwhile the war had broken out in the course of which Lodi was destroyed by the Milanese in 1111. Extraordinary storms, taken for a chastisement by God, turned people's minds again to Grossolano ; a conference of the nobles, clergy and people elected by the assembly, brought the matter up again for discussion and a decision taken by them replaced Grossolano by Jordan II in 1112.

In effect the popular party won the day, as it had done in the great days of the ' Pataria.'

At this time, to complete the story, the question of the investitures again gave signs of life. When Grossolano on his return in 1113, tried to rely on imperial favour, the Pope granted his recognition to Jordan, who after bloody fights, drove his rival out of the city and remained alone, recognised by everyone, in the face of all claims of imperial rights.

The Fourth Lateran Council gave in full canonical form its ultimate sanction to these happenings and Grossolano was able to return to Savona, but not without having made a declaration on his part against the Emperor.

In 1117 the Bishops and cities of Lombardy were gathered together in a Council or General Assembly, and in these solemn circumstances the title of ' consul ' appears for the first time.

The assembly was convoked by the Archbishop and the consuls ; but it is not to the Archbishop, but to the consuls, captains, the whole militia and the entire people of Milan that the leader of the opposition to Henry V, the Archbishop Frederic of Cologne, addressed words of praise and encouragement.

In 1117 a diploma sent to the Bishop and nobles of Lodi, dependent on the Archbishop (under the aforementioned grant of Conrad) also in temporal matters, is still signed by the Archbishop besides the consuls. But in 1125 Archbishop Ulric himself decided that, if the Bishop of Lodi were obliged to answer before him in spiritual as well as in temporal matters, the Bishop of Tortona had to answer in spiritual matters alone. When three years later Conrad of Swabia came to Milan, recognised by the people as King of Italy and received with all honours, there is no evidence that Archbishop Anselm V took any part in deciding these grave matters, but only heard of them during his absence from Milan ; and his chief chaplain, sent by him to explore the situation, found the assembly already sitting for its deliberations.

THE SIGNS OF THE TIMES

We can now summarise the various signs of the times. The people have the upper hand ; the Council or General Assembly decides in public affairs, even against the Emperor and the Archbishop ; the Archbishop himself is constantly losing ground, even to the extent of disappearing from the political government, his authority being restricted to spiritual matters ; ministers and deputies are elected by the Assembly itself ; the consuls have, at first together with the Archbishop, and later alone, the mandate and general representation. This is the upshot of the last struggles and comprises the full meaning of the ' Commune.'

While in the foregoing events it is not easy to trace any influence which the classical ideas of the Roman ' Municipium ' may have exercised on the formation of the new Commune, there is not the least difficulty in observing in them the causes of the rapid decline of archiepiscopal power and the rise of the people.

The lack of moderation of Archbishops like Landolf and Aribert had aroused the reaction of the nobles ; the prepotence of these incited that of the people. The people, who in their first conflict with the nobility and the Emperor had occasion to test their strength, had increased and disciplined it by uniting and co-ordinating it in practice. Concubinage, simony and the investitures, while bringing several of Aribert's successors and the nobility into discredit and showing the weakness inherent in all bad causes, had also produced heroic leaders for the people, the support of Rome and above all the enthusiasm and invincible

conscience of a good and holy cause ; and while
the incessant troubles of these conflicts made it
impossible for the Archbishops to govern, it placed
the people in the position of arbiter and trained
them to act for themselves.

The question has been asked whether the
possession of political authority by our Archbishops has been good, or perhaps bad for our
country.

The question would be very embarrassing, if we
considered the maintenance and increase of the
religious spirit and the effectiveness of ecclesiastical
discipline in themselves. But if we bear in mind
the personal excellence, the munificence, the true
charity of so many of our Archbishops, the importance and the manifold advantages that could not
but accrue to the city by their position as Metropolitans and doyens among the Italian magnates ;
if we remember that under their rule the men were
formed who with them and under their guidance
proved able to defend so successfully the first
' Carroccio,' it would be difficult to establish and
accept the assertion that their possession of such
power was an evil for the country.

THE CONDITIONS OF THE CHURCH IN MILAN
IN THE TWELFTH CENTURY

Having arrived at this fullness of the times,
when the Church in Milan with her Archbishop
retired from the political sphere and returned to
the Sanctuary with the treasure of so great a past,
purged and cleansed in the fire of reform, the
moment has come to consider what she had become
in what most truly belonged to her : in the extent
and exercise of the spiritual authority, in the clergy
and the hierarchical developments, the sacred
buildings and the practices of the cult, in pious and
charitable foundations, in her influence upon ideas
and the life of both individuals and society.

The ecclesiastical province is no longer as large as it had been. We noted the curtailments which had resulted from the constitution of the ecclesiastical provinces of Ravenna, Aquileia and Mayence. Still, it covered a considerable area. Up to the first years of the twelfth century, sixteen Bishoprics formed part of it: Brescia, Bergamo, Cremona, Lodi, Novara, Ivrea (Aosta had become part of the Metropolitan See of Tarantasia), Turin, Alba, Asti, Acqui, Tortona, Vercelli, Genoa, Savona, Albenga and Ventimiglia. More than a century back, the Bishopric of Bobbio had been added, if it belonged to Milan since its foundation in 1014 as it certainly did in 1059. In 1132 Bobbio was lost to Milan owing to the creation of the Metropolitan See of Genoa, followed soon afterwards by those of Savona and of Albenga. It was a loss compensated to some extent by the decree of Alexander III in 1162 that no further suffragans were to be removed from Milan, and by the creation in 1174 of the episcopal See of Alessandria which was made subject to Milan.

Apart from the prerogatives of honour and of jurisdiction which Canon Law conferred on the Metropolitan, the Archbishop of Milan must have enjoyed and exercised many other special rights, as the legend could arise that his suffragans at one time rendered him a service of honour and assistance, taking, to use the common phrase, ' their turn ' week by week. It was an obligation, as the legend asserts and as may well be believed, that proved extremely inconvenient for the more distantly placed Bishops, like those of Ivrea or Aosta, with the result that some measures of relief had to be devised.

It is not easy and perhaps impossible to define the limits of the diocese in the twelfth century.

It is known that, as at present, the diocese was divided into parishes. At the head of the parishes

were the parish churches, or so-called ' baptismal '
churches as being those in which at first baptism
was administered ; from these sprang up later
smaller parishes, as the churches and chapels of
ease in the parishes, originally served by the parish
clergy, received priests of their own and were
assigned their own areas, not, however, without
ties of hierarchical and administrative obedience
to the parish churches.

At the head of these parishes and of their clergy
were placed priests of eminence, first with the title
of Custodians, later of Archpriests and Provosts.

Every parish church had or was held to have a
school, and there was a large number of hospitals
and hospices, refuges for the infirm, hostels for
travellers and pilgrims, especially in the neighbourhood of monasteries.

Starting with the ninth century Canonries began
to spring up by the side of parish or other notable
churches, where the clergy concerned led a communal life according to the canons, whence precisely came the name of ' Canonry ' and ' Canons.'
Though it is impossible to establish the number of
parishes in the twelfth century, we find in the
thirteenth century no less than fifty-seven parishes
which together formed the diocese, with twenty-five
hospitals and about 2000 churches and more than
sixty Canonries.

Our information concerning the city itself is a
little more precise. In a document of Archbishop
Jordan of 1119, eleven mother churches are mentioned : Sta Maria Maggiore, Sta Tecla and S.
Giorgio within the walls ; outside the walls, Sant'
Ambrogio, S. Lorenzo, Sant' Eustorgio, S. Nazaro,
S. Stefano, S. Dionigi, S. Naborre and S. Martino,
this last-named in place of the ' Porziana ' which had
been handed over to the monks at the beginning of
the eleventh century. The more notable among the
minor churches or chapels numbered no less than

ten. Parishes were gradually formed in the course of the ninth and tenth centuries, each church being assigned its proper surrounding area.

The convents of nuns within the walls of the city since the days of Aribert amounted to seven, with perhaps as many abbeys of monks. There are numerous hospitals and orphanages for children, refuges for poor pilgrims, men and women separately, and for ecclesiastics. At the end of the thirteenth century there were about 200 churches in Milan, some small, some large, of which at least seventy were Canonries, with at least eleven, perhaps fifteen, hospitals attached to them.

A sort of sacred citadel had gradually taken shape within the centre of the city. There stood the two old venerable Basilicas, Sta Maria Maggiore to the East and Sta Tecla to the West. The former always remained the primary Basilica, but as early as the ninth century the Chapter used it only during the winter months, passing from the one to the other with curious ceremonial. Hence came the terms ' Winter Church ' and ' Summer Church,' which frequently occur in old texts. Six minor churches surrounded the larger : to the North the church of S. Raphael, to the South that of S. Uriel (the name of the angel in Esdra IV, an apocryphal book which, however, St. Ambrose quotes as Sacred Scripture), to the South-east S. Michael, S. Gabriel to the North-west, and to the South-west S. Giovanni with the Baptistery for men, to the North-east S. Stefano with a Baptistery for women. Near by in a little convent lived the nuns deputed to officiate at the baptisms in S. Stefano, to meet the requirements of the most delicate feelings. When later the nuns were transferred to the convent of Vigelinda in Sta Radegonda, they still preserved for a long time the memory of their ancient function. Living almost like nuns and charged with the menial services in the churches, were the ' scriptane,' so-called perhaps because their names were entered in a register for the purpose. Near the little Church of S. Gabriele stood the house of the ' decuman' priests, and the tall campanile of Sta Maria ; near the Church of S. Michele was the house of the Ordinaries and the old Archiepiscopal Palace, also called ' Ambrosian Palace,' or ' House (*domus*) of St. Ambrose,' whence the Church was also called *San Michele sul Domo*, and ' Domo ' or ' Duomo,' the Cathedral itself. The old palace which had been destroyed in the days of Barbarossa, was rebuilt by the Archbishop St. Galdinus.

All these churches, rectories and religious houses depended directly on the Archbishop. But as early as the time of Anspert, the Monastery of S. Ambrogio had sought the protection of the Emperor, and in 1099 the aforementioned priest Liprand had obtained the protection of Rome for his little church, perhaps, among other reasons, to use it as a refuge in those turbulent days. These were examples that were widely followed, and the result was that the archiepiscopal authority was gradually diminished by numerous exemptions of this kind.

HIERARCHICAL ORDERS WITHIN THE CLERGY

Mentioning ' Ordinaries ' and ' Decumans,' I have indicated the two principal orders into which the city clergy of Milan was divided. The first and highest was that of the ' Ordinaries ' (*ordinarii* or *de ordine*), or ' Cardinals.' Originally these terms meant usually priests destined—or, as the expression went, ' ordinati,' or ' incardinati '—for a particular church. In the tenth century this title was still given to priests attached to baptismal or parish churches of the diocese. But later the name became peculiar to the main clergy of the Metropolitan Church. More than that : ' ordinarii,' properly so-called, were only the twenty priests of the whole

Order or greater Chapter. In this Chapter, under
the presidence of the Archpriest and Archdeacon,
all the ecclesiastical orders were represented :
priests, deacons and subdeacons. From among its
members the ' cimiliarcas ' or treasurer, the ' vice-
dominus ' or deputy or vicar-general of the Archbishop, and the ' custodians ' of the most important
churches were elected ; by its vote and generally
from among its members the Archbishop himself
was chosen. Together with the Archbishop, the
' Ordinaries ' signed all diplomas and decrees ;
took part in the solemn functions at the principal
churches, a custom which still in part survives ;
they shared largely in the administration of the
diocese, in the great wealth and many privileges and
honours beyond those which belong by right to
any Cathedral Chapter ; they all were nobles.
There was a staff of notaries, lectors, schoolmasters
(' mazeconici ' was the corrupt name for them) and
clerics for the service and the liturgical chant, and
the custodians, whom St. Charles later replaced by
the ' ostiarii.' Each of these orders, as also that of
the subdeacons, had a head of its own, called
' primicerius ' ; the ' cimiliarcas ' was the chief of
the custodians. All these heads entered the Choir
equipped with the ferula. The viscount who super-
intended the laymen, and the head of the ' scuola
dei vecchioni ' remained outside the Choir, and they
still survive as real relics of the ancient times, with
their women companions ; and, even though they
cannot for certain be regarded as an institution of
St. Ambrose, they recall times going back as far as
his, when at the offertory of the Capitular Mass,
they offer in their curious costumes as representatives of the faithful, the bread and the wine for the
Holy Sacrifice.

A special order was formed of one hundred
priests, who, because they were distinguished by
carrying a special ferula, came to be called the

H

' clergy of the hundred ferulæ'. Their more ancient title was that of ' decumani,' or ' decomani '—a word of uncertain etymology. They also claimed to have been instituted by St. Ambrose, to the number of seventy-two, in memory of the seventy-two disciples; their number was increased to one hundred by St. Simplician, although there is no documentary mention of them before the ninth century, which, however, does not mean that the institution began only then. Twelve were attached to Sta Maria Maggiore; twelve to Sta Tecla ; the remainder was distributed among the mother churches and the principal chapels. Some special distinction of uncertain origin was enjoyed by those of S. Ambrogio and S. Nazaro, and the disputes over precedence between them and the Canons of the Cathedral were as famous as they were everlasting. The ' decumani ' belonged to the people and held benefices or ' obediences' of their own, and had their own badges. They were presided over by a ' primicerius ' who was also the head of the whole city-clergy and of those attached to tribunals, apart from the Ordinaries ; he was therefore also referred to as the ' primicerius of the Church of Milan,' and enjoyed such authority, especially on the penitential tribunal, that he came to be called ' coepiscopus,' or ' subepiscopus.' The ' decumani ' were also suppressed by St. Charles when their *raison d'être* had ceased to exist, but they left many marks and remnants of their former existence. A comprehensive representation of the various orders of the Milanese clergy with their distinctive badges, a relic of the sculpture of the ninth century, is still to be seen on the wall on the south side of the little Church of Sta Maria, called ' Beltrade,' or ' Bertrade,' from the name of its ancient foundress. It represents the customary procession from the Duomo to the little Church, carrying an image of the Blessed Virgin called ' Idea ' (the title of the mother of the gods, Cybele) sculptured in marble ; according to a rather hasty humanist, it is a witness to the tenacious persistence of the classical tradition, but really is one of the many instances of pagan names and rites which had continued in the tradition and popular usages with a Christian meaning and in Christian form.

All this hierarchical development gives some idea of the wealth of the Milanese clergy. It was indeed very considerable, though not yet altogether exempt from public charges. It was not the least of the incentives to a relaxation of discipline and customs, and ended by provoking the salutary reaction, described above. This relaxation had barely left untouched the regular dress itself which presented in the persons of our priests such uniformity and such distinct characteristics as to make them at once recognisable both as priests and as Milanese priests even abroad, where many of them went for purposes of study. Seeing the number of the clergy, the hierarchical development and the great wealth of the churches, it is no wonder that the Milanese clergy, especially on solemn occasions and after the severe discipline imposed by Aribert, presented a spectacle of grandeur and splendour of decorum which staggered even Peter Damian, when he came as Legate from Rome. Nor is it any less wonder that the services were as frequent as they were splendid and remunerative. Of course, the distributions both in kind and in money benefited not only the clergy, but also the poor and infirm. Naturally also, the magnificence of the cult helped greatly to implant and to keep alive a religious sense in the people and to refine their customs. Especially the religious festivities were often accompanied by generous donations to the poor, by general pardons and God's truces. They also promoted commerce, markets and fairs which coincided with them. While we find for a long time survivals of ordeals and pagan memories and customs, we find also the

long persistence of ceremonies as pious as they were
educational, like the washing of the feet of the old
men on Maundy Thursday, carried out by the
Archbishop and still in use to-day, and the washing
of the lepers, which the Archbishop also carried
out on Palm-Sunday. This ceremony is mentioned
by Baroldo, a verger of the Cathedral, who lived
at the beginning of the twelfth century during the
early years of the Commune, and left us most
valuable information on the feasts and rites and
usages of the Ambrosian Church.

FROM THE COMMUNE TO THE SIXTEENTH CENTURY

At this point my task might be said to be completed, except that this same Church, whose fortunes
we have followed thus summarily, continued, as I
observed at the beginning, to be the Ambrosian
Church. Still, the gap separating the periods has
been to some extent filled ; the fortunes of the
Church are increasingly distinct from political
events which belong henceforth to other times ;
moreover typographical necessities impose utmost
brevity in dealing with the third and last stage of
our road. I confine myself, even more than before,
to mentioning the most outstanding names and
events, in the succession of Bishops, the backbone
of the history of the Church in any place.

Jordan was followed by Ulric (1120–1126), and
by Anselm V. Pusterla (1126–1135). It was under
his rule that Genoa and Bobbio were separated
from the ecclesiastical province of Milan ; under
him also the animosities of the Ambrosian churchmen over the Pallium reawakened, together with
the political disputes over the coronation of Conrad,
nephew of Henry V ; as the result Anselm was
excommunicated and went over to the Anti-Pope
Anacletus II, from whom he received the Pallium,
until, with the victory of the party of the legitimate

Pope Innocent II, he was driven out of the city
(1135). This was the time when St. Bernard came
to Milan as Legate, was received with immense
enthusiasm and was even offered the Archbishopric.
He refused, but the effects of his visit were the full
reconciliation with Rome, the first impulse to the
foundation of the Abbey of Chiaravalle (Milanese),
and the election of Robaldo of Asti who on the death
of Anselm in 1136 took over the administration of
the diocese. Under Uberto, or Oberto (1146–1166),
the glorious events of the First Lombard League took
place ; in 1162 Milan was destroyed by Barbarossa,
only to rise even greater from her ruins. Galdino dei
Valvassori di Sala (1166–1176), formerly Chancellor and Archdeacon and the trusty friend of
Oberto, became, by direct designation and reserva-
tion of the Pope, Archbishop and Cardinal Legate,
brought back the Milanese refugees to the ruins of
their beloved city, co-operated effectively in the
rebuilding of it, combated by preaching the heresy
of the Cathari and died while preaching, deeply
lamented by the population and raised by Alexander
III to the honour of the altars as early as 1176.
He was succeeded by Algiso da Pirovano (1176–
1185), then by Uberto Crivelli, who retained for
life the See of Milan even when he had become
Pope Urban III ; then by Milo of Cardano (1187–
1195), formerly Archpriest of the Metropolitan
Cathedral and then Bishop of Turin, a generous
and munificent benefactor of the clergy, of the
poor and the sick ; then by Oberto II of Terzago
(1195–1196) who restored the Church of S. Ambrogio which had largely fallen in ruins ; then, by the
last Archbishop of the twelfth century, Filippo
Lampugnani (1196–1206).

Cardinal Uberto II Pirovano (1206–1211) was
succeeded by Gerardo Sessa from Reggio, an
illustrious person, who had been honoured with
important missions, who restored ecclesiastical

discipline in the Milanese and its suffragan dioceses, but died in Cremona in 1211, even before he had been consecrated. He was followed in 1213 by Enrico Settala, whose election had been placed by the Chapter in the hands of Pope Innocent III ; he died in 1230 after a toilsome pontificate, filled with the struggles for the liberty and honour of his Church, the expulsion of the heretics, and the vindication of his metropolitan rights. By way of compensation, the rule of Enrico also records the new peace concluded in 1225 between the nobility and the people, one result of which was the admission of nobles to the benefices of the ' Decumani,' and of members of the people to all the dignities of the ' Ordinaries,' with the exception only of the Archiepiscopal position itself. It marked a fresh victory of the people, even though almost all the practical advantages accrued to the nobility. It was during the rule of Enrico that St. Dominic twice came to Milan and obtained from him the Church of S. Eustorgio, whose secular clergy was transferred to S. Lorenzo in 1220. Under him, too, in full accord between the civil powers and the Archbishop, the first tribunal of the Inquisition was set up in Milan to stem the invasion from all sides of heretics under diverse names and with still more diverse errors and abuses, threatening the civil no less than the religious order. During his rule both Franciscan friars and Franciscan nuns came to settle in our city.

Guglielmo Rizolio (1230–1241) bears a name which has come down to us as of highest praise. It was he who launched decrees and censures against the Cathari, whom the Podestà of Milan, Oldrado da Tresseno, sent to the stake ' as he ought,' says the inscription at the foot of his equestrian monument in the Piazza Mercanti, ' ut debuit uxit ' ; what seemed a matter for reproach to Fiamma, the chronicler of the fourteenth century, had appeared to Guglielmo's contemporaries an occasion for praise. Yet it was then, and often afterwards, rather the outcome of a phase of customs, ideas, needs and laws, different from ours ; a harsh measure, even though intelligible, and, however deplorable in itself, certainly not to be imputed as a crime to either the Republic or the Church.

The Franciscan Leo of Parego (1241–1257), over whom the electors compromised, elected himself and was well received by the people. In the days of his rule the martyrdom of Peter of Verona occurred ; so did the establishment of the Franciscans at the Basilica Naboriana. His time also saw the great increase in the Order of the Umiliati, who, looking back on a history then of perhaps three centuries, had deserved so well, and were to do so even more, of the industrial and commercial development of Milan, until the Order collapsed under the weight of its accumulated wealth and easy abuses, when it was suppressed by St. Charles in 1571. He put an end to the disordered and scandalous life they were leading, after he had just escaped from their murderous attempt on his life. To the time of Leo also belongs the emergence of Martino della Torre, and the revival of the struggles between the nobles and the people, he himself following the party of the nobles.

Amidst the clash of the parties it was Urban IV, not the Chapter, that elected Ottone Visconti (1262–1295), more a soldier than a priest, a statesman rather than a Bishop. Yet, distinguished even as Archbishop, Ottone inaugurated the solemn entries, introduced the Carmelites, Servites and Celestines, endowed churches and convents munificently both during his life and on his death, supported the Crusade proclaimed by Nicholas IV, instituted the Lenten stations and the theological prebend of the Metropolitan Chapter, provided free medical and surgical treatment for the poor, and reinforced the ecclesiastical discipline in three brilliant Provincial Councils. After bitter fights, during which Milan fell under the interdict, Ottone, as the generous victor over the party of Torre at Desio in 1277, remained in possession as Archbishop and Lord of Milan, but divested himself of this Lordship and made it hereditary in his own family, as his predecessors had entrusted it to the Commune. Again the men of the people were excluded from the higher orders of the clergy.

The intrigues of the Milanese Cardinal Peregrosso secured for a short time the See to his nephew Rufino da Lucca (1296), who sent a vicar to represent him, and after barely a year left the place to Francesco Fontana of Parma (1296–1305). He witnessed and perhaps favoured the expulsion of Matteo Visconti and ceded the See to a Torriani, Cassone or Castone, in 1308, who, sharing the forced exile of all his family, went to the vacant Patriarchate of Aquileia in 1318 and left behind a distinguished memory on the occasion of a Provincial Council held at Bergamo in 1311.

Another Visconti, Giovanni II, was elected at Milan, but Pope John XXII opposed him with Aicardo, a compatriot of Aribert's. Aicardo was recognised by Matteo Visconti in 1320, Giovanni II found support in Louis of Bavaria and his Anti-Pope Nicholas V, who appointed him his Legate, while the legitimate Pope excommunicated him. The death of Aicardo in 1342 re-established peace. Giovanni Visconti, re-elected and now confirmed by the Pope, made his solemn entry into Milan, where, after the death of his brother Luchino (1349), he remained as Lord of the Duchy. As the founder in 1335 of the magnificent solemnity on the occasion of the procession of Corpus Domini which has been in use until recently ; possibly even of the procession and feast itself ; founder of the Certosa of Garignano, the friend of Petrarch, the admirer of Dante, as

Bishop and warrior, Giovanni sums up and represents fairly well all the tendencies of his time, when amidst the shadows of the passing Middle Ages, the heralds of the dawn of modern times appeared.

On the death of Giovanni Visconti the Lordship of Milan was definitely and for ever separated from the Archiepiscopal See. The influence of the Archbishops on political events became steadily less. The influence, on the other hand, exercised in favour of charity, of peace, of higher education in the light of a Divine Faith, of the evangelical law and Christian discipline, remained ever strong and beneficent.

After Roberto Visconti (1354–1361) and Guglielmo Pusterla (1361–1370), Simone Borsano, a distinguished cardinal (1375) and canon lawyer, was elected in 1370, but remained constantly away from the See, occupied as he was on important missions ; later he became schismatical, having followed the Anti-Pope Clement VII, and was deposed. He was succeeded by Antonio da Saluzzo (1380–1402) under whom, in 1386, a beginning was made of that marvel which was to become our Duomo.

He was followed by another Franciscan, Pietro II Filargo (1402–1409), a man of great erudition and a great preacher, who was the diplomatic agent of Galeazzo Visconti. He had previously been Bishop of Vicenza and of Novara, and in 1404 was made Cardinal and later Pope Alexander V by the Council of Pisa without any legitimate justification, except to spread the notorious Western Schism. He chose as his successor in Milan the person of his fellow-Franciscan, Francesco II Creppa, who was confronted by Giovanni III Visconti, appointed by Gregory XII, then no longer Pope ; wherefore, when Francesco had died, in 1414, and Giovanni had been deposed at the Council of Constance,

Martin V gave the See to Bartolomeo Capra, formerly Bishop of Cremona, a diplomat and administrator, a friend of literary men and a writer himself (died 1433). Martin V entered Milan solemnly in person and consecrated the High Altar of the new Cathedral, in 1418.

Worthy of remembrance as a promotor of studies and as having restored the Ambrosian Rite is Francesco Piccolpasso of Bologna (1435–1443), followed by Cardinal Enrico Rampini (1443–1450), Giovanni IV Visconti (1450–1453), Niccolò Amidano (1453–1454), Timoteo Maffei (who was elected but renounced the See in the same year, 1454), the Augustinian Gabriele Sforza (1454–1457), who together with his brother Francesco Sforza can be called the founder of our Great Hospital, and Carlo of Forlì (1457–1461).

This rapid succession of Archbishops was broken by Cardinal Stefano Nardino (1461–1484), one of the best of our Bishops. The founder of the Amadeisti, for whom he built the Church and the Convent of 'la Pace,' he was also a munificent benefactor of the Cathedral which he presented with rich furnishings, and a new Palace for the Archbishop and for the Ecclesiastical Tribunal. His enlightened beneficence has a monument also in Rome in the Collegio Nardino which he there founded.

He was succeeded by Giovanni V Arcimboldi who, however, renounced the See in 1488, after a short time in favour of his brother, Guidantonio (died 1497), who left behind him salutary disciplinary directions and large endowments for the furtherance of religion, promoted the building of the Duomo, decorated the Archiepiscopal Palace, and introduced the monks of St. Jerome to Milan. His nephew and successor, Ottaviano Arcimboldi, died in 1497, even before he had been consecrated.

Ippolito I d'Este (1497–1519), a man of high

worth, a magnificent prince and Mæcenas, lacking neither in piety nor in pastoral zeal, began his rule under excellent auspices, when barely nineteen years of age. But one might almost say that the Church suffered harm by his exceptional merits. Made Cardinal in 1509 and called to Rome, he never returned to his diocese and governed it, as well as he could, from afar by means of a vicar, until he finally renounced the See.

The same system of administration was followed for nearly thirty years by his nephew Ippolito II. He could, at least at first, adopt no other. He obtained our Archiepiscopal See in 1519, soon after reaching the age of ten, one of those wretched abuses which the conditions of the time rendered possible and the Tridentine Reform was soon to end. Meanwhile the See had received the Society of the Barnabites, and in 1550 Ippolito renounced it in favour of Giovannangelo Arcimboldi, Bishop of Novara, with the right of regression. Our Church cannot forget the name of the latter. Not only did he come in person, but issued excellent directions for the discipline of the clergy and for a Christian life, which had much suffered during the previous effective vacancy of the See ; he invited the co-operation of the Observant Friars Minor ; transferred in 1553 the Confraternity of St. Catharine of Siena from the decaying, and then actually ruined, Basilica of Sta Tecla to the Duomo, as one of the many confraternities and ' schools ' which had multiplied amazingly, so that every Church had one and sometimes more than one attached to it to the great advantage of the maintenance and development of a Christian life among all the orders of the population.

Especially deserving were the Guilds of the Christian Doctrine and of the Blessed Sacrament.[1]

[1] See for details the Essay on ' The Guilds of the Blessed Sacrament,' p. 210. (*Translator's note.*)

Having been founded during the first half of the sixteenth century, the former were reorganised and promoted by St. Charles and his successors, and helped wonderfully to spread and inculcate a precise knowledge of the truths of the Faith and of Christian duties among the people. They contributed to create that religious sense, as embracing as it was enlightened, vivid as well as solid, that is hereditary among our population even now and serves so effectively to render them well-behaved and peaceful. The Guilds of the Blessed Sacrament were really providential for both the religious spirit and for the poor. Having arisen towards the end of the fifteenth century, they prepared in the beginning of the next the ground for the institution of the ' Quarant' Ore,' a practice that was soon to become universal. And what the Guilds had done for the laity, the pious associations did for the clergy among whom examples of these are to be found as early as that same fifteenth century.

Giovannangelo died, only too early, in 1555, and for the second time Ippolito II took over the administration, if not the actual See. After another renunciation and after the death of Filippo Archinto, Bishop of Saluzzo, this happened a 'third time. Filippo was a man of real worth and saintliness who would certainly have proved a great Archbishop, if the intrigues of the Royal Administrator of vacant Benefices had not prevented him from occupying the See. This Administration was an institution of some age which went back to the end of the fourteenth century and was abolished by a decree of Massimiliano Sforza of August 9, 1515 ; it was, however, re-established by an agreement between Clement VII and Charles V in the form of the ' Royal-Apostolic Administration ' vested in a single person, and lasted in this form until the days of Joseph II.

ST. CHARLES AND CARDINAL FEDERICO BORROMEO

When Ippolito II for the last time in 1560 renounced this See which he had never actually visited, he perhaps never suspected what he was actually giving up. He who succeeded him in that position was St. Charles Borromeo. It was high time that the helm should be grasped with decision by a strong as well as loving hand. Not that the Church in Milan was really what the orchard of Renzo (in Manzoni's ' Promessi Sposi ') proved to be : great remains, even great treasures of a Christian life still existed, and the solid and complex ecclesiastical organisation had neither crumbled nor ceased to function, but many and serious were the evils that needed speedy and energetic remedies. The new Archbishop was equal to the task. First through men like Ferragata and Ormaneto, then in person (1565–1584), by means of six Provincial Councils and eleven Diocesan Synods, of pastoral visits, instructions and decrees, by new lay and ecclesiastical institutions, by the reform of such as already existed ; by calling in the aid of new religious societies ; defending the freedom of the Church, the one surviving liberty ; by concentrating on this all the energy which, while he had been Secretary of State, had been equal to the government of the Universal Church ; lavishing the immense wealth of his mind, of his heart, his riches, and himself ; setting an example of every virtue and saintliness ; redeeming with the priceless treasure of true Charity and an absolute rectitude that perhaps slight excess of energy which even he incurred by natural temperament and the harshness of the times—St. Charles brought it about that from his death onwards this Church, which had been that of St. Ambrose, became the Church of St. Ambrose and St. Charles.

Upon Charles, after Gaspare Visconti (1584–1595)

who continued, however feebly, his work with a
Synod, followed Cardinal Federico Borromeo, in
every way worthy of his great predecessor, who
found his panegyrist in that other glory of Milan,
namely Alessandro Manzoni. After having rivalled
the zeal, the pastoral activity and the saintliness of
his cousin, whom he saw raised to the dignity of
the altars in 1610, he perpetuated his memory in
that incomparable monument which is the Ambrosian Library.

DOWN TO NAPOLEON I

I do no more than mention the names of his
successors : Cesare Monti (1632–1650) ; Alfonso
Litta (1652–1679) ; Federico Visconti (1681–1693);
Federico Caccia (1693–1699) ; Giuseppe Archinto
(1699–1712) ; Benedetto Erba-Odescalchi (1712–
1737) ; Gaetano Stampa (1737–1742) ; Giuseppe
Pozzobonelli (1743–1783).

Several among these were men and Bishops of
high worth, notably Cesare, Alfonso and the two
Federicos, to the first of whom, Federico Visconti,
it fell to hold the last Diocesan Synod which has
been held among us (1687).

Meanwhile the Italian rule had been followed by
the short French domination and, after that, by the
longer and more oppressive rules of the Spaniards and
the Austrians. With political oppression had come
the Cæsaro-Papism of Madrid and of Vienna and
its perpetual interferences that led to constantly
renewed disputes over questions of juridical competence ; it culminated in the ecclesiastical reform
mania of Joseph II and his arbitrary ordinances, his
interferences with the cult, with church discipline,
with territorial divisions, with the seminaries, with
the chapters, with convents, with ecclesiastical
property, with everything.

This was but the wretched foretaste of even more
wretched events. Filippo Visconti (1784–1801), a

gentle and charitable man, who had suffered under the oppression of Josephine legislation, witnessed the invasion of the French Revolution, with its sacrilegious plunderings, its profanations, the overthrow of the ancient order of things, which was swept away by that torrent. He died at the age of eighty, far from his See, at Lyons, where he, together with the flower of his nation, had been summoned by a decree of the minister to vote the Constitution which it pleased the founder of this Republic to impose on it.

He was the last of the Milanese patricians who had succeeded to the See of Milan since the time of St. Charles. For it had certainly become a custom that the Archbishop of Milan should be chosen from among the patriciate of the city, but it was a custom only in fact and by courtesy. The very manner in which it occurred time after time, made it impossible for it to become a custom properly speaking and of right. No one made people feel this more brutally than Joseph II who in this matter, too, insisted on everything being subject to his will.

In the year 1804 the French Republic became an Empire and in the year following the Cisalpine Republic became a Kingdom. In Milan, Cardinal Giovanni Caprara, of Bologna, had been willing to accept the See in 1801, and although he did not reside there, his rule assumed great importance for the Church here, in view of the public events in which he took part.

A skilful diplomat, he had been the Legate of Pius VI at Vienna, with much distinction, if not with much success. The dignity of Cardinal and the Bishopric of Jesi were the reward for his services ; he was raised to the See of Milan by Pius VII, at the wish of Napoleon I, by virtue of the Concordat concluded with full powers of the Pontiff by Caprara in 1801 to regulate the ecclesiastical affairs of France. If he was not sufficiently prudent and determined in accepting the subjects of the new dioceses, he made up for this by the energetic note of August 18, 1803, protesting against the famous ' Organic Articles ' which the arbitrary will of the Emperor had added to the Concordat, falsifying thereby its spirit and application.

The Concordat with the Italian Republic, concluded on September 16, 1803, was also the work of our Archbishop. The Milanese ecclesiastical province, after losing earlier the Church of Turin, erected in 1515 as a Metropolitan Church, and with Turin also Mondovì and Ivrea, had been compensated to some extent by the creation of the Bishoprics of Casale (1474), Vigevano (1529), and Crema (1579) ; by virtue of the new Concordat it found itself reduced to the Dioceses of Brescia, Bergamo, Pavia, Como, Crema, Cremona, Lodi, Novara, Vigevano ; to these were added in 1818, Mantua and Ventimiglia which latter was transferred later to Genoa.

Of the Chapters, those of the Metropolitan Churches and Cathedrals were recognised and preserved, but on a much reduced scale. So were some of the more notable other Chapters, which were limited here to those of S. Ambrogio and of San Giovanni of Monza. All these measures and others concerning the clergy, religious corporations and ecclesiastical property, were sanctioned by Napoleon and applied by himself, when he spent three days here in Milan in 1805. On that occasion a scene was enacted which seemed to recall the great days of the Ambrosian Church and of her Metropolitans.

The Emperor Napoleon I was crowned here as King of Italy with the Iron Crown on May 9 by our Archbishop, who invoked on him the names of St. Ambrose and St. Charles. The external splendour rivalled and perhaps exceeded that of past times ; the Emperor was a son of Italy ; yet the

Christianity of Charlemagne was not reborn in him, nor was he amenable to the restraint which the power of our Archbishops, and of the Italian nobility and later the people themselves had imposed even on Charlemagne. The people were but a flock destined for the massacre of ambitious wars ; that power was but a memory and the hand of the successor of those fierce Metropolitans trembled. Still more trembled his heart which inspired him with the unworthy counsels that drew from the prisoner of Savona words of noble anger and worthy in every way of the Bishop of Bishops. Caprara redeemed to some extent his weakness by the generous benefactions of his last years, benefactions which he continued even at his death, in 1810, when he appointed our Great Hospital as his universal heir.

The higher and lower clergy who, even after the manifold oppressions and reductions, still surrounded their Archbishop on May 9, 1805, recall to our memory the mass of churchmen that had passed by during this long stretch of time, searching if there are other figures emerging in addition to those mentioned. The answer is given by whole books, like the *Martyrology of Milan*, *La gloria dei santi milanesi*, the *Biblioteca degli scrittori milanesi :* they reveal whole crowds of saints on the one side, of writers and men of learning on the other. If among these crowds there are many who form the herd, by no means small is the number of those who would do honour to any literature.

THE GLORIOUS INHERITANCE

Our thought, returning from so long a past, turns to the present, recalls and compares. How many changes ! yet—how much permanence ! Sta Maria Maggiore exists no longer ; but the image of the Blessed Virgin rises on the top of the Duomo which stands on the very spot of the ancient Basilica and seems with its vast fabric to cover and

I

protect all the relics and memories. The old Church of Sta Tecla has fallen too, but survives in its Chapel within the Cathedral. The numbers of the clergy are reduced, but the offices for the greater part continue to exist, as do the honours and titles. Triumphantly the melodies, the rites, the prayers survive the centuries. The ' scuola dei vecchioni ' still stands like a sentry at his post. The old mother churches are still there, often restored and rebuilt, the old Chapels of former times are there with their relics and their traditions ; the old Sant'Ambrogio still stands with its long and splendid history, with the tomb of its great Bishop about to receive solemn centenary honours ; there are still, even after much and often thoughtless destruction, many names that keep alive the memory of the great past of this still Ambrosian Church. The manifold benefactions survive which offer succour for every misery and are gathered round the churches as part of them, promoted and regulated by the laws of the Church, finding among the Ambrosian clergy and its Archbishops their most active and generous supporters. There survives, more precious than any other treasure, because it is the root and principle of them all, that deeply Christian sense, that solid religious life which has so large a share in the life and the kindliness of our people. There still survives and continues to function, orderly and unbroken, that ancient organisation of a rule by ' gates ' and ' regions ' and churches and parishes, proving itself marvellously adapted to the needs of the present time.

Perhaps we, too, like our forefathers, feel that there is in all this something deeply rooted, a homely treasure that still exists, still capable of yielding fruit.

SAINT CHARLES BORROMEO
FROM THE PORTRAIT BY CRESPI
AMBROSIAN LIBRARY, MILAN

BIBLIOGRAPHICAL NOTE

I have deliberately omitted all notes ; almost every line would have required a footnote, and many notes could have been only quotations or references, which would have caused insuperable difficulties of printing.

For the same reason I have had to abandon the idea of giving, I will not say a complete bibliography of the subject-matter, but even the mere references to books and documents which, as they helped me, might also help the reader, who might wish for further information on various points of the road covered. Of course, men of learning and professional scholars have nothing to learn from my paper ; except for the very small amount of new information which I may have given, they will have immediately detected that I have availed myself of the old treasures already gathered by the Bollandists, by Muratori, Giulini, Sassi, Oltrocchi, Frisi, Fumagalli, Mazzuchelli, and that I have drawn upon those collected in the *Monumenta Germaniæ*, the *Corpus inscriptionum latinarum*, the *Codex diplomaticus Longobardiæ*, the *Spicilegium Cassinense*, as well as on the historical and liturgical works of Catena, Schupfer, Paolucci, Ferrai, Duchesne, Ceriani, Lapotre, Magistretti, down to the bibliographical and historical notes still in progress of publication in the *Analecta Bollandiana*.

Readers may also be helped by the general and special bibliographies, which are now more than ever indispensable to every student.

Translator's note to p. 65.

' Carroccio ' means a large cart. It was a heavy vehicle, decorated with the city colours and drawn by oxen, carrying on a mast the city-banner. Sometimes also an altar was set up on it. It accompanied the army in its wars and formed its rallying-point in battle.

II

ESSAYS ON ST. CHARLES BORROMEO

The following Essays were contributions made by Mgr. Ratti to a Review, ' San Carlo Borromeo,' founded by him on the occasion of the third Centenary of the Canonisation of the great Archbishop and Patron Saint of the City of Milan. The review was published from November 1908 till December, 1910, in twenty-six numbers, illustrated.

The articles, based extensively on material found in the Ambrosian Library by the researches of Mgr. Ratti and enriched by his intimate acquaintance with its treasures, form an interesting cycle of contributions on the person, the times and the contemporaries of St. Charles.

Three of the shorter articles, reprinted in the Italian edition, have been omitted here, as relating perhaps too exclusively to Italian matters.

ST. CHARLES BORROMEO AND BARONIUS

IT is not accident, nor is it merely to inaugurate the section (of the review) devoted to incidents of the life of St. Charles and to his contemporaries, that we here offer to our readers a sketch of the characteristic figure of Cardinal Cæsar Baronius and some account of him.

The third centenary of that great founder of Church History and indeed of the History of Christian Civilisation, as his last biographer so happily called him (P. G. Calenzio : *La vita e gli scritti del Cardinale Cesare Baronio*, Roma, 1908), coincided with the foundation of our review. It is a centenary which is still, in a sense, being celebrated pending the preparation of the volume to be published on this occasion. Baronius was the good angel of the canonisation of St. Charles ; his aid was invoked in that connexion by Cardinal Federico Borromeo who loved him and whose affection was returned by Baronius with an almost brotherly love ; it was to him that the city of Milan appealed to urge the Holy See to pronounce the decision that was to give to her a new Patron, and it was he whom the city thanked in particular when her desire was about to be granted.   Indeed, since the year 1601, Baronius had devoted himself heart and soul to the cause of the canonisation of Charles Borromeo, had acted as the spokesman of Cardinal Federico before Pope Clement VIII, and was to do so again before Leo XI.   It was Baronius who transmitted, on July 21, 1601, the order of the Supreme Pontiff to the Vicar-General of Milan not to forbid either candles or votive tablets or any other mark of veneration ' which may be presented at the tomb of Cardinal Borromeo to his saintly memory,' adding, by order of the Pope, the words of the Psalm : ' Scitote quia Dominus sanctum suum mirificavit,' as Aringhi informs us in the manuscript Life of Baronius.

This letter and others of Baronius on the same subject were published in 1614 in Milan by the Rev. Marco Aurelio Grattarola, formerly procurator of the cause of canonisation, in his book : *Successi maravigliosi della venerazione di San Carlo.*

Without Baronius and without his first authoritative impulse, which he followed up by every kind of encouragement, Giov. Pietro Giussano would never have written that first great biography of St. Charles, which almost at once received the honour of being translated into Spanish, French and German. It was translated into Latin by Bartolomeo Rossi, who was an Oblate of St. Charles, and was enlarged by notes of Baldassare Oltrocchi, Pro-prefect of the Ambrosian Library.   It still remains, even with due regard to the works of Aristide Sala, Canon

Sylvain and others well worth consulting on anything connected with St. Charles.

Nor is this all : born in the same year, 1538, and in the same month of October, the one in North Italy at Arona, the other in the South at Sora, both destined to achieve world-fame and to testify once more to the amazing productivity of our country, our Saint and Cardinal Baronius were linked by close bonds of friendship, affection and mutual appreciation.

A further link between these two great men was another great man of the first rank, St. Philip Neri for whom St. Charles had a great veneration and who treated Baronius like a son. Our Saint had already taken possession of his See, when Baronius began to achieve fame by his erudition and his apostolic labours in the Chiesa dei Fiorentini in Rome, labours alternating with the humblest domestic duties in the little community of the ' Oratory,' grouped round Philip Neri. The most constant of these duties was that of cook, wherefore he was accustomed to sign himself ' coquus perpetuus.'

Our saintly Archbishop wished very much to have him in Milan, and negotiated to that end with Fr. Philip. There was a moment when the matter was thought to be settled : the parents of Baronius wrote to their son in great distress ; but Fr. Philip knew his men too well. Baronius was able to write back to his father not to worry and to reassure his mother, because Fr. Philip had replied to the Cardinal of Milan giving a definite refusal and that ' the matter is altogether out of the question.'

The admiration and—one may well call it so—the veneration of Baronius for our Cardinal was such that he became after St. Charles' death the most active promoter of his canonisation ; during his lifetime he honoured him to the extent of dedicating to him that immense and truly immortal work of his, the *Annales ecclesiastici*. He says so himself in the splendid letter in which he dedicated the second volume of the *Annales* to Cardinal Federico Borromeo, a letter which forms the first, most glowing and authoritative panegyric ever written of our Saint, quite fourteen years before his canonisation. While giving due weight to the friendship and admiration which linked him with the young Cardinal Federico, he adds that this very friendship and admiration rest upon the fact that he sees in Federico the great virtues of his saintly cousin come to life again, that St. Charles had chosen Federico as his favourite pupil and the object of his most tender and affectionate cares, and that Federico had justified with admirable fidelity the forethought and hopes of his saintly master. It was the friendship of Cardinal Federico for Baronius which caused him to add his picture to those of the great men who in their almost still living presence and in their works were destined to fill his Ambrosian Library, and to place a carefully executed copy in his favourite magnificent residence at Senago, where it still hangs for our admiration.

ST. CHARLES AND THE ALCIATI FAMILY

We say ‘and the Alciati family,’ for there were two Alciati, both of them glories of Milan, Andrea and Francesco, the former the uncle of the latter. The first enjoyed so high a reputation among his contemporaries that he was called ‘the Great’ ; the second, though he, too, was an outstanding man, was simply called ‘Alciatino’ (the little Alciati).

The former, Andrea, was a professor, much sought after and the object of successful competition among many universities, Italian and foreign. He left a large number of works both printed and in manuscript, full of erudition of all kinds : history, law and archæology. He still gives his name to a little street in the heart of Milan and has been quite recently the object of study and minute research ; for the so-called *Silloge Alciatina*, a collection of ancient inscriptions, has kept the learned world busy in the past and is likely to do so still in the future.

The other, Francesco, who grew up in the shadow —or perhaps rather in the light—of his great uncle, after having been professor or, as was then said ' lector,' of Canon Law in the University of Pavia, was created Cardinal with the title of S. Maria in Portico. His ashes rest in Rome in S. Maria degli Angeli, the later title of our Cardinal Federico Borromeo, and were honoured by a monument adorned with a marble bust and the following inscription : D.O.M. — ET MEMORIÆ FRANCISCI ALCIATI MEDIOLANENSIS—TIT. S. MARIÆ IN PORTICU— S.E.R. PRESBYTERI CARDINALIS—VIRTUTE HUMANITATE OFFICIO — I.V.SCIENTIA ET CETERIS OMNIBUS DIS- CIPLINIS FLORENTISSIMI—CARTHUSIENSIS FAMILIÆ PRO- TECTORIS—VIXIT AN. LVIII M(ENSES) II. D(IES) XVIII— OBIIT AN. SAL. M.D.L.XXX. KAL. MAII — VIRTUTE VIXIT—MEMORIA VIVIT—GLORIA VIVET.

It was Francesco, the ' little Alciati,' not Andrea ' the Great,' who had at Pavia the good fortune to have among his audience and his students our future saintly Archbishop, and to become his first panegyrist, when the young Borromeo was made a ' Doctor utriusque juris ' in the Episcopal Palace of Pavia, for the Bishop of Pavia was Chancellor of the University and conferred the degrees in his own residence. Still, there was also a tradition of friendship between the Borromeo family and the Alciati, which went back to the ' great ' Andrea. In a letter to the famous Paolo Giovio of Como, of the year 1549, Andrea speaks of a dinner which he enjoyed together with Giovio and other students, in the house of the Borromei here in Milan. This letter has been the subject of much discussion : Francesco Alciati himself was the first to deny its authenticity for reasons which need not here even be indicated, all the less so, as they have recently been shown to have been mistaken, and as the friendship between the families of the Borromei and the Alciati is confirmed by other documents. It is certain, for instance, that our Saint, when still a boy, acted one day as the guide of the ' great ' Andrea in some archæological researches in the Rocca d'Angera ; it is also established that Francesco Alciati entrusted some private affairs to his famous pupil. And even when he had been created Cardinal (certainly not without the friendly influence of the Borromei) and was settled in Rome, Francesco remained the eager and trusted correspondent and almost diplomatic agent of our saintly Archbishop after his transfer to Milan, so much so that the latter, practical man as he was, considered that the mere honour of rendering such service neither should nor could appear a reward sufficient in itself, and every year made a present of several hundred *scudi* to his eminent colleague.

There can be no doubt that it was the friendship with the Alciati, and especially with Francesco, then professor at Pavia (for Andrea had died in 1550), that counted for much in the choice of that town for the studies of Charles as a young man. There was also the advantage of being in the vicinity of Milan, for Charles might have pursued his studies more quietly, and more sheltered from the dangers and the disturbances of war, in other University towns. Indeed, pressing invitations came from Padua and Bologna, from relatives and friends of Charles, who were studying there ; and, the future Cardinal Federico was later sent to Bologna.

It cannot be urged as a reason for the choice of Pavia that Charles would have found a house of his own there : for the ' Collegio Borromeo ' was to be established by him there only later, and he himself lived in hired lodgings during his time of study. He lived first near the Church of San Gabriele which stood near the Vicolo Porta Marica, formerly San Gabriele, which runs into the Corso Cavour ; then near the Church of Santa Tecla, on the Largo Jacopo Menochio, still to-day called by the common people Piazetta Santa Tecla ; then in a house belonging to the Beccaria family opposite the Collegio Borromeo ; and lastly, in a house of the family of the Gambarana, at the corner between the Corso Vittorio Emanuele and the Corso Garibaldi, on the right coming from the latter : a real *Odyssey* of which the housebreaker and housing schemes have left no trace other than the towers which still to-day are called after the family of the Beccaria.

ST. ANDREA AVELLINO AND ST. CHARLES

On November 10 of this year (1908) occurred a further centenary of another great friend of St. Charles's and of a great Saint who, thanks to St. Charles, intermittently brought to our city the benefits of his active presence and continued them for many years with kindly solicitude even from afar. Again, as in the case of Baronius, the South joined hands with the North. For St. Andrea was born in the kingdom of Naples in Castronuovo, a village in Lucania, in 1521 ; to judge by his surname the family had come from Avellino. His baptismal name had been Lancellotto and he kept it until the year 1556. Then, ordained since 1547, he took the habit of the Theatine Order and the name of Andrea, it is said, out of the special devotion he had for the Holy Cross, of which the Apostle St. Andrew was both the martyr and the fervent poet, as can be seen from the account of his martyrdom.

Handsome of person, infinitely more beautiful of soul, not lacking in fortune, but rich indeed in intellectual gifts, after having, like our St. Charles, taken his degree *utriusque juris* and practised for some time in the ecclesiastical courts, he first became a priest, despite many temptations and other inducements of every kind, and later became a religious in obedience to a higher call from God. At the time he displayed so delicately tempered a mind and so tender a conscience that he was bound to be embarrassed by living in the world ; after some slight untruth had escaped him in the exercise of his duties, the words from the Book of Wisdom : ' The mouth that lieth, killeth the soul,' decided him to take the great step.

He was one of the saints most active and helpful in the great work of the Catholic Counter-Reformation, which the Protestant Reformation had intensified here in Italy, too. I say here in Italy too, for that great work was being no less actively pursued elsewhere, notably in Germany and in Switzerland. It is excellent that its history is now beginning to be written.

Already as a simple priest Andrea had, on the instructions of the Archbishop of Naples, devoted himself to the reform both of the clergy and of the laity with such zeal, that he became the object of hatred on the part of the wicked, to the extent of being persecuted and even beaten and wounded, in proportion as he won the incredible affection and veneration of the people at large. The flourishing discipline and the activities of the Theatines attracted him to that Congregation, which had only recently been founded ; and as he himself reached a higher perfection of his life, he devoted himself with ever more abundant results to the task of the sanctification of others.

It is no wonder that St. Charles and several others among the zealous and saintly Bishops of that time, desired to have him and his fellow-religious in their dioceses. St. Charles and Milan succeeded in securing him in 1570 : he came with several of his companions and our Archbishop went to meet them outside Porta Romana and brought them to the house which had been set apart and prepared for them with much care at Sta Maria near the Church S. Calimero. Not content with this, St. Charles, knowing them to be vowed to the strictest observance of poverty, assisted them with a subsidy of twenty-five gold *scudi* a month, until on one occasion he had the money returned to him with an expression of deepest appreciation, for the benefit of other poor people, on the ground that the charity of the faithful had provided sufficient for the plainest and strictest needs of the congregation. In the year 1575, after long negotiations and many difficulties, overcome only by the patience and generosity of St. Charles, it was possible for the Theatines to be moved and to be established near the Church of Sant' Antonio which owes it to them that still to-day it is among the most notable artistic treasures of our city. There the good fathers, having deserved so well of the Milanese, and much beloved by them, became the object of the highest admiration and gratitude for the heroism which they so lavishly displayed during the Plague of 1576.

But St. Andrea had been recalled as early as 1571 and had been sent elsewhere to continue the good work ; he did not return to Milan for several years. St. Charles, who had formed a real and intimate friendship with him, kept up the connexion by letter. It is a correspondence as moving as it is edifying. The great Archbishop addresses him as his ' Padre D. Andrea,' as he might a brother, and St. Andrea opens in his letters to him his heart

' as in confession.' Charles had gone to his reward fourteen years, while Andrea, full of years and merits, was still labouring for the good of souls. He died in 1608, like our Saint practically without having been ill, as valiant fighters like to die, on the battlefield with their weapons in their hands. On November 10, as he was beginning Holy Mass with his customary devotion, at the foot of the altar, he had a stroke : three times he repeated the words : ' Introibo ad altare Dei ' ; then he fell : a few hours later he was dead. His body is even to-day the object of veneration in the Theatine Church at Naples. I have said that he died practically without having been ill ; in a short note to an intimate friend of his, one of the last of his letters, of October 13, 1608, which is preserved as a relic of the Church of Sant' Antonio, the Saint, foreseeing his near end, writes : ' I have not been well since Thursday, and I have not called in any other doctors nor shall I do so. I beg you for the sake of Christ's Passion not to abandon me ; you know that I wished to die in your arms.'

His printed works fill seven stout volumes, of which two contain his letters, beautiful to read. He also left true and excellent disciples. The name of Lorenzo Scupoli and his well-known book *Del combattimento spirituale* bear witness to his Master and his ways.

The tenth of November of this year, 1908, celebrated with splendour in Naples, was solemnised also in our city and especially in two Churches : at Sant' Antonio, where, in addition to the Chapel dedicated to him, everything recalls the saintly Theatine, and in the Church of the Madonna del Castello, where a humbler but no less devotional Chapel, nor less dear to the piety of the Milanese, is consecrated to his memory.

THE LIFE OF ST. CHARLES IN A GREAT MODERN INSTITUTION

A great institution of our time is flourishing and bearing wonderful fruit quite close to us, however little known and (what is worse) little imitated among us ; an institution which looks back on barely more than fifty years of existence, and yet has produced an immense amount of good, especially among the younger generation, who, eager as never before to read, are also more than ever in need of good reading-matter.

I refer to the ' Society of St. Charles Borromeo,' the ' Verein des heiligen Karl Borromäus,' or the ' Borromäusverein ' for short. It may deservedly be considered as occupying first rank among the Societies that have the object of encouraging and promoting the diffusion of sound, instructive and pleasant reading-matter. It forms for that reason a most important part of that truly remarkable and enviable organisation of the many and diverse societies, the ' Vereinswesen,' which is one of blessings and glories of German Catholics. This organisation makes its influence effectively felt in all forms of individual and social—especially social —life.

The ' Borromäusverein ' was founded in 1844 with the consent and approval of the German Episcopate, by four excellent men, August Reichensperger, Prof. Dieringer (the author of a fine Life of St. Charles), the learned, indefatigable and heroic confessor of the Faith, Conrad Martin, Bishop of Paderborn, and Baron von Loë.

The name of our great and sainted fellow-citizen was chosen precisely on account of the zeal he had displayed against bad literature and for the diffusion of good reading-matter, so much so that in 1579 he had set up a ' Seminary Press ' of his own for that purpose.

The ' Borromäusverein' began work in 1845, directing its efforts especially towards the formation of libraries in the Catholic parishes of Germany, to distributing good books among its members and giving them the possibility of purchasing good books by means of catalogues issued every year by the Society. For many years now, the libraries of the Catholic Workers Union and its reading-rooms have also been assisted by the ' Borromäusverein,' especially with gifts of books.

The members are divided into two classes, full members and associates. The former pay a sub-scription of 6 marks, the others a subscription of 3 or even only 1½ marks. In 1899 the membership amounted to 77,144, distributed among 2044 local societies ; quite 26,244 contributed subscriptions of 6 marks.

The Society is nowadays represented in all the dioceses of Germany, most strongly in those of Cologne, Münster, Bonn, Treves, with extensions in Luxembourg and the German parts of Switzer-land. The headquarters are in Bonn. Even some years ago—we take the facts from information supplied by Dr. I. Felton in the *Ecclesiastical Encyclopædia* of Wetzer and Welte, 2nd ed. 1901, Vol. XII, Freiburg i. B.—it was estimated that the Borromäusverein had distributed books to a total value of four million marks and was maintaining more than 2000 libraries, besides having promoted or subsidised the publication of a number of important works. At the present time, its member-ship exceeds 100,000 ; the other figures have risen not in arithmetical, but almost in geometrical pro-portion. At the same rate the name of our Saint Charles Borromeo, a Milanese name *par excellence*, has, evermore blessed and venerated, been spread over the vast territory of a great nation.

When I reflect what manner of thing books, es-pecially to-day and above all for youthful readers, have come to be : truth or error, virtue or vice, food or poison, life or death, I in truth do not know what greater posthumous homage could have been rendered to our Patron, or to what greater benefit he could have lent the protection of his name. If we further reflect that not only this great German Society, but numberless other beneficent institutions in every part of the world—indications at least of these will be given when the occasion occurs—are linked with the name of our St. Charles, it would be difficult to find another name that does greater and more worthy honour to our city all over the world.

ST. CHARLES BORROMEO AND CARDINAL GUGLIELMO SIRLETO

The reform of morals and the liberation of reason were the great catchwords which Protestanism had inscribed in glowing colours upon its banners. The effect was, in part, to set free the lowest greed of princes and peoples, of clergy and laymen, and in part, a revolt against every authority, human and divine. If this was, in its way, a triumph of the true Church, it was a most sorrowful triumph, which no one could desire, and no one could but mourn. But divine Providence had another, better vindication in store, by raising up two bands of men, the one no less admirable than the other : a band of Saints and a band of Scholars, who cast lustre upon the Catholic Church in the century of Luther, Zwingli and Calvin. On the one side, it was a new flowering of sanctity, one and identical in substance, but of the greatest variety in the form ; in substance rivalling that of the best Christian centuries, in the variety of its forms admirably adapted to the changed conditions of the times. Under the direction of legitimate authority, it constituted a genuine, profound and universal reform of head and members, from the highest ranks of the hierarchy to the lowest, from the clergy to the Christian people. On the other side, there was a real and widespread blessing of genius, of erudition and of learning which men of eminence placed at the service of the Church and of Faith, proving irrefutably that Faith and Reason, obedience to authority and the cultivation of true learning can and do go hand in hand, not only without necessary conflicts, but rather in perfect harmony. It was a phenomenon which but yesterday, as it were, re-occurred in men, uniting genius and faith.

One of the brightest stars of the Faith and of learning in the fifteenth century was Baronius of whom we have already spoken. We shall meet several others yet. Here we wish to recall the memory and personality of Cardinal Guglielmo Sirleto, partly because by the accumulation of research and learning he was one of the greatest authorities in the great currents of ideas and events that agitated his time, partly because he entertained with the young Cardinal Borromeo the closest relations, no less appreciated by him than they were influential in moulding St. Charles' life.

Born in Guardavalle in Calabria in 1514, as the son of a humble country doctor, he came to Rome in a state of utmost poverty, after having studied in Naples. He had already a brilliant career behind him, when our Saint was called by the Pope, his uncle, to Rome and was created cardinal.

The astonishing talent and the no less astonishing erudition of the young Calabrese soon showed themselves, set off and rendered all the more attractive by the uprightness and integrity of his personality. The learned Cardinal Marcello Cervini, later Cardinal Librarian and then Pope Marcellus II, took him into his service. The Cardinal, when

K

he was charged with presiding over the Council of Trent, found in Sirleto a valuable councillor in all the questions which came up and were discussed at this Council, and employed him afterwards as collaborator in preparing the edition of the Bible in the Vulgate version, which had been decreed by the Council.

When Cervini became Cardinal Librarian of the Church, he chose Sirleto as Librarian of the Vatican Library. Rarely has a post and an office fitted more perfectly the inclinations and gifts of the man. Sirleto examined, studied and described one by one the manuscripts, especially the Greek manuscripts, while he also found time to compose learned commentaries on the books of the Old and the New Testaments, commentaries which have been the object of recent study.

Pope Marcellus II died in 1655, after a reign of only twenty-one days. But the career of Sirleto was not thereby brought to an end nor even delayed. Cardinal Federico Borromeo, who had occasion to know and to admire him, has devoted a page of his memoirs to the episodes which won him the favour and confidence of Paul IV who succeeded Marcellus.

The first of these episodes goes back to the very first day when Sirleto arrived in Rome, without a farthing, his only possessions being some books. When evening came, the young man, who had perhaps been disappointed in his expectation of some fortunate encounter on which he had pinned his hopes, had regretfully to sell one of his books, to obtain food and lodging. He received three *soldi* from a bookseller. But he had barely left the shop, when a beggar held out his hand to him : Sirleto gave him one of his *soldi*. Another beggar, encouraged by the success of the first, also implored help : he also got a *soldo*, so that the one remaining coin had to suffice for all the needs of the poor,

generous youth. But his reward came speedily ;
the next day, Cervini, having seen him in the
Vatican Library and having observed how he read
and translated the Greek of an ancient ccdex,
took him into his service.

The other episode is similar to the first and like
it, displayed the kind and charitable heart of Sirleto.
When he was Librarian of the Vatican Library, he
was returning home from the Library, alone and
absorbed in thought, when an unknown man of
wild appearance, sword in hand, fell upon him
with threats, attempting to rob him of his cloak.
Sirleto, torn between fear of the robber and em-
barrassment at having to walk home without his
cloak, slipped from the man's grip, and gentle and
humorous speaker as he was, began mildly to
protest ; as the other insisted, he promised him the
cloak with such innocence and such engaging words,
that his assailant, dropping his threats, started to
walk along with him. So Sirleto, plucking up his
courage, reproved him in all friendliness for having
given himself over to the life of a footpad, while
the other began to excuse himself, explaining that
only misfortune and necessity had driven him to it,
as he had been born of a good family. They
ended by coming to an agreement, by which the
robber left Sirleto in possession of his cloak and
Sirleto promised to give him four gold *scudi* on the
next day, at the same place and hour. So he did,
and did even better : for having obtained from the
wretched man the promise, which he kept, of turning to a better life, he gave him for several years
every week a certain sum of money. When the
affair became known at court, the ' alms of the
cloak ' became proverbial.

Paul IV not only maintained Sirleto in his office
and his honours, but promoted him to the position
of Protonotary, and entrusted him with the education of his nephews. One of them, Antonio Carafa,

owed his position as the head of the Commission
charged with editing the Bible in the Septuagint version, to the solid knowledge of Greek
which he had received from Sirleto. There was
no question of importance which the Pope did not
hand over to Sirleto for preparatory study. Thus
the latter came to compose his learned treatises on
Simony and on the Feast of St. Peter's Chair, and
to gather the data for the eventual claims of the
Holy See in the matter of the succession of the
Empire which had been reopened by the abdication
of Charles V.

On the death of Paul IV, Sirleto retired to the
house of the Theatines at S. Silvestro on the Quirinal,
where, dividing his time between spiritual exercises
and his favourite studies, he still found enough
leisure to teach others Greek and Hebrew.

Pope Pius IV visited him there immediately after
his election, to invite him together with other
learned and experienced men to assist his young
nephew, Charles Borromeo, whom Pius intended
to appoint his Secretary of State despite his extreme
youth.

A man of great judgment and of wisdom matured
by experience, Pius IV, even while he discerned with
sure touch the eminent gifts of his nephew, yet knew
but too well that mere native talent is unable to
take the place of positive knowledge and of the
experience of men and things, at least in the majority
of cases and especially in difficult situations.

Our young Cardinal became Sirleto's most diligent, affectionate and grateful pupil, and while,
after the schooling he had received from Sirleto, the
pupil rose swiftly to the height of his career in
Rome, a new phase began also for his master which
was to bring him the reputation so richly deserved
by his excellence and learning.

When the Council of Trent was resumed for the
third time—it had been the great work of Pius IV

and of his nephew the Cardinal—Sirleto, though he remained in Rome, took so direct a share in it, that Cardinal Seripando, the first of the Papal Legates to represent the Holy See at Trent, had occasion to say that Sirleto alone in Rome had done more for the good of the Council than fifty prelates might have been able to achieve in Trent.

When the Council had closed, Pius IV, yielding willingly to the insistence of his Cardinal Nephew, created Sirleto a Cardinal on March 12, 1565. The Pope's attention had been called to the extreme poverty and the obscure birth of Sirleto ; but the Nephew replied : ' I ask Your Holiness only for the Cardinal's hat for Sirleto ; the rest will be my concern.' And so it was ; it could be said with perfect truth that Sirleto had risen to the dignity of Cardinal ' on the shoulders of Cardinal Borromeo,' but the shoulders were worthy of the burden.

In September 1566, Pius V nominated Sirleto Bishop of San Marco in Calabria, whence he was later transferred to Squillace. In obedience to the decrees of the Council of Trent, Sirleto went to reside in his See and set actively to work in the government of his diocese.

But in Rome his absence was regretted and the lack of his learning soon felt. He was recalled in 1568, nominated Cardinal Librarian in 1570, and later, as a member and often as president of Congregations and Commissions, he was charged with the most varied and difficult affairs : such as the final revision of the Roman Catechism, the revision of the Missal and of the Breviary, the emendations of the Martyrology, the preparatory work for the emendation of the texts of the Vulgate and the Septuagint, the editing of the works of the Church Fathers, notably those of St. Ambrose, under the direction of the ' Sapienza,' the University of Rome, the protectorate of the Basilian monks and of the

Greek College in Rome, the new edition of the Acts
of the Council of Florence and the translation into
Greek of the catechism, of the canons and decrees
of the Council of Trent, and numberless other
matters for the promotion of the Union and reform
of the Greeks, the reform of the Gregorian calendar,
and lastly an enormous correspondence with the
whole learned world of Europe. Sirleto attended
to all these matters with incessant labour, all day
long and for a good part of the night, and this—
though it seems almost superhuman—despite his
weak health and frequent periods of illness.

It is no wonder that during the Conclave of
Pius V, Sirleto, thanks mainly to the efforts of St.
Charles, very nearly was elected Pope, and that
also during the following Conclaves of Gregory
XIII and Sixtus V many were the votes cast in his
favour.

Sirleto died on October 6, 1585, assisted by St.
Philip Neri. Sixtus V attended the funeral of so
great a man in person and afterwards pronounced
his panegyric in Consistory.

It is interesting for us to observe what a man, so
wise and so learned, thought of St. Charles, whom
he himself had taught and knew as few others.

Sirleto expressed his mind and opinion soon after
the death of our Saint. ' He lived—he said—
bodily upon the earth but in his soul in heaven.
The flesh was in him but a mere appearance ;
visibly a man, but angelic by Grace, he was a
model of Christian piety, a mirror and champion
of the episcopal and cardinalitial dignity. He was
a splendid ornament of the Church of God ; he
was the salt, the light, the city placed upon the hill,
the burning candle of the Gospels ; salt by reason
of his life and practice, light by reason of his
learning and preaching, city by reason of his defence
and the help he gave all good causes. He shone
in the Church by faith and wisdom, life and rule ;

by his faith like a martyr—martyrdom passed him by, not he martyrdom,—by his rule like a shepherd.'

And after having compared him with the great just men of the Old Testament, he concluded : ' An unshakable worker for truth, he never did but what tended to God. And God's spirit infused such strength in his mind as to render him everywhere unconquered and invulnerable. This faithful servant, when his work was done, eager to enter into the sight of God, into the solemn communion of all the Saints, was called to Heaven : a sorrowful day for us, but happy for his passing. For, after he had defended and loved the dignity of—as it were —all the soldiers of Christ and having emulated their example, it was but just that he be presented before the Throne of the Lamb by all the legions of the Saints.'[1]

Sirleto also expressed his appreciation in highest terms of praise, as might be expected from such a judge, of the mentality—to use that favourite word of our day—of St. Charles and of his love of study and learning ; he expressed it not only in words, but in an action more eloquent than any speech. A man of study and erudition himself, whose only treasure all through his life had been his books, he had intended and arranged the gift of his rich library to Cardinal Borromeo. As Cardinal Borromeo had died before him, less than a year before Sirleto went to his reward, his books, by a kindly disposition of Providence, ended by increasing the treasures of that Vatican Library which he had distinguished by his labours and loved so much.

------

[1] St. Charles died on November 3, 1584. (*Translator's note.*)

THE RECORDS OF ST. CHARLES IN SANTA PRASSEDE IN ROME

We gather up the memories which still keep our Saint vividly present to us in the Church of Santa Prassede in Rome, his final and favourite title. Milanese and all those who hold the memory of our great Patron in affectionate veneration, will be able to derive all the more benefit from their visits, now rendered so easy, to the Eternal City, goal of so many journeys and pious pilgrimages. We devote ourselves to our task all the more gladly, as those memories are wholly or almost wholly omitted in so many guide-books.

We give first place to a painting of the Saint which is to be found now in a corridor of the cloister, and in the days of St. Charles was placed on one of the pilasters by the side of the High Altar, where in the cardinalitial churches the picture of the titular Cardinal is usually displayed. Its workmanship and its original position put it beyond doubt that the painting was contemporary with the living man ; we can even with perfect certainty date it as belonging to the time when St. Charles changed his title from San Martino to that of Santa Prassede. The features of the likeness, which still show the bloom of youth, correspond with this date.

The faldstool, or pontifical chair, to be seen in the Chapel dedicated to St. Charles, as well as the mitre and mozzetta, recall to us the sacred functions which St. Charles loved to celebrate in his church.

In the same chapel stands the table ' on which ' —as a tablet informs us—' St. Charles Borromeo, titular Cardinal of this Church, used to serve food to the poor.'

On the side walls, two large paintings, the one by Parocel and the other by Stern, recall to us the two great devotions of the Saint, towards the

Blessed Sacrament and the Passion of our Saviour. In the one picture the Saint, supported by two exquisitely painted angels, is seen in an ecstasy before the Blessed Sacrament exposed on the altar ; in the other painting, he is seen kneeling before a representation of Jesus Christ after the deposition from the Cross, surrounded by angels who carry the instruments of the Passion.

On the reredos painting, Saint Praxedes, as it were, accompanies her great Titular to Milan and presents him to our admiration in the days of the great plague to which his heroism gave his name. St. Charles lies prostrate, with a rope round his neck, before the Crucifix, imploring mercy for his people ; in the background figures of the people stricken by the plague are visible in various attitudes ; above, an angel sheathes the sword of Divine Justice.

In the reception hall, we see the Saint in the first glow of his apotheosis. The austerities of his penances, the labours of his apostolic work have caused the bloom of his first youth to disappear from his face, thinner now, yet expressing his kindness, and have replaced it by a nimbus of lasting glory. The writing beneath says : ' B(eatus) Carolus ' : we are here dealing with the year 1606, when the public acts of veneration were for the first time permitted and encouraged by the Holy See.

The completed apothesosis, his canonisation, and with it the title of Saint and the liturgical cult follow four years later. This too is represented vividly in Santa Prassede by two reliquaries, one of them in the form of a graceful little temple, where some of the wearing apparel of the Saint is preserved ; the other, in the shape of a crystal phial, carried by angels and surrounded by lilies, contains a particle of his skin : ' Ex cute et pelle S(ancti) Caroli Borromœi Ep(iscopi).'

Indeed he was a living temple of the Holy Spirit and the unspotted purity of his life made him the minister and irrefutable model of the salutary general reform.

Cardinal Pico della Mirandola, of the family of that famous man of learning who seemed almost a miracle to his contemporaries, recorded in 1730 in a monumental inscription in the Choir of the Church the great works by which St. Charles benefited his titular Church and the fame which the glory of his sanctity imparted to it :

SANCTO CAROLO BORROMŒO—CARDINALI SANCTÆ PRAXEDIS—QUOD HANC ÆDEM TITULI SUI—INNUMERIS SANCTORUM RELIQUIIS—INSIGNEM—EXIMIO PIETATIS STUDIO PROSECUTUS—RENOVATA EXPOLITAQUE TEMPLI FACIE—SUPPLETIS IN ATRIO COLUMNIS—E MARMORE STRATIS ALTARIS GRADIBUS—ET ABSIDE INSTRUCTA —STATUIS PICTURIS LAQUEARE—ALIISQUE ORNAMEN- TIS AUXERIT—AC SANCTITATIS SUÆ—CELEBRITATE ILLUSTRAVERIT—CARDINALIS PICUS DE MIRANDULA— TANTI NOMINIS CULTOR—AC TITULI SUCCESSOR M.P. —ANNO DOMINI MDCCXXX.

It was but right that the memory of our saint should be preserved with special care in the place which he loved above all ; it was but right that he should continue to live in some measure in a spot which held so large a place in his life ; and this justice has not been denied him.

ST. CHARLES AND ST. PHILIP NERI

St. Philip Neri is one of the most characteristic and at the same time attractive figures in the history of Christian Saints, a history richer in such figures than any other. Endowed by nature with an exuberant, jocular and somewhat whimsical spirit, he remained thus in his dealings with everyone, even when he had reached the highest levels of sanctity. St. Charles, great judge of men that he was, gave his opinion of him, when, coming out of St. Philip's room, he said to the latter's pupils and sons : ' Philip is a man of admirable sincerity and singular sanctity.' Philip used these natural gifts of his in a remarkable way to draw souls to goodness, to render the Christian practices of piety and austerity attractive, and to conceal in his humility the extraordinary and wonderful things which divine Grace operated in him.

He was called to be and indeed became the apostle of Rome. With an astonishing intuition he directed the care and zeal of his apostolate to the youths of his time, as well as to the clergy.

Children and young men were the objects of his tenderest affection and he in return was loved by them like a father. He could not appear in the streets of Rome without being at once surrounded by a crowd of boys. He knew them all by name ; a wonderful story-teller, he kept them hanging on his lips ; he took them for walks, gathered them together in the gardens of Sant' Onofrio beneath the famous oak of Tasso, joked and played with them with wonderful skill and patience ; ' provided they do not offend against virtue and God (he used to say), I would let them break their sticks over my head.' And meanwhile he instructed, corrected and educated them.

He realised as few others, that times had changed : he realised that the best apologetics against Protestantism with its appeal to the past and to the very beginnings of the Church, was the defence offered by historical fact, and he urged Baronius to write his ' Annales.' He realised that the paganising atmosphere of Humanism, on the one hand, and the rationalistic current of the Protestant Reformation on the other, had led to a cleavage between society and the Church and her clergy. He realised that to make society again Christian, it was necessary to go out to it ; and he became the founder of the ' Oratory,' of the Oratorians, of what we would call a ' modern ' Order, a Congregation of secular priests, who, as has been well said, without leaving the world, live outside it, without monastic enclosure yet live in retirement, who without vows are vowed to a great mission, without bearing externally distinguishing marks are distinguished from others by the sanctity of their lives, preach the beauty of virtue by the gentleness of humility, co-operate in the cure of souls with zeal and prudence, and devote themselves to scientific studies.

Philip had been born in 1515 in Florence of a respectable family. His singular goodness had earned him, even as a child, the nickname of ' Pippo buono.' He passed some time in San Germano near Montecassino, in the house of an uncle who was in business. But God destined and called him to greater things : he followed his call and came to Rome. In Florence under the Dominicans at San Marco he had pursued his earlier studies, displaying ever more the remarkable gifts of his genius. Now at the University of the ' Sapienza ' and under the direction of the Augustinians, he devoted himself to philosophy and theology. And meanwhile under the guidance of a saintly teacher, Persiano Rosa, he gave himself up to pious works, to mortifications and charity, especially in the interests of the pilgrims, the sick, and the erring. Even while still a layman, he became an apostle.

He was ordained in 1551. The ardour of his sanctity and charity burnt with an ever brighter flame. After spending the whole day in caring for all kind of misery, hearing confessions, preaching, in pilgrimages to the catacombs and holy shrines, in the catacombs of San Callisto he passed the night,

not in rest but in more intimate converse with
God, in meditation and contemplation, in which his
love for Christ and the souls redeemed with his
Blood, found ever fresh fuel.   The news of the
wonderful deeds and then of the glorious death of
St. Francis Xavier in the Far East, turned his
thoughts and desires to missions ; but God's voice
told him that for him ' India was Rome.'

First at San Gerolamo della Carità, then at San
Giovanni dei Fiorentini, finally and definitely, at
Santa Maria della Vallicella which he rebuilt
larger and on a finer scale in 1575 (the ' Chiesa
Nova '), the ' Oratory ' gathered and established
itself round Philip ' in the hands of Mary,' as he
used to say.   Philip himself became its first Superior,
though he resisted and was overcome almost by
force.   But in 1593 he resigned the direction which
passed into the hands of his favourite pupil, the
great Baronius who was almost a son to him,
while Philip remained the father and venerated and
beloved councillor of all and in everything.   By
then the Oratory had become a centre and a
training-ground for a vast amount of good works.

Philip and his spiritual sons were working
miracles of conversions and sanctification by their
new preaching, sincere in its form and truly
apostolic in substance, and by their indefatigable
zeal in their sacred ministry.   Church music was
reformed, thanks to the work of the celebrated
Animuccia and the even more famous Palestrina,
and added new splendour to the sacred services.
Novel and wonderful events bore witness to Divine
intervention, reaching their peak when Philip on
March 16, 1583 recalled Prince Paolo Massimo,
a boy of fourteen, from death.   It can be said, that
in Rome, where everything is great and famous,
there was nothing greater or more famous than
Father Philip, in the eyes of all far and near, of
great and small.

No less than five Popes—and what Popes !—
Pius V, Gregory XIII, Sixtus V, Gregory XIV,
Clement VIII, regarded him with filial love and
veneration, even to the extent of reverently kissing
his hands. That Philip was offered the dignity of
cardinal, is a fact and intelligible enough ; Gregory
XIV actually sent the red hat to Vallicella :
Philip sent it back to him, with a joke, humbly
refusing.

He died on May 26, 1595. His beatification in
1615, his canonisation in 1662 officially confirmed
the odour of sanctity which had surrounded him
already for so many years and after his death had
not only remained, but had constantly grown and
been attested by many proofs.

And the small humble Oratory also grew, until
it became an immense tree. In the eighteenth
century quite a hundred houses existed in Italy
alone, and every Catholic country, even the
distant America and India, had its branches. In
England, in times not far distant, Cardinal Newman
cast lustre on it, and to-day distinguished men
headed by Cardinal Capecelatro, uphold its honour
in Italy.

St. Charles could not but be among the admirers
and friends of St. Philip and soon belonged to his
circle in a very special manner. Even in the first
years of his position of Cardinal, when as the
Cardinal Nephew and Secretary of State he was the
first personality in Rome after the Pope, he was
seen more than once visiting San Gerolamo della
Carità in search of St. Philip, remained in long
conversations with him in his humble cell, embracing
and kissing him with fraternal affection, kneeling
before him and kissing his hands with filial reverence, while St. Philip even then had the intuition of
the saintliness of his distinguished visitor.

The pictures which decorate the little cell, now

transformed into a Chapel, recall vividly these scenes of friendship. A simple inscription gives the information : ' Here St. Charles Borromeo often visited our Father St. Philip, recited with him the Divine office and sometimes on his knees kissed his hands while our holy Father (St. Philip) saw the splendour of sanctity shining in his face.'

Our Saint had chosen Father Philip as his intimate councillor, not only in matters of his own soul and his sanctification, but also in matters pertaining to his high office and as an instrument of his inexhaustible charity.

St. Charles availed himself most extensively of the help of St. Philip and of his disciples especially in the Church then called Sant' Ambrogio dei Lombardi (now San Carlo al Corso) and in the hospital attached to it, which together formed the meeting place and centre of the numerous Lombards in Rome. He often went there to listen to and observe their apostolic preaching, occasionally preaching himself in the presence and at the invitation of St. Philip. He thus became one of his most perfect and diligent pupils, to the great edification of all Rome, matched only by the astonishment aroused by the novel sight of a Cardinal—and such a Cardinal—becoming a preacher.

When St. Charles had transferred his residence to Milan, he kept up a continuous correspondence with Philip of which many precious remains are preserved in the Ambrosian Library. He entrusted to St. Philip the spiritual care of his sister, Anna Colonna, who justified it in every way ; he was with St. Philip at the death-bed of his uncle, the Pope ; together with him, though in a different way, he worked for the election of that saintly Pope, Pius V.

The election of Gregory XIII and still more the Holy Year of 1575, brought these two friends together again, and set before the eyes of Rome and of its numberless pilgrims the spectacle of these two kinds of sanctity, of two men who regarded each other with so much affection and were in such noble rivalry with one another.

St. Charles, whom St. Philip called ‘ the most rapacious robber for carrying off his best men,’ had wished, since the institution of the Oratory, to have some of its most promising members in Milan. We have referred elsewhere to his efforts to secure Baronius, and how St. Philip could not be induced to give him up. The insistence of our Archbishop continued for a long time ; so did the humble but firm refusals of the priest : again a proof of their mutual esteem and personal firmness.

At last in 1575 two Oratorians were conceded to Milan and did a great deal of good there ; but continuous and constantly fresh difficulties arose. Just before that sadly famous outbreak of the plague, Philip, by a decision which seemed afterwards to have been prophetic, deaf to all pleadings, recalled them to Rome, wherefore St. Charles called him a ‘ man without pity.’ Philip replied by saying that it was not the business of Cardinal Borromeo to despoil other people’s altars in order to cover his own. Later on, the Oratorians came back to Milan and remained for some time, but again departed, never to return.

More than external and accidental difficulties, a divergence of views concerning principles between St. Charles and St. Philip had been the obstacle. St. Charles wanted helpers in the external and official administration of his diocese ; St. Philip wanted men who should work in retirement, wholly devoted to their own and other souls’ sanctification. St. Philip insisted that his men should continue to belong to him and to the Oratory ; St. Charles, as he himself wrote to his agent in Rome, Cesare Speciano, desired ‘ that everything should remain in (his) decision, as (he) desired nothing else but the formation of a company of men ready to carry out any wish of (his), but composed of fathers of the Oratory.' He later created such a company for himself in the Diocesan Congregation of the Oblates.

Such conflicts—and there were others, harsher than those mentioned—so far from loosening the bonds of friendship between the two Saints, helped rather to tighten them ever more. When St. Charles returned to Rome in 1579, he gave such solemn and touching proofs of it that they have remained for ever memorable. St. Charles insisted on nothing less than that St. Philip should examine the rules of the Oblates which he had prepared with the utmost care, with prayers and fasting, and he himself went to beg St. Philip to do so, bringing the manuscript in person. After much protesting and declaring his own incompetence, Philip played one of his pranks on him. He told him with a great air of mystery, that he knew the very man for the task among the Capuchins of the Convent of S. Bonaventura ; they ought to go and consult him and abide by his decision. The Cardinal wished to see him at once and took Father Philip with him in his carriage to show the coachman the way. On arrival, St. Philip who during the drive had told the Cardinal the most wonderful things about his man, had Brother Felix called, a lay-brother who could neither read nor write and always worked in the garden, when he was not out begging for the convent. His external appearance seemed only too evidently to display the inner man : St. Charles believed himself the victim of a practical joke ; and so indeed he was, at least in form. But not in substance ; for that poor lay-brother was a Saint. He had come from Cantalice, a little village in Umbria ; born in 1515, he died in Rome in 1587 in the odour of sanctity, and ended by becoming famous for his goodness, patience and charity, for the matchless and irresistible kindliness with which he replied both to gifts and refusals, to kind words and insults alike : ' Deo gratias,' wherefore everybody called him ' Brother Deo gratias.' He was beatified in 1625 and his canonisation followed in 1712.

St. Philip knew him well and insisted that, there and then, he should listen to the rules written by the Cardinal, and give his judgment on them. He did so, and suggested certain improvements, so important and so well presented, that the Cardinal willingly accepted them.

After the death of St. Charles, among the chorus of voices that proclaimed him a Saint, that of St. Philip was among the loudest and most authoritative. The fathers of the Oratory were the most eager promoters of his canonisation, foremost among them Baronius. The affection of St. Philip for St. Charles was transferred with truly paternal tenderness to his young cousin, Cardinal Federico Borromeo, who returned it with filial devotion. An exchange of letters between them, and the printed and manuscript recollections of Cardinal Federico supply touching details of this mutual affection. Federico went and stayed at the Oratory as in his own house and in the bosom of his own family ; Philip was his confessor, counsellor, superior and father ; his priests were like brothers to him.

It was from Philip's affection that he drew the courage which, as he himself says, he needed, when the Pope appointed him to the See of Milan ; in the person of his saintly cousin, Philip pointed out to him the model to follow in every act and moment of his pastoral life ; and at the hands of Federico, who by a kindly disposition of Providence happened to be in Rome, St. Philip received the Blessed Sacrament as Viaticum, with memorable proofs of his faith, humility and love.

To the quite special affection of Philip for Cardinal Federico, we owe the small ingenious portrait in coloured wax of finest modelling, for which, according to a reliable tradition, St. Philip, who had been refractory to everyone else's prayer, finally resigned himself to sit, to satisfy his beloved Cardinal who refused to leave Rome without taking with him a picture of his kind and saintly Father.

ST. CHARLES AT TRENT DURING HIS LIFE AND AFTER HIS DEATH

From January 1562, when for the third and last time the Council of Trent really and effectively reassembled, until December, 1563, the date of its final closure, St. Charles can—indeed must—be said to have been in Trent in mind and heart ; and the contacts, so close and continuous, sustained and eager, which he maintained with that great Council, were contacts which linked him with that city that had the honour to be its venue.

A little later, in November 1565, the capital of the Trentino had also the good fortune to be visited by him in person. He had been sent there as the Legate and representative of his uncle the Pope, at the request of Cosimo de'Medici, Duke of Florence, to meet the Archduchess Joan, daughter of the Emperor Ferdinand I, coming to Trent with her elder sister, the Archduchess Barbara. For the marriages between Barbara and Alfonso II d'Este, and of Joan and Francesco de'Medici, son of Cosimo and sharing with him in the government of Tuscany, were to be solemnised at Trent.

At Trent were also two members of the family of the Madruzzi, Cristoforo, Cardinal and Bishop of Trent, and Lodovico, his nephew, a disciple of St. Philip Neri and after some years also Cardinal and successor to his uncle, both linked in close friendship with St. Charles. A telling and, for the history of that time, peculiarly important proof of this friendship is the copious correspondence between these three eminent men, which has fortunately been discovered in our time, thanks to the ingenious and successful researches of Dr. Andrea Galante, Professor in the University of Innsbruck.

A further link with the Madruzzi family and Trent was the marriage of Fortunato, the brother of Lodovico, with Margherita von Hohenems, the daughter of Chiara de'Medici, sister of Pius IV, and therefore (maternal) aunt to St. Charles.

Yet another friend of our Saint in Trent was Father Franz Spaur, one of the first six men who bound themselves by solemn vows to the Congregation of the Somaschi, after it had been approved by the Holy See ; Fr. Spaur died in the odour of sanctity in the Collegio di San Biagio in Rome in 1585 (see N. Toneatti, *Calendario Ecclesiastico per l'anno* 1857, p. 174 ; Margotti, *S. Pietro e l'Italia*, II, p. 53).

St. Charles should have gone a second time to Trent, in 1568, and had received instructions from Pope Pius V, by Brief of May 15 of that year, in order to compose the serious conflict which had arisen between the Archduke Ferdinand of Austria and Lodovico Madruzzi, in whose favour Cardinal Cristoforo had resigned from his Bishopric. But St. Charles was prevented, partly by the very acute phase of the conflict at the time, partly by urgent calls of his own diocese, from returning to the city of Trent, though not without making his influence felt in favour of the just claims of Madruzzi.

It is almost needless to say that our Saint made extensive use of the very wide faculties which his position as Legate gave him, to forward wherever he passed and especially at Trent, the constantly more practical application of the decrees of the Council, particularly in religious houses to which his visits brought great spiritual and material benefits.

It is no wonder that, even after his death, his memory remained, or rather became ever more alive in Trent and its surrounding parts.

In the convent of the Poor Clares of San Michele, in the suburb of Santa Croce, which had been visited by him, the place is still pointed out where he celebrated Holy Mass, vested, so a local historian, Marini, says, in a chasuble ' of the poorest and most abject stuff,' but at once and ever after religiously preserved as a precious relic.

Another relic ' ex visceribus S. Caroli Borromoei ' is preserved in the Cathedral. It is kept in a reliquary, in the form of a monstrance without rays ; on the foot it bears in relief the Madonna with the Child, St. Charles with the Crucifix, the figure of an Emperor with the orb in one hand and a sword in the other, and a lion rampant, probably the armorial bearings of the donor, a Count Lodron. The upper part is worked in floral relief patterns among which five *putti* support the Cardinal's hat, the mitre, the pastoral, the pallium and the word ' Humilitas.'

A letter, in a handsome silver frame, is preserved as a relic in the Basilica of Santa Maria Maggiore, dated October 18, 1561, addressed to the Cardinal of Trent ; only the signature is in autograph ; the letter deals with the provision of the provostship of Missaglia. Another letter is kept in the Civic Library of Trent ; it is of July, 1560, addressed to the same Cardinal ; it is a mere note of courtesy, written by some clerk's hand, but contains a polite and cordial postscript in the Saint's autograph.

One of the well-known pictures of the Saint is taken from a magnificent painting preserved in the Episcopal Seminary of Trent. Another comes from a coloured copper engraving, that belongs to the Diocesan Museum of the town. What is worthy of note is that the small town of Trent sets an example to very many cities, some much larger, like our own, of a Diocesan Museum which gathers up, and will gather up more widely and diligently all the sacred treasures of the town and diocese. The considerable number of them makes a brave and instructive show, as can be seen from the splendid catalogue published by the Rev. Professor Casagrande, the Director of the Diocesan Museum.

Another picture of St. Charles which is justly held in great esteem is also preserved at Trent: it is a replica of that of which we have spoken in No. 4 of our review ' S. Carlo Borromeo.'

' In our Diocese we have remains of St. Charles everywhere: churches, chapels, pictures . . .' with these words the aforementioned Director of the Diocesan Museum of Trent closes the list of items of information he kindly sent us, for which we are happy to be able to thank him publicly. Worthy of special mention are the paintings which embellish the altar and the walls of the Chapel dedicated to St. Charles in the Church of the Inviolata at Riva di Garda, a real jewel of art which two years ago was the object of the loving and ingenious care of our Professor L. Cavenaghi, who has since become famous for having rescued the Leonard da Vinci's ' Last Supper ' from certain ruin.

MARCO GEROLAMO VIDA DA CREMONA, BISHOP OF ALBA

The attention, affection and veneration of all the Bishops who had gathered for the first Provincial Council of Milan to support the young Metropolitan Borromeo, were concentrated upon a handsome old

man, tall of stature, with a flowing beard and a
face expressive of intelligence and kindliness. The
repute of a life singularly devoted to his pastoral
cares, of a man of great learning and literary
eminence, of a great poet, had preceded him. He
was Mgr. Marco Gerolamo Vida of Cremona,
Bishop of Alba and he himself was even greater and
more remarkable than either his appearance or his
fame.

Born at Cremona in 1490, he died in his See of
Alba in 1566, according to general consensus on
September 24, according to a document in the
Secret Archives of the Vatican on the 27th. He
had studied with great success in Padua and
Bologna, and had soon become famous for his
Latin poetry, remarkable alike for the purity of its
Christian inspiration and its classical form. It
had made him known and welcome in the elegant
and cultured circles of his home town no less than
at the court of the Gonzagas in Mantua and that
of Leo X in Rome. As the writer, so was the man.
It could recently be said of him that ' he remains
still the *rara avis* among his contemporaries. . . .
The corruption which surrounded him for so long,
so far from infecting him, had not even touched
him, and in the midst of the elegant, but cynical
dissipation of the Medicean court, he continued to
be what he had been at Cremona and at Mantua, a
good and learned ecclesiastic ; in other words, he
realised in himself the ideal of the priest as the
Council of Trent endeavoured to produce him.'
Receiving from Leo X the Priorship of San Silvestro
in Frascati, he wrote in that verdant and pleasant
solitude his *Christias*, in six Books, which he published in 1535, his masterpiece and perhaps the
most beautiful attempt to compose a sacred and
Christian epic. Clement VII created him Protonotary Apostolic and designated him for the dignity
of Cardinal. He preferred the modest Episcopal

See of Alba, where he displayed his qualities of excellent Bishop and citizen during the Franco-Spanish war which brought upon Alba the misfortune of its siege by the French. He was three times in Trent with the Fathers of the Council, in 1545, in 1547 and during its final stage. It witnesses to the esteem in which he was generally held, that the Fathers sent him a letter urging his presence; so does his noble and important reply, which has been edited by Professor F. Novati in the *Archivio Storico Lombardo*, 1894, from which the above-quoted words are taken.

Vida became an active and zealous executor of the Tridentine reform, forestalling even the example set by St. Charles. After a pastoral visit, he proclaimed a synod which was later deferred owing to the disturbances of wars and out of regard for the increased poverty of his clergy; but as early as 1562 he published his *Constitutiones synodales*, in the preface to which he explains, almost with apologies, that he has used a plain and practically vulgar Latin in order to be understood and obeyed by all.

Between him and St. Charles ensued a noble contest of modesty and zeal. Our Saint consulted Vida on the occasion of his first Provincial Council; Vida, soon after the Council and about two months before his death, requested leave of his young Metropolitan to return to and remain for some time in Cremona to restore his shattered health and to commission the painter Giulio Campi to paint a picture, representing the Martyrdom of St. Laurence which he intended for his Cathedral at Alba.

A curious and little known or noticed episode occurred when St. Charles, out of kindly and humble deference to the famous literary man, asked Vida for some suggestion or outline for his inaugural discourse at the Council. Vida, putting himself in the place of his Metropolitan, sent him a short and highly polished discourse in his best classical manner, spick and span. Our readers, even those (if there are such) who know St. Charles only from the pages of our review, will be able to judge whether he was the sort of man likely to recite by heart the speech of another. We possess, in fact, the discourse delivered by St. Charles ; it is printed in the *Atti della Chiesa Milanese ;* it is a fine example of sacred eloquence, but it is utterly different from that of Vida. The strange part is that this latter was, now almost twenty years ago, published from the original preserved in the Ambrosian Library, as ' having been delivered at the first Provincial Council in the presence of St. Charles.' Vida wrote and published many other works, beside the *Christias* and the *Constitutiones synodales: Scacchia ludus* (Rome, 1527) ; *Poeticorum Libri III* (Rome, 1527) ; *Bombycum Libri II* (Lyons and Basle, 1537) ; *Hymni de rebus divinis* (Louvain, 1552) ; and in prose : *Dialogi de reipublicæ dignitate* (Cremona, 1556), without mentioning other minor works and a correspondence still largely inedited and not without importance for the history of his time. Professor F. Novati, mentioned above, has given us a fine sample of it in his ' Sedici lettere di M. G. Vida, Vescovo di Alba ' (*Archivio Storico Lombardo*, 1898–1899). The works of Vida gathered in two volumes, were published again in Padua in 1731. There are numerous editions of his poetical writings : Cremona, 1550 ; Leyden, 1559 ; Oxford 1722, 1725, 1733.

Many, like Marcheselli, Tadisi, Tiraboschi, Lancetti, have written about him ; even writers in other countries, like De La Tour, Le Fèvre-Deumier ; yet it has been well said by Professor Novati, that Vida still awaits his biographer. Professor Novati has proved himself so capable a judge of his great fellow-citizen and so well informed on everything regarding him, that we desire and hope that he himself will be in the near future Vida's biographer.

Then the reason will disappear which justifies the lament and reproach contained in the words of Niccolò Tommaseo (*Dizionario Estetico*) : ' One of the men most undeservedly ignored by the ungrateful learning and the miserable elegance of our day, is Gerolamo Vida, priest, citizen, worthy Bishop, and friend, who, in a time of faint-hearted passions and low desires, loved generous causes generously, and wrote, prayed and battled ; more truly a poet than Fracastoro, because warmer in his affection and richer in imagery, and a master of language and verse.'

CASTELLINO DA CASTELLO

Here is a man of whom the words of Dante might well be repeated :

' . . . e se il mondo sapesse il cuor ch'egli ebbe

assai l'*onora* e più l'*onorerebbe* ! '[1]

Some of our readers might be tempted to say that the world honours him but little. But such a remark would be neither just nor true : the life and the merits of Castellino were recalled to the memory of the public not so very long ago, in 1884, and his works, or rather his great work, namely the *Schools of Christian Doctrine*, at least in their first and principal phase, have had a monument in a notable volume to which we refer below. In our Duomo, about the middle of the wall on the right-hand side, a modest but eloquent inscription indicates the place of his tomb, which was allowed—and little

------

[1] *Dante : Parad.* VI, 140–142. The italics in the original, indicate that the author has replaced ' loda ' and ' loderebbe ' of the quotation by ' onora ' and ' onorerebbe.'

(*Translator's note.*)

more need be said—to be placed there by St.
Charles who had removed so many other tombs
from the precincts of the Cathedral. The inscription
reads :

> CASTELLINUS DE CASTELLO
> Sacerdos Mediolanensis
> Eximia Vir Pietate
> An. MDXXXVI Die B. Andreæ Solemni
> Doctrinæ Christianæ Scholas Instituendi
> Auctor Primus Fuit
> Obiit die XXI Septembris
> An. MDLXVI

In 1881 a marble tablet was set up near the corner
of Via Alessandro Manzoni and the Vicolo San
Giacomo, which reads :

> Il Sacerdote
> CASTELLINO DA CASTELLO
> di Menaggio
> qui fondava nel 1536
> la prima Scuola Elementare Festiva
> pei Fanciulli Poveri.

The two inscriptions need to be read together :
a Milanese by reason of his residence and his work
here, Castellino was a Comasco, as his birthplace,
Menaggio, belongs to that part. A street there still
bears his name, and several families of the name of
Castelli still exist, from whom, on the evidence of old
documents, his name ' da Castello ' is derived.

Christian Doctrine, which was the main subject
of the schools which he founded, constituted their
particular and essential value. But this instruction
in Doctrine was combined with the first elements of
knowledge generally. It can indeed be said that
Castellino, vigorous and effectual opponent of
ignorance in the matter of religion, was at the same
time an opponent of ignorance generally, or as we
now say, of illiteracy.

He was, of course, not alone in pursuing this great work ; he had many collaborators. But the credit for it goes back in the first place to him, and he remained for quite thirty years the directing mind ; from him came the impulse which constantly grew in strength, as the work expanded and assumed immense proportions. With him and obedient to him were his spiritual sons ; they were numerous and even before beginning the work, had established themselves in their own quarters.

Much is spoken and written nowadays about the Catholic Counter-Reformation, set up against the Protestant Reformation. Castellino, and with him Milan, can claim one of the first places (first in time and importance) in these great and glorious events.

He first called his work the ' Society of Christian Reform.' This title suffices to throw into relief the farsighted and historically opportune conception of this humble priest. But he did not cling to the title and, when it aroused apprehension by its novelty, he adopted at a meeting held in 1546 in San Sepolcro—in the priests of San Sepolcro he found at once his most helpful collaborators— another, which touchingly displays the spirit which animated him and his helpers : ' Servants in Charity of the Little Ones ' (*Servi dei puttini in carità*). They also called themselves the ' Society of the Christian Life,' or the ' Guild of Christian Religion ' (*Collegio di religione cristiana*), but they made no change in either their principles or their action except in constantly widening and intensifying their work.

The efficacy of the work of Castellino was truly remarkable.

His first school was opened under a portico which stood behind the Church of San Giacomo e Filippo, then situated at the corner of the Via Alessandro Manzoni and the Vicolo San Giacomo, where the above-mentioned tablet is now set up.

At the time of his death, September 21, 1566, his schools had spread not only through all the quarters in Milan and the larger and smaller towns of her territory, but also to Genoa, Vigevano, Verona, Piacenza, Mantua, Parma, Lodi, Cremona, Novara, Bergamo, Brescia, Rome, Asti, Ascoli, Venice, Savona, Turin, Ferrara, Sora, and Como. I have mentioned these larger towns in the order of priority in which they welcomed the work of Castellino. These places, and numberless others, were visited by the disciples of Castellino, who did not stint themselves, bringing their own methods, their books, yet modifying them with great wisdom to adapt them to varying needs. Castellino himself often went ahead of them to start the first furrow, or followed them to superintend and direct their work. On a return journey from Genoa in 1541, he completely lost his eyesight, and later other infirmities afflicted him so that he passed the last eight years of his saintly life on a bed of suffering. Yet his vigorous spirit never failed him, nor the confidence, full of gratitude, of his own people. Having been elected Prior-General in 1539, then Prior-General for life in 1554, he continued his labours indefatigably, assisted first by Sub-Priors, then, after 1558, by Deputy Priors-General. On September 16, 1565, a year before his death, displaying an energy which seemed a miracle to everyone in a man who had been bedridden for seven years, in order not to miss an important gathering at S. Michele al Gallo, he had himself taken out of bed and carried there.

Though Popes, Cardinals, Bishops and the most distinguished prelates of his time, and the best men among princes and rulers were soon won over to his cause, neither he nor his helpers were immune from opposition and tribulations. There is nothing more wonderful or more attractively heroic than the spirit which Castellino had succeeded in fostering in his disciples. At a particular time apprehension was also aroused in Rome, where two Milanese, a certain Cusani and Pensabene, had introduced the 'schools'; the very development which the work had enjoyed, caused alarm, in view of the simplicity, seemingly too ingenuous, of the 'workers' (as they called themselves) who were, for the greater part, there as everywhere, laymen.

'Good news, my brothers, good news'—so wrote Pensabene on July 13, 1564, to his brethren in Milan—'rejoice with us over the good news; we have been rejected as wretched and useless instruments . . . O my brothers, what better news could we give you than that we have been despised for the love of Christ? What greater prize or favour could we find in this life? Because our meek and gentle Jesus, too, is so kind and generous as never to weary in conquering by courtesy.' But the clouds soon vanished before these invincibly humble and reverent souls, and as the Council of Trent (cp. Sess. V and XXIV) had given them all encouraging signs of sympathy with their work, so also the favour of the Popes became indeed boundless.

St. Charles felt for Castellino the admiration which is paid to great men and the veneration which is reserved for Saints. And he was in truth a Saint: he had given up his whole life to the most saintly and divine work of Charity, and the voice of the people called him the 'father of purity.' When he died, on September 21, 1566, the little sapling he had planted thirty years ago under the portico of the Church of San Giacomo, had grown into a gigantic tree and was pushing its roots and spreading its branches over the whole of Italy and was about to cross even her frontiers to overshadow every Christian land. He himself, keeping step with the times and conditions, had more than once recast and perfected the regulations and the

Rule which directed the great work. When St. Charles took it over into his great heart and his strong hands, he held nothing more dear and precious, and perhaps no other cause received more generously the benefits of his apostolic zeal and of his genius for government. As early as 1546 Castellino had predicted that a great light was about to rise in Milan which would dispel the darkness : now that light had risen and he was able to say in his turn : ' Nunc dimittis, Domine, servum tuum in pace.'

ST. CHARLES, BENEDETTO ARIAS MONTANO AND GIOVAN STEFANO LAINATI

Giovan Stefano Lainati !

A man may know or think he knows much more than Don Abbondio (in the ' Promessi Sposi ' of Manzoni) and still consider himself entitled to ask, as Don Abbondio did about Carneades : Who was he ?[1] Yet many have written about him with much praise : our Fr. Morigia in *La nobiltà di Milano*, p. 167 (Milano, 1595), A. Possevino, S.J., of Mantua in the *Apparatus Sacer ad Scriptores veteris et novi Testamenti*, vol. III, p. 251 (Venezia, 1606), G. Ghilini of Alessandria in the *Teatro d'huomini letterati*, vol. II, p. 153 (Venezia, 1647), F. Picinelli in the *Elenco dei letterati Milanesi*, p. 329 (*Milano*, 1670) and F. Argelati of Bologna, in the *Biblioteca Scriptorum Mediolanensium*, vol. II, col. 800. It is true there is no reference to him in Hurter's *Nomenclator litterarius theologiæ catholicæ* which is almost the only work that is nowadays usually quoted. At any rate, it is certain that he was not just anybody, either as man or as scholar.

He was a saintly priest and provost of the Collegiate Church of Santa Maria Fulcorina, of which

---

[1] Allusion to the opening of Chap. viii of Manzoni's *Promessi Sposi* : ' Carneade ! Chi era costui ? —ruminava tra se Don Abbondio.'—(*Translator's note.*)

all that now remains, is the name of the road leading from the place still called ' Cinque vie ' to Santa Maria alla Porta, and some remains in house No. 12 of that road ; for the Church was suppressed in 1799. The good priest himself describes in a letter to St. Charles, of August 15, 1565, the condition in which he found the Church and the rectory when he came to take possession : ' When I came, moved only by Christian charity, to Santa Maria Castagnola (so the Church was called by the common folk), I found it roofless, without any furnishings, the bells buried in the ground in various spots. I have therefore had to re-roof it, to make new fittings and even to fight to get gradual possession of the rectory '—for the house had not only ceased to serve as rectory for 300 years, but had been occupied by intruders, had become the meeting place of some of the worst elements of the population and had been allowed to get into a condition bordering on ruin. So the saintly priest had gradually repaired everything, reducing himself to a condition of genuine poverty, and yet had succeeded in winning the blessings of all the poor and sick, so that when he died in 1576, his funeral assumed the proportions of a public event in the little place. Among other reputations, he enjoyed also that of being a most effective exorcist.

He was also a man given much to study and his labours resulted in a work which even to-day might prove useful, especially for priests and preachers, if it were better known and less difficult to find.

He himself refers to it in the letter quoted above : ' I have also composed a book, a very large volume, of comments taken from the works of St. Ambrose, on the gospel texts of every day, both according to the Ambrosian and the Roman rites. Without exaggerating, I can say that this book has been praised by all the theologians who assert that the Church is in need of such ; even Bishop Martino who was Bishop of Segovia and is now Bishop of Toledo, seeing such a work, has given it full approval.'

Bishop Martino here mentioned is Martino Perez de Ayala, who was present three times at the Council of Trent, distinguishing himself greatly by his philosophical, theological and linguistic erudition and by his eloquence. He had been a student at Toledo (not Bishop there, as Lainati wrote by mistake) and at Louvain, had been made Bishop of Guadix in 1548 and had been transferred first to Segovia in 1560, then to Valencia in 1564; he had died in 1566. He was the author of many works, chiefly philosophical and catechetical, and his work *De divinis, apostolicis atque ecclesiasticis traditionibus*, enjoyed fame among theologians.

It was on the occasion of his first visit to the Council of Trent that he stopped in Milan and made the acquaintance of the Provost of Santa Maria Fulcorina. He formed so high an opinion of him that, when he went to Trent the third time, he passed through Milan in order to see him again, enquired after him with affectionate solicitude, almost wondering whether he would still find him alive.

On that occasion, under date December 29, 1563, at Milan, he issued to Lainati a certificate to the effect that he had seen and carefully read a good deal of his volume and considered it as a work *Ecclesiæ valde utilem et plane dignam quæ ab omnibus Sacræ Scripturæ studiosis legatur et complectatur.* The good priest was fully justified in saying that the learned Bishop, having examined his work, had given it full approval.

In company with the Bishop as his consultor and companion, Benedetto Arias Montano also came to Milan. His name would probably not have been unknown even to Don Abbondio. Arias Montano, born at Frejenal in Estremadura in 1527, died in 1598 in Seville. He and his learning enjoyed the

M

highest reputation among his contemporaries, and
his fame has not passed away even now nor is it
likely to do so as long as the world remembers the
Polyglot Bible which was published at Antwerp
by the Plantin Press in 1572, under the auspices of
King Philip II, who had entrusted Arias Montano
with its preparation and publication. (It is for this
reason that it is often referred to as the ' Polyglotta
Regia.') Arias Montano was singled out for this
work by his vast erudition and learning in the most
diverse spheres of knowledge and especially by his
familarity with many languages, dead and living,
particularly oriental. His published works are
many and varied ; but it is in the history of biblical
and philological study that his name is written in
golden letters. This polyglot edition of the Bible,
by no means without merit, even though not free
from defects and mistakes, brought Arias Montano
not only praise and satisfaction, but also polemics
and controversies into which this is not the place to
enter. He was denounced to the Roman Inquisition and had to make several journeys to Rome,
but eventually in 1580 triumphed over all his
critics.

The publication of the volume of Lainati's we
owe to that same Plantin Press and to Arias Montano.
The volume appeared with the name and armorial
bearings of St. Charles on the title-page, because
Montano was indebted to the help of St. Charles
for obtaining the manuscript. It is to this somewhat curious combination of circumstances that
we owe our knowledge of the relations between our
Saint and this great Spanish scholar.

All this is confirmed by a letter which Arias
Montano addressed to St. Charles on January 24,
1578, which we publish here from the original
preserved in the Ambrosian Library.

ILLUSTRIOUS AND MOST REVEREND SIR,

I have arrived in the Netherlands safely, delivered by the Grace of God from the perils of the journey, though slightly indisposed as the result of a most bitter winter and of the various inclemencies of the weather of the regions through which I have passed. Now, with the help of God, I am somewhat recovered ; in any case, wherever I may be, I am at Your Grace's service and anxious to have occasion to serve you. By order of the King I shall be for some time in these states ; I therefore beg of Your Grace, if there be anything in this country in which I could be of service to you, you will entrust me rather than another with its care, for none of even your foremost and most devoted servants will exceed me in my desire or intention, however far behind others I may be in health and talents. I also beg of Your Grace to commend the rest of my life to God, because my greatest wish is to withdraw from harrowing toils and to live in the manner I have indicated to Your Grace, where in study I might serve God and do something useful for my contemporaries and for posterity.

I have begged of Your Grace to instruct the Provost of Castigniuola (*sic*), the Priest Stefano di Leinà (*sic*) to send me to Flanders the Homiliary which he has compiled from the works of St. Ambrose both because of the devotion which I have for this saintly man, and because I hope that the work will prove pleasing and helpful to the faithful. For, while I am here in Flanders, I shall find the means to have it corrected, approved and printed, since among the various kinds of business I am engaged on here, is also that of attending to matters of doctrine and publications. When I passed on my return from Milan I spoke to the aforementioned about the matter ; and he told me that he had not yet copied it and had the original no longer ; wherefore, fearing lest it be lost, which would be a great and irreparable misfortune, I have begged and encouraged him to set to work and to send it to me. And knowing that the authority and helpfulness of Your Grace and your devotion to sacred things and the general well-fare might forward this matter, I beg you humbly and urgently to induce the aforesaid Provost to send me the said copy as soon as possible so that I might have it printed, corrected and approved in the first place by the censors who are here appointed for such a function by the authority of the Church and of the King ; and that this might be, before I leave this country, for I should not like to suffer the disappointment which the Archbishop of Valencia, Martinus Ayala, the author of the book *Traditionum apostolicarum and ecclesiasticarum* experienced, who wished to see that book printed and then died without having seen it, though he had read and approved it, when he was with me in Trent and Milan. Furthermore, I beg of Your Grace to hold dear the said priest Stefano ; on account of his good life, known for so many years with such great simplicity and good example, the said Archbishop loved him like a father and venerated him as servant of God, and I love him similarly and know that Your Grace holds such goodness and piety also in affection. The manner of sending the work will be easy by the kind offices of the family Gallina, honoured merchants in Milan who know of me and have correspondents and relatives in this country ; it is through them that I send Your Grace this present letter. I beg you to offer my respects to My Lords Count Sfortia [*sic*,] brother of the Illustrious Morone, and Count Borrumeo [*sic*] the younger, whose acquaintance I made in the house of the Governor on the 2nd day of last November and to whom I am deeply indebted for their great kindness and courtesy towards myself.   Given at Antwerp, 24 January 1573.

Kissing Your Grace's hand
I remain
Your Grace's
chaplain and most devoted servant
BENED. ARIAS MONTANO.

A tergo ;

All' Illmo et Rev.^{mo} S^{or} il Card^l
Borromeo mio S^{or} osser.^{mo.}
MILANO.

The references in this letter to Lainati and his book and the good offices of our Archbishop, are amply confirmed by the letter, addressed to the ' Christian Readers,' full of praise of Milan and the Milanese (or ' Ambrosians,' as Arias calls them), which this learned man prefixed to the volume. The actual preface and introduction properly speaking he had left to Pietro Galesini who makes a great display there of his erudition and also a little of his personal vanity in ten long pages on the vicissitudes and the earlier homiletic writers of the Church of Milan.

The volume of Lainati was published in Antwerp in 1575 under the following title :

Volumen/homiliarum/e Sancti Ambrosii/episcopi et doctoris/ libris contextum/opera et studio/ Stephani Leinatii, presbyteri mediolanensis, et/ Ecclesiæ Sanctæ Mariæ ad Fulcorinum præpositi ; /usui/S. Mediolanensis Ecclesiæ/accomodatum/ Ad amplissimum et optimum S.R.E./Cardinalem/ Carolum Borromoeum Archiepiscopum Mediolani.—Here follows the coat of arms of Borromeo— Antverpiæ/Ex Officina Christophori Plantini/ Architypographi Regij/M.D.LXXV.

The title indicates sufficiently clearly the scope of the work.   It is a handsome folio volume of 300

pages, with, in addition, 14 pages filled by the
frontispiece and the above-mentioned preliminary
matter. It is a genuine compilation from St.
Ambrose's works, put together by Lainati with a
learning, skill and industry which Montano had
good cause for admiring. In connexion with each
Gospel text, as they follow one another for every day
in the Ambrosian Missal, Lainati has gathered from
the various works of St. Ambrose the passages which
fit to each as a homiletic explanation. He has been
so successful in this, as Montano observes, that the
passages collected look as if this had been the very
intention of St. Ambrose. Only a short appendix is
devoted to the Roman Missal.

The letter published above bears every trace of
the intimate and friendly relations existing between
our Archbishop and the learned Spaniard, especially
the passage where Montano speaks of the confi-
dences he made to him concerning ' the rest of
his life.' Some light is thrown on these relations
also by two letters of Speciano, who was the
diplomatic agent of St. Charles in Rome, to his
employer.

' Il Cavaglier Arias Montano,' as Speciano calls
him in a letter of June 11 (F. 92 inf. f. 253v),
arrived in Rome at the beginning of the month
1575, and put up at Santa Prassede.

Our Archbishop had evidently recommended
him warmly to his agent in Rome, for the latter
writes in another letter of July 6 : ' I am showing
the Cavagliere Arias Montano such kindness as
my natural lack of charity permits, and, inasmuch
as we have arranged for him what he wanted, and to
judge by what he says, the lodgings at Santa Prassede
seem to meet his wishes in every way. He has
declined to exchange them for the house of the
Spanish Ambassador (' Imbasciatore Catholico '),
although the Ambassador pressed him much and
came to see him expressly for the purpose at Santa

Prassede. The same has happened with the Bishop of Badajoz.'

Our review, devoted as it is to St. Charles Borromeo, could not but recall so notable a work as Lainati's, to which our Saint could in justice lay some claim, or pass over his close friendship with one of the brightest luminaries of science of his century.

ST. CHARLES AND THE SPIRITUAL EXERCISES OF ST. IGNATIUS

The biographers of St. Charles are agreed in asserting that what may well be called his conversion began with a set of ' spiritual exercises.'[1] They also are in agreement in saying that it was his pious custom to make them regularly once, if not twice, a year. That he made them the first time according to the manner of St. Ignatius, can hardly, it seems, be a matter of doubt, since he did so under the direction of Fr. Ribera of the Society of Jesus. But we can hardly say more than that about the relations of the Saint to the Exercises of St. Ignatius, if we confine ourselves to the documents which, as far as I know, have so far been published. It is, however, true that the III Provincial Council (Part I) of 1570 (cf. *Acta Eccl. Med.*, Part I, vol. ii) lays down for candidates to the order of Sub-Deacons, what in fact corresponds to the notion of real and proper ' Exercises ' and, moreover, in the manner of St. Ignatius rather than of others, including a retreat to a place specially set apart, complete freedom from all other occupations and cares, a

[1] We use this term because, as is well known, certain pious practices and forms of prayer and especially of meditation are still called by that name and were even more commonly called ' spiritual exercises ' at the time of St. Charles. It is important to bear this in mind to grasp fully the thought of our Saint, whenever in his letters or elsewhere he deals with Ascetics.

general examination of conscience and confession covering the whole preceding life, wholesome meditations and other pious practices (*aliisque spiritualibus exercitationibus*) : all this under the guidance of a spiritual director, who has, of course, been approved by the Bishop ; the whole lasting for a month, or more or less according to the prudent advice of the director himself.

The same practice is to be followed by the Deacons before Ordination, and is also prescribed, at least as a pressing recommendation (this time by the Apostolic Visitor) for those who have reached the Priesthood, especially if they are advanced in age and have never previously taken part in spiritual exercises. Young clerical students on their entering the Seminary or returning there after their autumn vacations (cf. *Acta Eccl. Med.*, Part V, vol. iii, *Institutiones ad . . . Seminarii regimen*, beginning) are to take part in exercises for at least a week under the direction of the Father Confessor of the Seminary.[1]

From the draft of a letter of St. Charles to Mgr. G. B. Fontana (the draft bears no date, but is certainly of September 1579) it is evident that he had begun to build a house specially destined for

---

[1] A Venetian priest by name Bennato (as he signs himself), author of a number of ascetic works, composed on this brief text of instructions for the Confessor of the Seminary a whole book under the title : ' Il direttore spirituale de' Seminari secondo lo spirito di S. Carlo Borromeo. Opera utilissima a'Maestri de' Novizi ne'Chiostri ed a'Direttori della Gioventù ne'Collegi, ed a tutti li Confessori. Con l'Aggiunta delle Meditazioni per gli Esercizi Spirituali proprie ed adattate al loro stato e condizione." In Venezia, appresso Simone Occhi, MDCCXLVII ; pp. xxiv.-467 ; about 0.15 × 0.9 m. The contents correspond only in part with the title, but it seems worth while recording the book on the occasion of the third centenary of our Saint.

these exercises. He writes there : ' As regards the place specially set apart for the exercises, I have received the plans which you have sent me. The building can be continued in the way in which it has been begun. . . .' There can be no doubt that he speaks here of real and proper exercises, for he goes on to say : ' but I am afraid that, the refectory being in common, this might cause some distraction to those who are making the exercises.' This was perhaps the first house expressly built for this purpose. Bartolomeo De Rossi (*De origine et progressu Congregationis Oblatorum*, p. 69 ff, Milan, 1739) states that it was built near the Seminario della Canonica, now the Royal Higher Technical Institute, at one time the House of the ' Umiliati ' which after their suppression was handed over to the Seminary. He also gives a short description of it : it contained an extensive series of cells, used down to his time for their original purpose by the new recruits of the Seminary and for the Ordinands, under the direction of the Oblate Fathers, among whom he speaks with special praise of P. Antonio Moro and P. Giuseppe Oldoni. But so far there is no mention of St. Ignatius, or of his method or of his famous book.

The draft of a letter of St. Charles to Cardinal Paleotti, fortunately almost exactly dated (September 1582), gives us all the information we can desire. He writes as follows : ' . . . As to the spiritual exercises which those destined for Holy Orders are to make, the time fixed by the Apostolic Visitor and by our Provincial Council was laid down as about a month, but in practice it is about a fortnight at the discretion of the spiritual Director and Confessor who guides those taking part in the exercises. In regard to the manner, we try to follow the Jesuit Fathers and to be guided by their rules which are in a way laid down by P. Egnatio [*sic*] in the little volume[1] which must be well known to Your Emin- ence. Your Eminence can therefore obtain all information from them.' The document could not be more informative, and is all the more significant, as since 1579 the Jesuits had been replaced by the Oblates in the direction of the Seminary.

There is some further information available, even if it does not add much in the way of detail. There follows immediately on the above draft that of a letter of St. Charles, apparently written directly after- wards, addressed to the Father Provincial of the Jesuits of the Venetian Province, in which he says that he ' is inclined ' to take Fr. Antonio di Nuvolara with him on the journey to Rome, on which he is about to start ' either by boat or by sedan-chair, to avail myself of his help in some spiritual exercises.' It is worth noting that the Saint prefers these means of transport on account of their greater convenience for spiritual occupations. It seems to me indeed that we too might be ' inclined ' to think that by these ' spiritual exercises ' St. Charles meant a short, but real course of spiritual exercises. It is also noteworthy from this detail that even after his conversion he preferred as directors in these exercises the sons of him who had been by Provi- dence their originator. Fr. Adorno, S.J., was with him, as he had been on other occasions, in that last retreat at Monte Varallo, whence he came to Milan to die. We have seen above how discreetly and politely he referred Cardinal Paleotti to the sons of St. Ignatius for ' all information ' as to the manner and practice of these ' exercises.'

[1] It is curious that the ' little book of P. Egnatio ' does not figure among St. Charles' books of which we have the catalogue in the Ambrosian Library. We shall see below that he had the Latin edition of Vienna of 1563 at hand, and perhaps because he had it so constantly at hand, that wonderful ' little book ' never was, nor was found afterwards to be, on the shelves with the others, when the inventory was taken.

But the best and most important part of the attitude of St. Charles to the spiritual exercises of St. Ignatius still remains to be given, even though we have to confine ourselves to short indications.

He not only knew and practised these exercises in their quite special form ; in his humility and his burning and heroic desire for good and with all his habits of self-discipline, he not only placed himself under the tuition of the sons of St. Ignatius as he had placed the students of his Seminary under them, and allowed himself to be directed by them in the manner and practice of these exercises, but he also wished to become a guide and master in this manner and practice himself. It was what we might expect from his temperament made to rule, and what we ought to expect from the delicate conscience and the insatiable eagerness and solicitude of a shepherd of souls. We possess actually a most interesting documentary proof of this in a MS. of the Ambrosian Library.[1]

On folio 1, at the top of the page, is written : *Exercitiorum spiritualium regulæ generales in ipso exercitio tradendo*. Another hand, that of Antonio

---

[1] It bears the mark D.325 infer. It is a paper MS., measuring 0.32×0.24 m., consisting of 28 written folios, recently paginated only on the *recto*. What is now the first, was to have been originally, if not the cover, at least the fly-leaf. It has only two pages and is fastened to the rest by means of a large clip. The first 15 folios are in the hand of a copyist of the sixteenth century with very few autograph corrections by St. Charles. Folios 16–25 *recto* are in the hand of another contemporary copyist, but with many more autograph additions of the Saint (notably folios 19 *recto*, 21 *verso*, 24 *verso* ; folios 25–28 *verso* are entirely written by St. Charles). The folios of 4 pages are not combined in sheets of five, but only two by two. An older hand, perhaps St. Charles' own, numbered them up to 10 on the first page only of every four. The last page of folio 10 is partly left blank and has at the foot a caption (*Regulæ*) without reference, however, to what follows. The first of the numbered folios (2 and 3 of the present pagination) bears the number 4 of the older pagination which suggests that there are 3 folios (or 12 pages) missing.

Olgiato, the first worthy Prefect of the Ambrosian
Library (1602–1647), has added : ' Hæc est manus
B. Caroli,' and just below : ' Quædam additamenta
sunt manu eiusdem B. Caroli in fine exarata.' This
is perfectly, if not wholly, true (see note on p. 167) ;
the authority of Olgiato is valuable, but in this
case almost superfluous, for the facts are evident
to any one who has any knowledge of the hand-
writing of St. Charles in the various stages of his
life.

On the same page, lengthways along the stitching,
again the hand of St. Charles has written : *Modus
quomodo tradenda sunt puncta et diversa exercitia spiritualia.* Here, too, a clearly eighteenth century hand
has added : ' Hæc est manus S. Caroli.'

Superfluous as this assurance may seem, as much
and even more so than that of Olgiato, the two
sentences, placed by St. Charles himself as titles
at the head of the MS., can be said to be of special
interest and importance. It is enough to recall
that the first edition of the *Directorium*, the manual
for those who give or direct the exercises of St. Ignatius, dates from 1591, thirteen years after the death
of St. Charles. It is true that immediately after the
death of St. Ignatius the first General Assembly of
his sons had charged Fr. Laynez with the task of
preparing a proper ' Directorium,' as for the other
activities of the Society, so also for the spiritual
exercises. But this great ' Directorium ' was never
actually composed and for a long time only partial
and experimental attempts at doing so were made ;
as for example, the instructions of Fr. Paul Hoffée,
Provincial for Upper Germany, in 1568, ' pro
magistro exercitantium '—precisely, as will be seen,
the idea of St. Charles. It had also been the idea
of St. Ignatius himself ; for no one understood better
than he the need of a director for those taking part
in exercises ; for it is an essential and characteristic
feature of the exercises of St. Ignatius, that they

cannot be made by any one alone, but that he requires a director who proposes them and directs him. Hence also the need of guidance and assistance for the director himself. The point is that the exercises of St. Ignatius as he conceived and ordered them, are not a matter of doctrine, but a method, which rests on the finest shades of experience and a marvellous, not to say miraculous insight in the deepest and most complicated psychological processes ; a method, moreover, which in most cases is indicated only by headings, more or less detached and apparently disconnected.

For this purpose St. Ignatius himself provided a manual for his exercises with scattered ' notes ' and ' rules ' which for the larger part concern the function and work of him who directs and gives the exercises.

He hoped by means of these notes and explanations which no one equalled him in giving, himself to train really capable directors from among his first disciples, and he himself had graded and classified the particular gifts of each : Le Fèvre, Salmeron, Villanueva and Domenech. St. Ignatius considered one of our own fellow-countrymen, Francesco Strada, as exceptionally gifted for conducting the exercises of the first week.

St. Charles turned to this first *Directorium* of St. Ignatius and by gathering together the various scattered parts, co-ordinating them and sometimes clarifying them by titles or notes, began to compose them into a single whole. Corresponding with the titles placed at the opening of the MS. in his own hand, we find there collected all those—but only those—directions, rules and notes which have a bearing on the office and functions of the director, while all others are omitted. The various texts and passages are taken and literally transcribed from the volume ' *Exercitia spiritualia: a Rev. admodum in Christo patre nostro M. Ignatio de Loyola, Societatis Jesu*

Institutore, et primo Generali præposito, auctore : Viennæ Austriæ, in ædibus Cæsarei Collegi dictæ Societatis : anno Domini 1563. It is a small volume in 32-mo of 141 fols., numbered in *recto*, with one folio unnumbered at the end. Our MS. bears on the margin the number of the folio of the printed book for every passage quoted.

As explained above, our MS. is incomplete : it ends with folio 15 *verso* with a blank space and a caption ' Regulæ' without anything to follow. The blank was reserved for a fourth note (' Quarto denique notandum est ') in the printed volume, which comes after the fourth week, assuming that it has been St. Charles' intention to insert this at all, for it concerns less the Director than those who take part in the exercises. The caption seems to leave no doubt that what was to follow was the rules concerning different ways of prayer, which in their turn would have been followed by those dealing with the analysis of spiritual motives and discretion, with notes on scruples and lastly by the rules for the formation of a fully Catholic mind. But, as said, if all this had actually been transcribed and put in order, it must have been lost together with the first three folios.

What follows in fact, is something quite else, yet interesting for the study of St. Charles. It consists of twenty-one meditations or exercises in the general sense of that term, all dealing with the subject of prayer, taking this word in the fullest extent of its spiritual and ascetic meaning.

It is a kind of preparatory exercise, except that no distribution into days is given, nor seems perhaps to have been intended.

A great part of the writing is in St. Charles' own hand. It runs without interruption or the appearance of any other hand from folio 25 to the end. But even in the earlier folios which are in a hand different also from those of the copyists previously found, the autograph writing of St. Charles appears frequently, completing, correcting, adding to the text or inserting notes on the margin.

It is evident at the first glance and confirmed by more careful scrutiny that he has really become a master in the disposition and arrangement of meditations in the manner of St. Ignatius. The subject is always clearly set out, then follows the preparatory prayer, the preludes, the various points, finally the colloquy or colloquies. I add the last, because, e.g., in exercise No. 15, a colloquy is added ' ad Mariam, quia dies festus eius Conceptionis.'

The interesting point is that the main lines, the structural lines, so to say, are always those of St. Ignatius ; but the building material is taken largely not only from the Scriptures, but also from the Liturgy, the Fathers, the Roman Catechism and from that favourite author of our Saint, Fr. Granata, and his book *Trattato dell' Orazione*.

The many pages which are not autographs in the MS., especially the earlier and more interesting part of it, may suggest that we are dealing here with a work not really due to his personal conception and instigation. But any such doubt is dispelled by the very titles given to the first part of it in the Saint's own hand, and the not very numerous but very important errors, showing the ignorance of the copyists, as well as by the corrections, additions and the extensive autograph sections. There is no shadow of any reasonable or substantial doubt that we have here a manuscript really due to the idea and initiative of St. Charles, even in those parts which are not actually written by him. This, of course, does not exclude the collaboration of competent friends which the humility of our Saint was wont to invoke.

It is probable that St. Charles was referring to this MS. and particularly to its first part, when he wrote to Cardinal Paleotti on October 20, 1584 : ' These " ricordi et regole " of the spiritual exercises for which Your Eminence asks me, are still in an imperfect condition and in their first draft.   Fr. Achille Gagliardo, S.J., has had them to go over and put them into better order, but has left them on account of his departure in the hands of Fr. Adorno. They can give Your Eminence an account of them, should you so desire, during their stay in Rome. The work has also been in the hands of His Lordship the Bishop of Verona, who has given great attention to some of the points.   For I must really, as soon as the occasion presents itself, take it up again at leisure perhaps with the assistance of Fr. Adorno.'

' The index to the works of Granata is not yet made, because we are waiting for the printing of the volumes ; the one which remains to be printed is the last which is now in hand.   And then the indexes will be made.'

St. Charles had either already obtained or hoped to secure the co-operation of the two Jesuits, Fr. Gagliardo and Fr. Adorno, as well as that of the Bishop of Verona, Agostino Valier, as we would expect, for St. Charles was wont to appeal to them by preference for help in such matters.   The title given as ' ricordi et regole ' of the spiritual exercises and the reference to the MS. as a draft, make a confusion with another work, the so-called ' Synopsis,' impossible.   This latter had then been put into its final form by Valier himself, while St. Charles was still alive, namely in December 1583, as appears clearly from Valier's letter to the Oblates which he sent with a copy of the ' Synopsis ' still in our possession in the Ambrosian MS. No. B. 46 *infer*. But the description, including the reference to the works of Fr. Granata, corresponds fully or almost so with the title and general nature of the

work here in question.   I say advisedly, ' almost so,'
because it lacks the part referred to as ' ricordi ' ;
but perhaps it was that which filled the three first
folios that are missing.   The ' occasion,' still less
the ' leisure ' to which St. Charles looked forward,
never presented themselves.   He did not know
that he was within a month of his death, and
we know how he employed that brief space of
time.   So we have of his work nothing but the
' first draft,' precious indeed, even though in itself
incomplete.

We have here to make reference to another
manuscript in the Ambrosian Library, bearing upon
the present discussion.   The MS. has the mark
D.240 *infer*.   It is written in different hands of the
end of the sixteenth century and bears on the
fly-leaf the title : *Esercizi di meditazioni sopra la
Creazione, Novissimi, Vita di Gesù Cristo, e Conoscimento
di Dio*.   This title is written in an eighteenth-
century hand, but gives a full indication of the
contents.   On the *verso* of the same folio the
hand of the Prefect Olgiato has added : ' Medita-
tionum initia istarum videntur excepta ex spiritualibus exercitiis B. Ignatii.'   And further : ' Inter
lucubrationes B. Caroli hoc opusculum repertum
est.'   A slip is inserted at folio 5 : ' Meditationes
piæ, istarum rerum initia desumpta ex spiritualibus Exercitationibus Beati Ignatii.   In lucu-
brationibus Cardinalis fuerunt repertæ.'
The reference to ' Cardinalis ' could only mean
St. Charles, if Bonomi, as it would seem, wrote
the slip.   In any case, that was how Olgiato,
an unimpeachable witness, read and interpreted it,
and indeed the derivation thus indicated from the
Ignatian exercises is obvious.
What, however, is no less obvious in it, is also the

work of others besides St. Charles : on folio 2, 2 *verso*, 13 and 16, it is expressly stated that the meditations are those of a Lombard Jesuit.

Though we are therefore dealing with writings of others, the Cardinal may have intended to make use of them and possibly himself suggested and ordered them—a fresh indication of the love and study he devoted to the exercises of St. Ignatius and of the method he adopted for their application.

This was moreover natural, not to say happily inevitable. A book like the *Exercises of St. Ignatius* which almost at once established itself and was adopted as the wisest and most universal guide in spiritual direction, as an inexhaustible spring of deep and solid piety and an irresistible stimulus and the safest guide to conversions and to the highest spiritual perfection, could not but occupy the first place among the favourite books of St. Charles whose characteristic genius and noble aspirations, in a word, whose whole mind, found in it so perfect an expression.

ST. CHARLES IN THE WRITINGS OF CARDINAL FEDERICO BORROMEO

There is no one possessing greater authority or competence to give us information about St. Charles than Cardinal Federico Borromeo, his beloved cousin, disciple and almost son, his successor in his office and in his work ; and we can add at once that no one has spoken of him in terms of higher praise than he. The figure of the man, the Bishop and the Saint stands out and assumes new life in the recollections which Cardinal Federico set down in his published and unpublished writings, without—as far as is known—having ever had any intention of writing a formal biography of him. It is our hope to achieve this same result by submitting to our readers the pages which follow, taken

QVI FVIT INSVBRVM DOMINA FEDERICVS IN VRBE
ANTISTES PHŒBI PRÆSVL IN ÆDE FVIT.
TEMPORA VELAVIT MVREX: FEDERICVS AT OSTRO
DOCTA ROMANO LVMINA MENTE TVLIT
ERGO QVID MIRER COCCVM VEL CRINE TIARAM
MIROR QVOD FACTIS ORNAT VTRVMQVE SVIS.

CARDINAL FEDERICO BORROMEO
1564–1631
ARCHBISHOP OF MILAN
FOUNDER OF THE AMBROSIAN LIBRARY

bodily from the writings of the great Cardinal. Even Manzoni's admiration, expressed in those noble and famous chapters of the *Promessi Sposi*, has not availed to make these writings known as much as they deserve.

I translate what follows from the elegant Latin of Cardinal Federico, excepts where the extracts have been already translated better than I could, by Manzoni or others, to be mentioned in due course.

I abstain from further remarks ; for if by way of introduction I were to characterise the texts most worthy of note, I should risk saying in my own words all or almost all that the reader will find in the words of Cardinal Federico himself.

If his words are read and pondered, I have no doubt but that the reader, too, will seem to see the beloved and venerated figure of the man, the Bishop, and the Saint in all the vividness of that living personality whom Federico knew. So it seems to me that the best and the only introduction to the following pages are the words of that voice which spoke to St. Augustine from on high : ' Tolle et lege ! Tolle et lege.'

———

One of the works in which Cardinal Federico speaks most directly and at length of his great cousin, as of a second father, is the short ' Commentary to his studies ' (*Federici Cardinalis Borromoei Archiepiscopi Mediolani, De suis studiis commentarius ;* Mediolani, Anno M.DC. XXVII). Chapter XVIII (p. 22) bears on the margin the suggestive note : ' What happened to me in the presence of St. Charles.' The text tells the following story :

' Being in Milan on the instructions of my mother, I was taken to call formally on the Archbishop, my cousin Charles, who not only welcomed me with great kindness, but as a sign of his benevolence presented me with an Agnus Dei framed in gold.

As this man of God gently enquired about my studies, my tutor who was present, gave him an account of how things stood, and added—what perhaps was his opinion—that I had not made too much progress, as I was lacking in natural gifts and intelligence and was rather slow in learning. My tutor had said this in my presence without the least *arrière-pensée* or malice prepense. I am telling what happened, as this can best give an idea of the prudence and kindliness of St. Charles. For he did not say as many another, less prudent, might easily have said : " Ah, well ; so this boy is really stupid ? He is not likely to come up to expectations and hopes ? " Nor did he rebuke me for my slowness, my bad memory or carelessness. Looking me in the face, he said to the tutor : " I don't think that is the case ; the shape of his head seems to me to promise something better." I have to set down his very words. Then after a short silence, he looked at me again and added : " His features are exactly like my father's." St. Charles' father was Count Giberto, brother to my father ; we were therefore cousins. That day I left St. Charles, not a little crestfallen and sad on account of these remarks which, made in the presence of so great a man, might have overwhelmed and dispirited even Quintilian or Cicero. And so we returned home.'

The younger cousin sets down later (p. 25) with gratitude and satisfaction what followed :

' In course of time, I was taken now and then to see Cardinal Charles who always received me with much kindness and seemed to take pleasure in my presence. It was he who suggested to my mother that she ought not to keep me longer at home ; and in fact, after the matter had been discussed with

him, I was sent to Bologna, the See of Gabriele
Paleotti, a great friend of St. Charles, created
Cardinal by Pius IV on his recommendation.'

Soon afterwards (p. 27) the Saint seems really to
occupy the place and position of Federico's father :

' So I, having reached the stage of dialectics,
went to Bologna, as my mother and St. Charles
wished. On my departure he gave me certain
directions in writing which, while I was in Bologna,
were lost through my great negligence, with
irreparable harm, nor could they ever be found
again. Among these instructions there was also
with many other excellent exhortations, the advice
that I should fight principally against that passion
to which I was most prone and under which I most
suffered, a counsel truly worthy of the prudence of
so great a man, which I cherished for ever after.'

The advice and benevolence of St. Charles
watched over his young cousin up to the end of his
studies.

' I spent my time '—he continues (p. 34)—' in the
study of letters, when St. Charles expressed the
opinion that I should leave the University of
Bologna and should go to Pavia. Having moved
there, I completed in due time the courses in
Philosophy and Theology to the best of my abilities.
While I was endeavouring to make headway in the
study of Philosophy and Theology, St. Charles
enquired from time to time about my progress,
often conversed with me and exhorted me to continue diligently. I remember that at that time I
had conceived a passion for sacred pictures of really
good workmanship. And having gone one day to
Milan and being a guest in the house of St. Charles,
I had a great wish to become possessed of a painting
representing the Nativity of our Lord, and when
someone present with perhaps excessive boldness

interposed on my behalf, I asked for the gift of it.
Then the Saint told me in the most kindly way, that
it was indeed a noble piece of painting and it was
not little that I demanded ; but, having with his
words, as it were, raised the price of the picture
and after keeping me for some time in suspense, he
then of his own accord made me a present of it.   I
later placed this same picture in our house and it
was indeed a souvenir to be jealously guarded in
memory of its donor, St. Charles.   Meanwhile I
completed the course of my studies and had become
the senior student at Pavia ;   as St. Charles had
meanwhile died, my parents were of opinion that
I should go to Rome, and so I went there.'

As soon as he had been made Archbishop of
Milan (p. 44), his mind was preoccupied by his new
duties, and especially by that of preaching.   Again,
the dominant note of his mind is St. Charles.

' No sooner had I assumed my new office than it
occurred to me that I ought to preach, partly as a
duty of my office, partly on account of the special
practice which St. Charles had introduced in the
Church in Milan.   For he had devoted an almost
unbelievable care to, and had practised, preaching
with the utmost zeal.   He had been so fond of
this duty of preaching that I am impelled to say
what may seem an exaggeration : namely that he
appeared to set no greater store by anything else in
a Bishop, and himself proved this constantly by his
example.'

Again, the name of St. Charles may be said to be
the starting-point of Cardinal Federico's activity
as a writer.   He himself assures us on this point
(p. 72).

' In the year 1610, six months before I went to Rome for the Canonisation of St. Charles, I began to write, and it is now seventeen years that I devote myself to this task, so great and so full of difficulties. When I began to write, I was forty-six years old, and I may well wonder whether I did not begin too late.'

But everything considered and even while admitting the advantages of beginning early, the great Cardinal did not deplore his late start.

———

Federico does not forget one of his own relatives who deserved well of his education, his uncle, Count Francesco, who had impressed on him among other things : ' Let your work be your recreation,' a lesson which he learnt excellently and later always practised, as his saintly cousin had set him in this an admirable example, which he more than once records. But when he wished, of his charity, to sing the praises of his late uncle, he thought all that need be said was, that St. Charles himself had given him praise from the very pulpit, a fact which we had not known before and would hardly have expected of St. Charles, as it concerned a relative of his. But in fact, he was referring to a great friend and father of the poor :

' I had an uncle, Count Francesco, who was so generous towards the poor that when he died, St. Charles himself had no hesitation of saying from the pulpit that a father of the poor had died with him.'

———

A fierce passage of Federico's book *De non vulgari existimatione et fama* (Mediolani, A.S. M.DC.XXIII,

p. 25), takes us back to the first years of St. Charles' great career.

After having loudly deplored the wretched fate of those ecclesiastics who in their eagerness to bestow wealth upon their relatives then become their victims, he adds in a noble outburst at the end of the book :

' With good reason St. Charles and all his House adore God and give Him thanks, and glory in the fact that neither houses nor wealth, nor feudal possessions ever came to the Borromeo family from the papal dominions, and that the sacred mantle of St. Peter is not to be seen in our house as a covering and adornment of mere flesh. For St. Charles, though he had become the heir to his brother, divided all that heritage among the poor of Christ, either by selling it or by giving it away during his lifetime or, when he died, by testamentary disposition. He left us nothing but the possessions of our forefathers, which belonged to us by the inviolable rights of our noble birth. Thus the wealth of that pontificate came to so glorious an end.'

A page in the volume entitled *De gratia principum*, and translated by the author himself into Italian under the title *La gratia de' principi*, refers to that same period. In Chapter XXIV he deals with ' the great familiarity and intimacy shown by Princes with their subjects,' and comments (p. 195) on the advantages which the subjects are not slow to derive from this practice, ' as if the most importunate and forward were also the best and possessed greater merits.' ' And because '—he adds—' some wise rulers were aware of the great advantage which such familiarity brings (to such subjects), they took very wisely the part of being continually on the defensive and covering and protecting themselves with the shield of dignity. One of these is believed to have been St. Charles, since it is to be observed that some, not so much to praise as to blame him, used to say that Cardinal Charles Borromeo never dropped the Cardinal ; and others were wont to say that he was a Bishop who never dropped the Bishop. And it was indeed as they have said. But whereas they thought themselves to be blaming him by this reputation, they in fact greatly commended him, for the memory of this praiseworthy habit of his, displaying not only supreme saintliness but also supreme prudence, has persisted down to our days. Encouraged by the example of such prudence, other rulers, both secular and ecclesiastical, have adopted this habit of not forgetting themselves. . . .'

In the next chapter of the same book he happens to talk about repartees and takes occasion to tell of an incident of the life of St. Charles which has been quite overlooked by his biographers. After giving some examples of rather bold and indiscreet repartees, he records one of Speroni (the famous Speron Speroni, it would seem) to St. Charles :

' Similarly not little blameworthy was the behaviour of Speroni, who when he had been asked by St. Charles, the nephew of the Pope, at table, whether Venice was as great as Milan, replied : "No, Monsignor ; Milan is as great as Venice." Which reply, apart from being too subtle, showed that the Cardinal's question had been less wise and prudent, even though not wrong in point of fact.'

Less on account of its size than for the sake of its contents, the book entitled *Museum* (Mediolani, A.S.

M.DC.XXV), occupies one of the foremost places among the works written by Cardinal Federico.

St. Charles is not forgotten but rather takes a place of honour in this brilliant and most interesting work (p. 5), in which Cardinal Federico describes the picture collection which he had added to his—the Ambrosian—Library, and displays not only his love of art, but also the refinement of his taste and the ripeness of his judgment. The name of St. Charles, linked with so many works, is also coupled with the fate of one of the most important paintings among the present treasures of the Ambrosian gallery : the ' Adoration of the Magi " by Titian (Sala E, n. 42). The Ambrosian owes this picture to him and to his love of great art. Like the previous passage, this reminiscence shows that, even in the sphere of art where Cardinal Federico earned so much credit and praise, it had been the example of his cousin which led and inspired him. I avail myself of the skilful translation of the *Museum* by Mgr. Luigi Grasselli, prepared for the third Centenary of the Inauguration of the Ambrosian Library on December 8, 1909, and published in honour of that occasion at the same time as a photographic reproduction of the original by Senatore Luca Beltrami, with an introduction and notes (Milan 1909).

' Beginning with the pictures, we find, placed in a conspicuous position, the "Adoration of the Magi." It is the famous work of Titian, who devoted special care to its painting to please Cardinal d'Este, the elder, who intended it as a present for Francis I, King of France, as we have perhaps stated elsewhere. When the Cardinal died, the picture came by purchase into the possession of St. Charles Borromeo. It is the usual fate of collections that form the embellishment of great houses, to be put up for sale and dispersed, like the bodies of their dead owners falling to dust. This picture was cared for specially, until after the death of St. Charles, when it was purchased on our instructions.'

A posthumous volume, *De sacris nostrorum temporum oratoribus libri quinque* (Mediolani, M.DC.XXXI), leads us from the home circle and the sphere of art to that of the literary and religious history of the end of the sixteenth and the beginnings of the seventeenth century, set out with a noteworthy wealth of information and judgments on it. We find there also, as might be expected, abundant indications on the studies, the gifts and the writings of St. Charles as a preacher.

At the end (p. 65) of the fine eulogy on the Franciscan Fr. Alfonso Lupi, a very famous preacher at the time of St. Charles, Federico records the opinion of St. Charles, who more than once had made use of his works ; this opinion does as much honour to the judge as to the object of his judgment.

'St. Charles once preaching in the Cathedral of our city, said of Lupi that he certainly possessed none of the qualities which we are wont to find in perfect preachers, and yet he possessed all the gifts of the orator. Taking eloquence in its strictest sense, Lupi was not eloquent. His discourse was not distinguished either by an abundance of learning, or by clearness of disposition, or by the elegant choice of words ; nor did he possess particular gracefulness. And yet, in some new and unusual manner he appealed most strongly to the minds of his hearers, whether by merit of his eloquence or by admiration for his learning or by the ordering and elegance of his whole preaching. So much did the spirit of inward piety succeed in filling the gaps which he might have shown ; and it seemed by divine disposition that those gifts which are so necessary to the orator were so fused and combined in him that it was impossible to distinguish one from the other.'

The third book of the same work begins as follows :

' Perhaps it will cause surprise, if in continuing the discourse I began on Sacred Oratory of our times, I have thought well to deal at the opening of this third book with St. Charles, Cardinal of Santa Prassede and Archbishop of Milan. It is no small honour to those who at the present time have devoted themselves to preaching, to have found among their ranks a colleague of so great a name, who by divine disposition and the authority of the Roman Pontiff, has been solemnly added to the number of Saints to the great joy of Christendom. But he possessed in the highest degree all those praiseworthy gifts which a true and great orator cannot lack, and his preaching was always of a kind to maintain worthily the honour of that name. This was perhaps overlooked by those foolish men who, essentially ignorant of that great art, paid attention only to his somewhat defective pronunciation or to his voice which was always veiled, or to his style which had not the least trace of that display, nor abounded in those frivolities which appealed to them so much. These benighted persons did not even reflect that antiquity itself easily bore with such defects when, combined or singly, they occurred in some of their great orators.'

So he continues, recalling the examples of Pericles, Demosthenes and St. Ambrose, and then says a little further on (p. 100) :

' The saintly Archbishop displayed such prudence and reverence in dealing with the dogmas and mysteries of the Faith, that, though since his youth he had had no practice in that part of Theology which is called Scholastic, nothing ever escaped him in that way that might deserve reproach or might offend the mind of his listeners ; a matter certainly worthy of our admiration. And also dealing with other subjects he always displayed the same circumspect prudence so that never a single of those words fell from his lips which, spoken by other preachers, become in so many cases hack-neyed.'

And having duly criticised certain ineptitudes of contemporary preachers, he turns again to his great cousin and continues :

' This wonderful man was admirable on account of many other things : his remarkable diligence in the study of Sacred Scriptures, his persistence in preaching for so many years, the continual work, his struggle with natural defects, his nightly vigils, his patience in learning by heart, if necessary, what he had written, the skill and industry of his studies and the many volumes written in his own hand, of which I shall have to speak in the sequel.

' He showed also, when he spoke to the people, great experience and knowledge of human affairs, which were the source of his astonishing maturity of judgment and counsel concerning the affairs and various things that make up human life.'

Soon afterwards Federico goes on to speak of the writings of St. Charles, as he had promised, and says :

' He showed great energy whenever it fell to him to elucidate some passage of Sacred Scripture, and he never descended to that foolishness which is peculiar to those preachers who attempt to state and interpret principles in the light of their own personal caprice. His commentaries on the Sacred Scriptures which he gave in great number and frequently, would have been better remembered, if his writings could have been brought to that perfection which they would certainly have been given, had he lived longer.

' For shortly before he died, he had given proof of how anxious he was to give them the final touch, and for this purpose he had chosen one of his household to take down the exact words when he preached, and had stated that he preferred that his sermons should reach the public in Latin rather than in his native speech. I believe he thought that Latin possessed greater dignity. In preparing his sermons he adopted the expedient of setting out the subject-matter in the form of a tree, arranging the arguments and texts as its branches, to assist, I think, his memory, which was greatly helped by this disposition. I saw to it with great care that these " trees " were collected—they came to fill eight volumes—after they had remained inaccessible for a long time and had almost been forgotten. They are now preserved with all due honour in the Ambrosian Library. For, if our minds are so set upon showing honour to so great a man as to consider it a great good fortune to come into possession of a fragment of his garments and of a picture of him, why should we not equally eagerly search for these relics of his mind, lest, like all human things, they be dispersed and perish? And, alas, these had already begun to suffer this common lot, and even then some of the writings of St. Charles had been lost, as I gathered from those whose duty it should have been to look after them diligently and faithfully. I do not know if it be true to say that fatal necessity exposes the fruits of our mind to damage and manifold injuries more than the works of our hands : surely it is because the judgment of man is almost blind when it is a question of estimating the worth of literary works, while the other works are more subject to the judgment of the eye.

'Concerning the literary remains of St. Charles, a man possessed of an erudite mind might do a great work by sifting and separating what is really his from the various things which he took over into his writings from the works of others. His really original contributions, arranged in various groups might be set out under different subjects. I have no doubt that it would be an undertaking of the greatest utility and of solid results which even a large number of volumes would be unable to yield. . . .'

In what high esteem Cardinal Federico held the writings of St. Charles, he states himself, in the book entitled *Meditamenta litteraria*, written towards the end of his life and published in 1633. Recalling (p. 85) one of his earliest books, the *Juveniles exercitationes* and some letters of St. Charles added at the end, he speaks thus of them and their author :

'For the rest, some letters of the saintly Cardinal and Archbishop Charles will add worth and honour to this imperfect and immature work. I believe that these letters have come into my hands by a divine disposition, and as I have found them, so I offer them gladly to others.'

Going on to speak of that famous orator and luminary of his times, the Dominican Fr. Luigi da Granata, he lets him be introduced and appreciated by St. Charles :

'Our blessed Archbishop found great delight in the books of Luigi da Granata, whose spirit and mind bore a certain resemblance to his own. We shall now speak of this man, in accordance with the chronological order, and the singular affection which St. Charles felt for him. Our monasteries perhaps hardly possessed a man in our times who preached with more apostolic zeal and spirit.' The learned Cardinal continues an eulogy of Granata for almost five pages, even though he notices in him too frequent quotations from profane authors and a lack of vigour and art especially at the opening and ending of his sermons.

At the end of the third book the Cardinal comes to speak of Toleto, the preacher of cardinals and popes, whose eulogy he skilfully summarises at the beginning by saying that, though he preached for many years before the fine flower of Rome, none was ever weary of listening to him. The name of Toleto gives him the opportunity to recall the reply he once had from him in the matter of preaching, and to make a last handsome mention of St. Charles :

'I, too,' he says (p.129), 'moved by his great reputation and about to embark upon my pastoral office and seeing that I too should have to preach, went on my own account to call upon that great man and begged him to give me, from his experience, some advice on the most useful manner of preaching. He replied that I should never speak too long and should never speak without preparation. And having given me these two pieces of advice, he fell silent. I would gladly have derived more instruction from the prudence of so great a man and did not refrain from begging him, but I obtained nothing further from his modesty. Later, forced by my office and to satisfy the wishes of the people of this great city, who, while the memory of St. Charles was still fresh and living, expected to hear his voice again through me, I had perforce to preach fairly often. If I have achieved some mediocre success in this art, I do not know whether I owe it more to my daily labours or to some gift of nature.'

Federico concludes his book by justifying himself in the eyes of those who reproached him in a friendly and respectful way for never having given encouragement to any outstanding mind in the art of oratory, as he had done in almost all the other arts and studies. His defence is in substance that eloquence is too difficult an art and requires too many gifts and talents to be found united in one person more than extremely rarely ; that he had indeed searched for suitable persons, and only discovered two, and that even these two, through some fateful calamity, had never been able to complete the course.

This opinion of Cardinal Federico on the subject of eloquence makes his judgments on the eloquence of his saintly cousin all the more important and significant.

———————

The volumes on ' Sacred Oratory ' (*Sacrarum Concionum*, vol. I and II, Mediolani, M.DC. XXXIII) and ' On Episcopal Preaching ' (*De concionante episcopo*, Mediolani, M.DC.XXXII) present us with a splendid picture of the Archbishop as student and orator, as a saint in the glory of his canonisation.

The first discourse on the priestly office, addressed by Cardinal Federico to his clergy gathered at the Synod of 1604, concludes (I, 108) with the following exhortation :

' Let each take converse within himself and promise a new life and new practice for the future. It is your Archbishop who asks you ; not indeed I, but the generous soul of him who never admitted the need of rest, except in death. It seems indeed

o

as if he were present among us and, still eager for work, encouraging us in our labours, and at the same time, with that severe expression of his, rebuking the unworthy habits of some, threatening the slothful and intimating to each his punishment.'

In the second discourse of the same Synod (l.c., p. 96) he turns against the ignorance of some of the clergy :

' I need not speak of the daily and nightly studies of our saintly Archbishop Charles, even though he bore on his shoulders the heavy burden of this Church and lived in the midst of a real whirlwind of cares.'

One of the letters dealing with public affairs and administration, one of the official utterances, which were issued from time to time by Cardinal Federico and collected by himself under the title *Patentes litteræ*, is the one (p. 36), dated October 31, 1625, which is reprinted in the new edition of the Breviary, substantially the same as St. Charles'.

With what gentleness and modesty he barely dares to hint at the imperfection of what the Saint had done !

' St. Charles,' he says, ' having undertaken the work of amending the Breviary, gave it the form which it still has. But he had done this work during the last part of his life ; if he had been spared longer, I have no doubt but that he would have given us a perfectly amended edition.'

The discourse, No. 14, delivered on the second day of the Synod of the year 1606, with the object of correcting the greed of some of the clergy, ends with the following peroration (Vol. I, cit., p. 123) :

' I address this assembly which for so many years was presided over and directed by that Blessed

Servant of God. I implore now sorrowfully that same Servant of God and Blessed to assist me, and to inspire your hearts with what I have tried so far to impress upon you. For I well see that my discourse is by itself unavailing, nor do I possess eloquence enough to inspire you.

'May he therefore be the master, the speaker to this vast flock and the shepherd of this assembly. Remember, o my sons, your great preacher and Archbishop, and listen to his voice from on high and obey his precepts.'

The discourse No. 22, of the first day of the Synod of 1611, the first to be held after the Canonisation of St. Charles (Vol. I, cit., pp. 177–184), ought here to be reproduced entirely, dealing as it does with the usefulness of example and particularly of the example set by St. Charles. But we have to limit ourselves to the most salient parts :

'What a man '—Cardinal Federico exclaims— ' and what a shepherd was he ! Worthy of how much admiration ! ' and after having sung the praises of his apostolic labours among the hills and dales and the huts of the poor that formed their setting, he adds :

'Woe to us, priests, woe to us, shepherds of souls ! . . . Not even the sweat of St. Charles's brow availed to water the barrenness of some. . . . But is he no longer alive here, before our eyes, as the model? Does he no longer live ?

'*Mortuus est pater et non est mortuus*. . . .

'Let us therefore, o my priests, reverently and humbly approach that shining tomb irradiated by so much light. My sons, let us go to our father ; flock, come to thy shepherd ; rivulets, rush to the stream, to that stream which flows with the abundance of heavenly waters. All roads are open to us, no access is barred to such devotion. Venerate him whom you loved so much ; ask him whom you knew so well and gather from the wealth of that saintly shrine. Contemplate that body which was the temple of the spirit, which you so often saw, broken with weariness and labouring for your good, finding no rest but in death ; lastly bear to pray also for me, who am but his shadow.'

But not a vain shadow. He himself, the Archbishop, seems to feel it and at the end of the discourse, pronounced on the second day of that same Synod (l.c., p. 192), he breaks out into this noble protestation :

' It shall never happen that I should forget my priestly office, or the olden days, or the former shepherds, above all St. Charles, my guide and my master. It shall never be that, as the minister of the altar and the custodian of sacred things, I should be found wholly unworthy of so great an office.'

In the first discourse, delivered at the Synod of the year 1616, deploring the carelessness and the lack of piety of some priests he rebukes them by recalling to them the Saint (l.c., p. 266) :

' Only too soon have you lost sight of the praiseworthy institutions of this Church and especially of those prescribed and decreed by its saintly Bishop, Charles. So easily have you, bad disciples of so great a master, been able to lose the memory of the sacred rites and institutions. . . .'

And the next year, on the first day of the Synod (l.c., p. 308), to spur on his clergy to the study of the Sacred Science, he says :

' There stands before you the recent memory of your Bishop St. Charles, who was hard and severe towards himself, and ceaselessly laboured for the salvation of his people ; and you, sitting there, and doing nothing, hope to reach your heavenly home in Paradise and to rejoice in his sight ? Your saintly Bishop permitted himself in this life only such brief moments of rest, that no one, my brethren, can imagine that he would have been willing thus to suffer anxiety and weariness for his whole life for any prize less than the life of the Blessed and the heavenly joys. Even squalor, and penance, and harshness against the flesh, and the labour continued day and night was beloved of the Saint, as if he could by no other means hope to escape eternal punishment and win the eternal prize.'

The tenth discourse in the volume II quoted above had been prepared by Cardinal Federico for Christmas 1610, the same year in which the canonisation of his cousin Charles had taken place. This fact is indicated in the very subject of his sermon : ' The birth of Christ and the Canonisation of St. Charles.'

The sermon opens in fact with a hymn of praise and thanks to God which may refer equally well to the supremely joyful and salutary event of Christ's Nativity or to the quite recent event of the Canonisation. Following on this, with a sudden transition, he mentions the anxious questions of Joseph in Egypt asking his brothers whether his old father is still living, and then he continues :

' In the same way I seem to hear you asking and enquiring the same of me, after several messengers, one after another, have confirmed to you the fact which you can no longer call in doubt. Is our father still alive ? Is our and your father still living ? I reply to all, breaking out in joy : O Milanese, our father lives indeed ; he not only lives, but lives crowned with glory in heaven and on earth. He lives on earth in the minds of the faithful, he lives among far distant peoples, for even there his memory is venerated. He lives on the lips of men, for they exalt him in praise and admiration. He lives in the churches and in the sacred buildings. No longer in whispered and murmured prayers, but in loud and universal song his praises are uttered and new altars and new churches are rising and are being embellished in his honour. Rome herself, having had her fill of triumphs and no longer capable, almost, of wonderment, is yet wrapped in admiration. But our Saint is also living in heaven and of his life there, no doubt remains ; the hope of the faithful, now crowned by the canonisation, has become an assured and constant faith. Henceforth we know that his name is written in the Book of Life of the Lamb, and that he has been received into the joys of Paradise, and there in radiance rejoices in the springs of everlasting glory, the palm of the Blessed in his hand. *Benedictus Dominus Deus Israel, qui facit mirabilia solus* for all this, because he has filled earth and heaven with His greatness and His glory. But it is only right that the greater flame and light should obscure and absorb the lesser. . . . ' And so the preacher goes on to speak of the Incarnation, returning at the end once more to his great predecessor and, after a bare reference to the example of his life and death, he concludes :

' May this Saint, in his life and in his death, so newly added to Paradise, remain for ever present to us, and may we all, living and dead, be his own beloved children.'

The aforementioned volume *De concionante episcopo*, opens with the name of St. Charles.

' While the great St. Charles of everlasting memory was ruling this, the Ambrosian Church, it fell to me by a singular kindness of Providence, not only to rejoice in his presence, but also to profit by his conversation, as far as my age and the heavy burden weighing upon the Archbishop permitted. At that time he often spoke to me and told me much of his studies and his spiritual life. Even as far as I was able to judge at that age, I could see that he was wholly absorbed in the task of preaching and spared neither labour nor any practice that formed part of that pastoral office. For this purpose he gathered much from the most diverse writers and arranged the vast mass of material, collected by constant work, in the form that he found most convenient ; and he had men appointed for the object of keeping careful note of everything. He preached with great frequency and always watched himself rigorously, lest he should forget any one of the rules, according to which he, in conformity with the ancient canons, had re-introduced and sanctioned this practice and discipline of preaching to enable the shepherds of souls to feed and sustain their flocks with the word of God. And in order to secure a constantly growing number of suitable persons who might effectively and worthily fulfil that office from among the youths who in colleges and seminaries were receiving instruction in letters, he was diligently enquiring which were those who by natural gifts possessed fluency of speech, and these he desired to devote themselves by preference to the study of eloquence. And if any one showed promise in this study, we found him encouraged by the Saint with prizes and honours to pursue ever more eagerly his study so as to fulfil the hopes which he had aroused. Even though I was then but a young man, I was able to observe and to admire all these great things ; and with wonderment I used sometimes to hear grave men and excellent priests belonging to the household of the Cardinal, talking among themselves and saying : that the principal duty of Bishops was that of preaching ; that their example ought to stimulate the parish priests ; that nothing was more apt to correct and guide and even to comfort the men of the people and to enrich them with heavenly gifts than the words that fell from the saintly and kindly lips of their Bishop. I considered these things as true indeed, for they were spoken by men whom I greatly esteemed and understood to be full of honesty and wisdom. But later by a providential disposition I knew even more clearly and with more certainty with how much truth these words had been spoken.'

And a little further on (p. 4), he says : ' Charles, therefore, a man of exceptional sanctity granted to our times, held this most important office of preaching in such esteem, that he applied to himself the words of Jesaiah (XII, 7) : *Quam pulchri super montes pedes annunciantis et prædicantis pacem, annunciantis bonum, prædicantis salutem, dicentis Sion : Regnabit Deus tuus.* And from Holy Scripture he used to take the words suitable for guiding his flock to the harbour of salvation.'

In Chapter X of the second book of the same volume, Cardinal Federico has occasion to recall the great tribulations which were caused to St. Charles by the tactlessness and indiscipline of a preacher whose name he does not mention. It was perhaps that unfortunate Fr. Mazarino whose name occurs so frequently in the life of the Saint. The passage is worth quoting as a picture of the times :

' I remember '—he says on p. 103—' that when I was a young man, there was a certain preacher, who more than once mounted the pulpit in order to criticise the decrees issued by St. Charles for the discipline of the Metropolitan Church ; and he always did so with overbearing insolence and audacity. It is almost unbelievable how many

minds were infected and poisoned by the sermons
of this man and how many people, both of the
nobility and the common folk, were in agreement
with his words. The objections to the Church
decrees were quickly taken up and some men,
who were hostile to the Bishop, eagerly followed the
critic and brought others over to their side, and on
account of his acrimony the people gathered in
ever-increasing numbers round him. The minds
eager for this sort of nourishment went so far, that
if the preacher even said something right or salutary,
they immediately forgot it, and when the sermon
was finished, only repeated and bandied about in
their conversation the insults hurled against the
decrees of St. Charles and directed thus openly or
indirectly against his person. St. Charles, seeing
that this was not an insult or injury directed merely
against himself, but against the common welfare
and the Church, after a long discussion of the matter,
decided finally to impose silence upon the importunate preacher and the man ceased to molest him
further.'

In the following chapter (p. 108) occurs another
episode hitherto quite unknown and characteristic
of the pastoral care of St. Charles.

' St. Charles of glorious memory, Archbishop of
this city, desired, as I heard when I was a young
man, that while a Bishop preached, all other preachers should during that time abstain from speaking,
and he requested for the purpose instructions from
the Apostolic See. But perhaps grave reasons prevented the Supreme Pontiff from meeting his
wishes. His intention was, I think, thereby to induce
all the Bishops, and even to force and oblige some
of them, to undertake this task. For they could not

have continued in their silence, when their people, as it were, hungry, gathered in great crowds around them. Nor does it seem in conflict with the principles of decorum, that all the subjects of the supreme Pastor of the town should hasten to listen to him, even those who profess a religious life in convents. The times of our forefathers and fathers had indeed no need for such a law, for they held their own pastors in great honour and gathered round them when they preached ; and the pastors themselves fed the flock committed to their care by preaching the word of God, with much greater diligence and solicitude. How greatly have these ancient customs been degraded and changed ! How different are our times from those former days ! '

And further (p. 132), Cardinal Federico records the heroic struggle which the Saint began against the difficulties which his very nature presented to his preaching.

' I wish moreover to record a detail which those who have reported the sayings and doings of St. Charles have perhaps not mentioned. That great man, not possessing by nature, great fluency and ready speech forced himself by assiduous work and study to overcome these natural obstacles, in such a way that nobody questioned that he had not given himself to this practice of preaching because of any delight or facility he had in speaking, but solely in order to fulfil his duty.'

———

We have deferred to the end the most precious passages : the saintly Bishop taken as a model by another saintly Bishop ; St. Charles as he came to life again in the work and the soul of Cardinal Federico.

We have gathered these extracts from a precious little volume in which Cardinal Federico jotted down in his own hand notes on the most varied things. He himself headed the volume : ' *Tumultuariæ tabulæ*,' or ' Random Notes.' It contains a little of everything : maxims of the highest kind side by side with practical notes on diocesan administration ; reflexions about and judgments on persons, institutions and events, side by side with quite intimate thoughts and intentions concerning his personal conduct, both of his inner and outward life : all of it subordinated in his mind to the spiritual rule of the Church of Milan to which the trust of Clement VIII had called him.

His formal election took place on April 24, 1595. It had been only in afternoon of the 15th of the same month that he had had the first intimation of it from the Pope himself. Thus he singled out that hour which proved so important and decisive for his life, immediately following the heading given above:

' On April 15 about 22 o'clock, the Supreme Pontiff Clement VIII had me called. He explained to me his intention concerning the government of the Church in Milan. My God, you know what thoughts I carried in my heart ! You know what manner of man I am ! Queen of Heaven, help me ! St. Ambrose, help me ! '

I translate this literally from the Cardinal's Latin. The rest of the little volume is in Italian.

There follows, still on the first page, a note which can be taken as the explanation of the title : ' Some thoughts have passed through my mind at this beginning which it may be better to let mature.'

———

How immediately his thought turned to his aintly cousin as to his master and model and how well he had learnt his lesson in his school and by his example, is shown by the second page of his recollections : a page splendid in its candid simplicity and in its very secretiveness ; I cannot but transcribe it entirely :

' 1. The principal function of the Bishop is alms ; therefore *dispersit dedit pauperibus*. Delighted, when nothing remains in the house.

' I propose to form a Congregation for the administration of the household, which shall keep accounts of all the ecclesiastical properties and expenses.

' 2. The furnishings should be poor, but abundant for the members of the household and for foreign visitors.

' 3. Hospitality shall be modest and conforming to the last intentions entertained by my cousin, the Cardinal of saintly memory,[1] though he had been unable to carry them out owing to his death.'

The Cardinal thus numbers up to ninety-three his notes of the first year of his rule. It is sufficiently clear that the memory of his cousin is present to his mind from the very first and that he applies to him the words : *dispersit dedit pauperibus*. The third note informs us that the Saint, however rigorous with himself, devoted care and thought to hospitality even in his last days.

Under No. 6, Cardinal Federico, in setting forth some wise principle of government, also gives us information on the methods of administration of his cousin, on the condition of the clergy as he had

[1] It is impossible to render the charm of the Italian expression used here and in the sequel by Cardinal Federico, who refers to St. Charles as ' il Cardinale Santa Memoria ' (as if ' Santa Memoria ' were his title). (*Translator's note.*)

found it and had then left it to his immediate successor, and how the latter had guarded and preserved and even improved that precious heritage, to hand it on to him, Federico.

'6. I shall employ Milanese and only rarely introduce men from outside. On this matter the Cardinal of saintly memory entertained similar ideas, though the outcome was different. Finding himself hard up for suitable persons, to keep things going until his own pupils should appear, he made much use of foreigners and appointed them to official posts. I am no longer in this position. There are workers in sufficiency and—what is important—they are hungering for work. Assuming that, I shall have to form a seminary for suitable men whom I can then promote and set to work. . . .'

As St. Charles had done, so also his worthy cousin proposes to manage his dealings with Rome :

'9. At Rome I shall recommend the affairs of my Church to a particular Cardinal who can on occasions carry on the negotiations of God's service.' What Cardinal Alciati had been to St. Charles, these same functions, and even more, Cardinal Baronius fulfilled for his cousin.

And side by side with this friendly Cardinal, Federico wished also to have some prelate as his diplomatic agent in Rome, and he makes a note following the rules to be adopted by the agent : 'To make a success of the young man, I have thought of bringing him to Milan to instruct him in all things by direct observation, and then to send him back to reside in Rome after having changed him *in virum alterum*.' The same procedure had been adopted by St. Charles.

A reference no less interesting than explicit to St. Charles follows soon afterwards :

' 12. The saintly Cardinal found the friars so refractory to his orders that he was obliged to cause them many humiliations ; whence they developed a considerable aversion to him, and this continued up to his death. Even now it has not disappeared from the mind of many who are convinced that the Cardinal felt a cordial distaste against them and did not like them at all. It will have to be my business to remove this false opposition. . . .'

The following is a charming page which presents the two cousins, as in a snapshot, in the exercise of their functions as rulers :

' 29. At congregations, so Mgr Morra (formerly Vicar-General of St. Charles) told me, the Cardinal used to preserve his position above the parties in controversies over jurisdictions, checking the ardour of excessive feeling on the part of the disputants. And indeed that is how the business ought to be dealt with : they eager, I with moderation ; they full of zeal without restraint, I with the tempering of discretion ; they as good soldiers, I as the general in Christ's militia. If they were not like that, they would be useless ; if I am not like that, I should be of no use.'

It has been a matter of common knowledge that St. Charles frequently went on pastoral visitations ; but it was not known that the motive was often, though not always, not simply the visitation, or the visitation only. It is his cousin who gives us the information :

' 36. I have been told, I have forgotten by whom, that my Cardinal in the midst of these exceedingly difficult disputes over jurisdictions often went on visitations to find some relaxation from them.' This is a piece of information which is sure not to be a matter of indifference to more than one Bishop. And how much affection is contained in the words ' my Cardinal ' !

Further on, Cardinal Federico supplies another piece of news no less interesting : St. Charles planned a compilation or collection of the Councils ; possibly he means that the Saint, already acquainted with the first edition of the *Atti della Chiesa Milanese*, edited by Galesini, planned a more complete collection ; in this case the edition of 1599, very much enlarged, which Federico ordered, would represent the posthumous realisation of one of the Saint's intentions.

' 42. I intend to bear in mind the completion of that compilation of the Councils which the Cardinal had planned to carry out.'

The remembrance of his Cardinal appears once again in a note dated June 29, 1595 (the above-quoted notes are certainly anterior to that date), where he mentions the farsighted plan of an institution of which he intends to avail himself in his administration of the diocese.

' 60. The Cardinal of saintly memory endowed doctoral benefices in the main Collegiate Churches of Milan ; . . . I shall make use of these Doctors to delegate to them the causes of extraordinary visitations.'

––––––––

We close our account with a piece of information that Cardinal Federico himself obtained during the last days of the Saint's earthly life and preserved for us in that little volume entitled *Ad aridam mentem epistola* (Mediolani, Anno M.DC.XX., p. 18) :

' Shortly before St. Charles passed away from this life, I remember being his travel-companion on some pilgrimage. And while we were riding along, he produced a little book which contained the Psalms of David with some notes and the summary of the psalms. Having pulled the book out of his pocket, the Saint told me that whenever he felt his mind and spirit languish, he was wont to have recourse to this book and draw from it fresh vigour and encouragement of mind.'

And, as it were, reflecting how much more he must feel the need of such encouragement, if so gigantic a personality as St. Charles felt it, Federico, turning to himself, continues : ' You have not touched even the confines of that perfection and sanctity to which we know he had risen. You have not yet consumed the greater part of your life in fasting, in penance of the flesh and exercise of the spirit as he had done ; nor do I know whether for you that divine fate is in store that by consent of the Church your name shall be added to the number of the Saints.'

Either the very obviousness of the truth deceives us, or every one of these stones which we have taken from the literary remains of Cardinal Federico is an unparalleled monument to the glory of our Father and Patron ; any word that I might add, could not but spoil it. This is really a case of : *saxa ipsa loquentur.*

THE CENTENARY OF THE CANONISATION OF ST. CHARLES IN LONDON

We are indebted to the kindness and courtesy of the Rev. W. F. Keogh, the Superior of the English Congregation of the Oblates of St. Charles, that we are able to offer our readers an account of the solemn celebrations which formed the echo in London of those that have taken place here.

This notice would be ampler and, we feel sure,

would be all the more welcome to our readers, if our space permitted us to make full use of the information so kindly supplied to us. As it is, we are obliged to confine ourselves to mere indications.

It is well known that the name and memory of St. Charles have been propagated in England, and indeed the whole Anglo-Saxon world, by the 'Congregation of the Oblates of St. Charles,' which, projected in 1837 by Dr. Wiseman, was finally constituted and founded by him, when he had become Archbishop of Westminster and Cardinal. He had been admirably assisted by Dr. Manning, who, originally a Protestant, had been received into the Church and ordained, and was later to succeed Dr. Wiseman, both in the dignity of Cardinal and the position of Archbishop.

The London Congregation was closely modelled upon ours here in Milan. Dr. Manning came to Milan expressly and went to Rho to gather full and detailed information, with which he returned to England, gratefully bearing with him several relics of St. Charles which our Archbishop had presented to him.

After the rule of the new Congregation had been approved by the Holy See, it was solemnly inaugurated by Cardinal Wiseman, with the assistance of five Bishops, on Whit-Sunday, 1857, in Bayswater, in the Church originally called St. Helen's, and after this event, St. Mary's of the Angels.

It is hard to do justice to all the good of which this place became the scene and the centre of diffusion. More than 2500 children frequent the schools run by the Oblates at Bayswater, and after 1869 missionaries went out from there to the most distant and difficult parts of India and Africa. Thus both in England and in the remotest spheres of the influence of the Congregation, with the name of Jesus Christ, went also that of His faithful servant, our saintly Archbishop.

P

It was in the Church of St. Mary's of the Angels that the Centenary of his Canonisation was celebrated from October 26 to November 4 of the year 1910. It was preceded by a Novena with sermons. The first preacher was the Archbishop of Westminster, the last, the Superior of the Oblates, Fr. W. F. Keogh ; the others the Revs. Robinson, Swaby, W. S. Laurence, Blake, Worsley, Hoare and Bennett. The subjects of the sermons comprised the principal virtues of St. Charles : Faith, Hope, the Love of God, the Love of one's neighbour, Zeal, Humility, Penance ; and, finally, his death. On November 3, followed the first Solemn Vespers, Address and Benediction ; on the 4th, Solemn High Mass *coram Archiepiscopo*, with a sermon by Rev. R. H. Benson.[1]

How eloquent and encouraging is even the bare recital of these events ! What a long way has been covered, since the days when St. Charles charitably received in his diocese and beneath his hospitable roof the English Catholics, driven out by the fierce and ferocious persecutions.

The English Catholics have not forgotten the kindness of our Saint towards their forebears, and have chosen him even to-day as Patron and Protector of those good works to which England will one day owe her full return to the Faith of her glorious and heroic fathers.

ST. CHARLES AND AMERICA

More than one reader will perhaps be surprised at this title. His surprise will be even greater, if we add that the subject is in a way inevitable and that we deeply regret not to be able to develop it at greater length. The New World has not only dedicated churches, altars and statues to our Saint ; the veneration which his name has inspired all over the vast extent of the lands 'which the Genoese

[1] See note on p. 209.

divined,' has its monument, so to say, in their geography.

Something of the same kind has occurred also in our country ; not only many springs in our lower Alps, which refreshed our Saint on his pastoral wanderings, have taken the name of ' St. Charles,' but several localities have been called after him. There are two boroughs in the Province of Turin, San Carlo Canavese and San Carlo di Ciriè, and not a few wards : one each in the Provinces of Milan, Novara, Sondrio, Genoa, Forlì, Ferrara, Perugia, Reggio Calabria and Palermo ; two in each of the Provinces of Como and Cuneo ; six in that of Alessandria.   So much is clear from the census of 1901 and subsequent information up to 1906.

The facts are even more striking and eloquent in America, and especially in the southern continent. Mountains and hills, rivers and lakes, straits and promontories, villages and cities bear the name of our Saint.   It is only natural ; for at the time, when the glory of our Saint reached its height in his Canonisation, many of the places had not yet come into existence, and therefore had no name.   Certain it is that his Canonisation could not have found a wider or more lasting echo.

Among other countries especially Mexico, Venezuela, Panama, Columbia, Brazil, the Argentine, Paraguay, Uruguay and Chile stand out.   The index of Stieler's atlas shows up to fifty localities and places which bear the name of our Saint, and even this index registers only the principal places.

The name of St. Charles shines no less gloriously, even the more gloriously for its beneficence, in many of the institutions which are flourishing in both North and South America.

We note among others the ' Institute of St. Charles ' founded twenty years ago in memory of

Mgr Scalabrini, Bishop of Piacenza, to assist Italian emigrants, which has spread in an astonishing manner especially in the United States and in Brazil. We remember with deep gratitude the encouraging message which the Rev. Vittorio Gregori of the 'Institute of St. Charles,' full of enthusiasm, sent us two years ago from the Sacred Heart Church in Boston.

We mention also the 'St. Charles College' near Ellicot City, Maryland, and the 'Schools of St. Charles for Boys' at St. Charles, Illinois, of which the Rev. Don Alessandro Bianchi, Doctor of the Ambrosian Library, brought us news and printed information.

'St. Charles' College' is a Grand Séminaire for the education of priests. It must suffice to say that it was begun in 1831 and then after slow and painful beginnings, refounded a second time in 1848 ; it counts at the present time 214 students and has had up to now quite 3903 on its books, coming mostly from the United States, Porto Rico, Cuba and the Philippines.

'The Schools of St. Charles' in Illinois are really a reformatory which might well serve as a model to ours. They were opened in December 1904 ; their object is the education of character and the training in easy and useful handicrafts. Boys of all countries and of various denominations are to be found there : at the present time there are 388, of whom 236 are Protestants, 139 Catholics and 13 Jews. The Catholics have their own Chapel and Chaplain.

By linking the name of our Saint with such great works of practical and beneficent education and using it almost as their ensign, they render homage to the great credit earned by him in this same field in which he was one of the first, one of the wisest and most effective cultivators on a large scale. It was this activity which rendered him one of the most eminent and providential benefactors not only of the Church but of civic life.

The Church, incomparable Mistress in this too, has paid her debt of gratitude by the highest and richest reward she can bestow, Canonisation. Of the World, so lavish in applause and honours often undeserved, and so far removed from the ideals which guided the heart of St. Charles and carried it to those heights of heroic charity, it may well be said :

> ' e se il mondo sapesse il cor ch'egli ebbe
> assai l'*onora* e più l'*onorerebbe*.'[1]

[1] See *Translator's note* on p. 150.

Translator's note from p. 206.

The *Tablet* of November 12th, 1910, reports :
'. . . Father Robert Hugh Benson preached the panegyric. Exterior opportunities and interior dispositions, he said, were given to St. Charles in overflowing measure. In worldly disposition he was placed by birth above most men. Born of a noble family, related to the Sovereign Pontiff, made Secretary of State to the Holy See, his hands were on the springs of earthly power which men crave. These advantages were of little value without the interior disposition of perfect union with the will of God. . . . The preacher compared the sixteenth to the present century. In a new form the same crisis was surrounding them. The world, the flesh and the devil were gathering forces for a great conflict and the new battle would be won in the old way, by the men of God who would use external opportunities, with will attuned in all things to the will of God. God did not directly interpose his will. He worked His will through the instrumentality of men. He trusts His honour to men to vindicate. That was God's plan.'

III

THE 'SCHOOLS' OR GUILDS OF THE BLESSED SACRAMENT IN MILAN

This paper formed Part IV of a work entitled : *Contribution to the Eucharistic History of Milan*, Milano, Giuseppe Palma, 1895, 8°, pp. 75. The essay had first been published in the periodical *La Scuola Cattolica e la Scienza Italiana*, issues of August and September, 1895.

The other three parts of the ' Contribution . . . ' had dealt with (i) ' the Feast of Corpus Domini ' ; (ii) ' the Quarant' Ore,' and (iii) ' the Oratories and Churches, Monastery and Charitable Institutions of Corpus Domini,' the whole having been published on the occasion of the Thirteenth Eucharistic Congress, held in Milan in 1895.

THE ' SCHOOLS ' OR GUILDS OF THE BLESSED SACRAMENT IN MILAN

No one will, I hope, expect to find here a complete nor even an outline history of the ' Schools ' or Guilds of the Blessed Sacrament. Such a history, were it but a collection of statistical figures, especially if it comprised all the guilds of the vast Archdiocese of Milan, would offer the most consoling reflexions to any one who has any faith in the Divine charity which our Lord shows us in the Blessed Sacrament.

————

We possess in the Ambrosian Library (E.S.I. 30), a precious little MS. written throughout in the same hand belonging to the end of the sixteenth century.[1]

[1] On the *verso* of the cover is written : ' Emptus ab haeredibus P.is Ab.is C. M. Masnaghi Ab. S. Mariæ Donæ apud Clavennam,' Another hand has added : ' Olim extabat in

It tells us that at that time ' in every parish Church, with the exception of two or three, there exists a Guild of " Corpus Domini," composed of persons in the parish. The object of the Guild is to supply the candles and the oil for the Most Blessed Sacrament, to see to the celebration of the Feast of " Corpus Domini," to accompany the Blessed Sacrament when it is taken to the sick, and to provide candles also for this purpose and, in short, to attend to everything that may be required in connexion with the Blessed Sacrament. And although for the greater part these Guilds have no revenues of their own except the few to be specially mentioned in some of the parishes, they are able to make complete provision for all the aforementioned objects, by means of alms collected in special boxes placed outside the churches of these parishes, and particu-

Domo professa Soc. Jesu apud S. Fidelem Mediolani ut constat ex alio exemplari huius operis anno 1728 ex hoc Autographo descripto.'

The Ab. Masnaghi in question was a friend of Canon G. B. Castiglione who wrote the ' Istoria delle Scuole della Dottrina Cristiana ' of which the Ambrosian Library possesses the autograph MS. The first part of it was printed in Milan in 1800. He left other MSS., among them a ' Bibliografia Milanese ' (cf. Porro, *Catalogo dei codici manoscritti della Biblioteca Trivulziana*, n. 825).

A note prefixed in Masnaghi's hand to our MS. here, states : ' Historical account of the churches, monasteries, confraternities and Pious Institutions of Milan.—MS. in my possession.— It was purchased by me as part of the papers of the late G. B. Castiglione who died on 2 March of the present year 1789.' He mentions this MS. of his in his ' Bibliografia Milanese,' p. 62, *a tergo* in the following terms : ' The autograph codex is in our possession. The author, who remains anonymous, lived towards the end of the sixteenth century, as he more than once indicates. The history of the churches, monasteries and Confraternities is fully set out. He is especially well informed on the subject of Pious Institutions, so that nothing better could be desired. He gives an account of their objects, resources, representatives, officers and alms. Unfortunately the information he gives is not retrospective.'

larly among the laity ; and in addition many of the Guilds have also Mass celebrated in the said churches every day, or on feast-days, each one according to its means.'

With the help of documents kept in the Archiepiscopal Curia and in the State Archives it would be easy to follow the rapid increase and spread of this pious Institution in the parishes during the rule of St. Charles and of his successors in office. His successors, it is true, found little left for them to do, after the miracle of St. Charles' activity.[1] Accord-

[1] We can easily observe two ways in which St. Charles proceeded in the matter of the Guilds of the Blessed Sacrament. At first he promoted the multiplication of these Guilds, giving to each its own rules, according to the place where it existed and the earlier organisations (Guilds of other names and for other purposes) which had been incorporated in it. So, for instance, we have the rules given by St. Charles in 1571 to the ' Guild of the Blessed Sacrament and the Blessed Virgin Crowned ' of S. Michele alla Chiusa (Arch. of the Curia, Sect X, *S. Lorenzo*, vol. xi, no. 26), printed by Pacifico Ponzio in 1577 ; so also the rules of the Guilds of *Charity*, of *Corpus Domini* and of *St. Joseph* in Arona, fused into a single Guild on April 5, 1578 ; and many other examples.

St. Charles' other preoccupation, in full harmony with his spirit and temperament, was to reduce all the Guilds to a uniform plan. He did so, at least as regards the Guilds of the City, by the rules inserted later in Part V of the ' Atti della Chiesa Milanese,' after the edition of 1599. In the *Acta Ecclesiæ Mediolanensis ab eius initiis usque ad nostram ætatem*, vol. III, col. 262 ff, I have reprinted the rules from the official *editio princeps* of 1583 (Milano, Pacifico Ponzio). But already the edition of 1582 of the ' Atti ' (inevitably incomplete, but valuable and now very rare), on folio 335, contains a general formula of the ' Rules of the Guild of Corpus Domini in the Parish Church of——.'

This twofold procedure is also apparent in the succession and the tenor of the decrees and orders issued by St. Charles to the Guilds. By the Prov. Counc. I (*Acta*, etc., Vol. II, col. 46) the institution of Guilds in the parishes was prescribed. By the Prov. Counc. III (*ibid.*, col. 246) it is laid down that the Guilds instituted or about to be instituted ' regulis utantur ad communem illarum huius Provinciæ Sodalitatum usum nostro iussu edendis.' The ' various Instructions ' say : ' In every

ing to the three synoptic tables attached to the
'Atti della Chiesa Milanese,'[1] there existed even
then fully 556 Guilds of the Blessed Sacrament
among 763 parishes. Out of 730 parishes, very few
have no Confraternity or Guild of the Blessed
Sacrament of their own, and even keeping the
average membership of each Guild at a low figure,
there must have been thousands and thousands of
members of both sexes.

Thus the laity in a body, but with order and
discipline, had been brought into a closer relation
to the very focus of Divine Service. The Guilds
in this way have maintained for centuries a whole
army of worshippers in the service of their Divine
King in the Blessed Sacrament, whether He
resides upon the Altar or goes out to comfort the
sick or moves in the splendour of a procession. Is
that not a great consolation?

But, as I said, I neither intend nor am able to
deal with all our Guilds. My intention is only to
give, more completely than has been done up till
now, information about the oldest among our Guilds
of the 'Corpus Domini' which flourished before
the time of St. Charles.

Parish, where the Guild of the Blessed Sacarement is not yet
instituted, it shall at once be formed with the rules which
will be prescribed by us.' The same order is repeated in the
Instructions for visits to the sick (*ibid.*, col. 1354), prepared by
St. Charles and published by his successor in the *Sacramentale
Ambrosianum*. But this mentions 'rules prescribed' (*regulis
præscriptis*). I am not aware that St. Charles published
rules other than those of 1583, which, as said, concern the
Guilds of the City. This is perhaps the reason why Card.
Federico found it necessary to issue a general rule for all
Guilds, as he did by decree issued by his Vicar-General,
A. Albergati.

[1] Cf. *Acta Eccles. Med. ab eius initiis usque ad nostram ætatem*,
Milano, 1892, Vol. III, after Part viii. The three tables are
to be found as early as in the editions of the 'Atti' of 1599;
but they contain many variants from the MS. tables which I
found only recently and was able to compare with the edition
here quoted.

If the rule of this genius for pastoral work constitutes a real high tide of action in the Church of Milan, the effects of which we still feel, we must yet not imagine that everything or nearly everything began with him.

The fact is that, despite the many and serious defects and disorders, the City and the Diocese and the Province were still held together in a vast and sound ecclesiastical organisation. An immense heritage of good, both among the laity[1] and the clergy, still survived triumphantly, in despite of human frailty and the tribulations of the most wretched times. The Milanese Church resembled, to my mind, not so much a devastated, barren field, as an immense old tree, uncared for, it is true, and gone rather wild, but by no means dead or even near dying, but still full of life, waiting merely for the touch of a skilful gardener to bring forth fresh flowers and excellent fruit. The proof of this will be given in the first volume of the aforementioned *Acta Ecclesiæ Mediolanensis*, etc., if God grants me life and sufficient strength for the purpose, for the materials are certainly not lacking.[2]

---

[1] A passage in certain ordinances of the Metropolitan Chapter of the year 1462 and renewed in 1471 (State Arch. *Culto, Funzioni sacre, Milano, Metropolit.* 2091), bears witness to the devotion of the laity to the Blessed Sacrament. It states : ' Tempore elevationis Sacramenti usque ad assumptionem omnes genua flectant cum magna reverentia sicut decet. Nam et laici hoc faciunt.'

[2] The Author here refers to the *Acta Ecclesiæ Mediolanensis ab eius initiis usque ad nostram ætatem.* Opera et studio Presb. Achillis Ratti ; Mediolani, ex typ. Pont. S. Iosephi (Raff. Ferraris, editore), in-fol.

Of this work, vol. II was published in 1890, and forms vol. 1 of the *Acta Eccl. Mediol. a S. Carlo condita.* Vol. III, dated 1892, forms vol. 2 of the same *Acta Eccl. Mediol. a S. Carlo*, etc. ; Vol. IV appeared in 1897 with the subtitle : *Acta Eccl. Med. a S. Caroli B. successoribus condita nunc primum in unum collecta et edita* (up to the year 1797). Vol. I is still unpublished. (Note in the Italian edition.)

Meanwhile I have presented in the preceding sections[1] some fragments of these materials. Further material is provided by our old Guild of the Blessed Sacrament.

When I use the term ' old,' I must observe that the adjective must not be taken in too wide a sense. Old Guilds, really old guilds existed in Milan, as is well known ; Guilds of the most varied names and purposes, both sacred and profane. But the Guilds of the Blessed Sacrament, as far as documentary evidence goes, are all of them later than the year 1486. It may be that they are later than the year 1491, which is the year when Blessed Bernardino da Feltre passed through Milan and preached here.

No one, however, has produced evidence of the institution by him of Guilds of the Blessed Sacrament here in Milan, similar to those which he had founded in Parma, in Orvieto, in Genoa, in Ravenna and was about to found in Brescia. The Bollandists (*Acta Sanct.*, September, vol. VII, pp. 874–983) do not mention any ; still less does the Rev. Pietro Moiraghi (*Vita del B. Bernardino Tomitano da Feltre*, etc., Pavia, 1894),[2] and not even the *Documenti rife-*

---

[1] See the paragraph following the title of this Essay. (*Translator's note.*)

[2] Neither the Bollandists nor Moiraghi even mention the Guild instituted by Fra. Bernardino at Brescia. The Archives of the Archiepiscopal Curia contain (Sect. xiii, vol. i, A) a beautiful little parchment codex in a handsome contemporary binding in stamped leather and wood, with metal clasps, on the flyleaf of which is written in an early sixteenth century hand : ' *Memoria como mi benedet cataldo la fece fare mensis Maii M.D.X.VII* ' ; the hand of Sisinio Francesco, Archivist of the Archiepiscopal Archives (1725) added : ' *SS.mi Corporis Domini Congreg. in Civitate Brixiæ.*' The MS. is all by the same hand, in good Gothic with the headings and initials in red. At the end a contemporary hand, perhaps that of the writer himself, noted : ' *Expletus est* 26 *maii* 1517.' It begins as follows :

rentisi al soggiorno in Milano di Fra Bernardino Tomitano da Feltre, published from the State Archives of Milan by the Cav. Pietro Ghinzoni, Feltre, 1881. It is certainly noteworthy that documentary evidence

' Questa siè la regola et ordine se serva et è da servare per la congregazione et università de la Scola de miser Iesu Christo posta in la giesia de sancta Maria de Bechis. In nomine Patris et Filii et Spiritus Sancti. Amen. A laude et gloria del omnipotente et eterno dio e del excelso e sacratissimo Sacramento del corpo de messer Jesu Christo et de la sua madre virgine Maria et del glorioso martyre sancto Laurentio et sancta Lucia.'

' Qua se comenza lordine, ovvero regula de li homini et donne che desiderano essere in la scola over congregatione de lo Sacratissimo Sacramento del corpo di miser Iesu Christo ordinata in la giesia mazor de Bressa per exortatione del venerabile frate Bernardino da Feltro de lordine di frati minori : et confirmata per Monsignor Paulo Zane vescovo di Bressa nel Mille quatrocento nonanta quatro adì primo de septembrio.'

Then follows in xxi ' capituli ' the rule, with, in addition, some prayers for the dead.

To judge by the very full information which has been furnished me by the courtesy—only equalled by the patience—of my friend, Rev. Dr. Giovanni Rampa, the rule of our MS. corresponds with that of the MS. G.VI.15 of the *Biblioteca Queriniana* at Brescia, which is also in parchment and written in Gothic script. It contains the ' Costituzioni ordinate adì 1 de Agosto 1541,' signed by ' P. Hieronimo di Faustino Capelano de la giesia de S. Bernardino de Roncadelle.' This P. Hieronimo seems simply to have adapted the rule of the Cathedral Guild to that of his own church, by inserting the names of the latter's Patron-Saints in the proem.

In 1615 the ' Regole et ordini generali della Scuola del SS. Corpo di N.S.G.C. della Cattedrale di Brescia ' were published by Marchetti of Brescia. These rules were common to all the Guilds of the town and the diocese. ' Among these Guilds,' states the Introduction, ' is the one founded in the Cathedral Church of Brescia by Bl. Bernardino da Feltre ; as this is the most ancient and principal Guild of all . . . etc.' Dr. Rampa also sent me the tenor of the decree issued by Bp. Paolo Zane (cf. Gradenigo, *Brixia sacra*, p. 359, where, however, no mention is made of the Guild) ; it is preserved in the Archives of the Chapter of the Cathedral of Brescia, in a vol. marked E, containing copies of episcopal decrees from 1433 to the middle of the seventeenth century.

exists in plenty for the time *after* the coming of Bl. Tomitano but fails us completely for the time *before* his arrival in Milan.

As for the documents themselves, the Parish Archives, excepting those of S. Giorgio in Palazzo, and—after some lapse of time—those of S. Lorenzo, contain very little prior to the time of St. Charles. The Archives of the Curia, notably in the volumes dealing with the Pastoral Visitations, give us very little more information. Less barren are the State Archives. They contain 140 documents of the so-called 'Fondo di Religione,' 115 older and 25 modern, with the title 'Confraternite del Santissimo e Santissimo nelle Chiese (A—Z).'[1] Both the number and the title sound very promising, calculated to revive and excite to its utmost pitch the energy and patience, even if flagging, of some poor researcher. But they fail to fulfil what they promised. His first illusion is quickly followed by disillusionment.

The ancient Church of *S. Marcellino*, formerly in Porta Comasina,[2] is represented by no less than 17 documents with the title : '*Confraternite . Comuni. Milano . S. Marcellino—Santissimo—Registri.*' I had actually reached the last, bearing the number 162. Up to then some older documents had turned up, but they concerned the Church, not the Guild.

[1] Of course, I have not been able to handle and examine in a relatively short time such a mass of materials (for the greater part, it is true, very easy to examine) without the help of the enlightened and inexhaustible patience of the officials of the State Archives, especially of the department of the 'Fondo di Religione.' I am deeply grateful to them and to the liberty granted to researchers once they have been admitted, naturally with all the necessary precautions. It is indeed highly desirable that this wise liberty be in no way modified or restricted, except in the interest of serious study, by whatever reforms may be judged useful or needed after the long period of direction under the distinguished and lamented author of the 'Storia Universale.'

[2] Cf. Lattuada, l. c., vol. V, p. 37.

Discouraged and weary I opened the folder. It contains three registers ; I turn over the leaves of the first : nothing ; the second : nothing ; I take up the third (it is numbered 3) and immediately after the fly-leaf, which states : ' Index of the Archives of the Guild of the Blessed Sacrament,' I find a note in the following terms : ' Archivium docet venerandam Scholam SSmi Sacramenti in Parochiali Ecclesia S. Marcellini P. C. Mediolani ante annum Millesimum Ducentesimum vigesimum sextum viguisse, etc.' I could not believe my eyes : surely, I thought, this is some crude mistake ; it is quite impossible. But then I reflected : why should it be impossible ? There were pious Guilds, under this very name, formed by laymen in Milan at least as early as 1142.[1] True, as far as we know, they were rather congregations of penitence and suffrage. But, then—we know so little about them. And, further, why should not these pious works have also included the cult of the Blessed Sacrament ? Had not in this way the Guild of the ' Raccomandati ' been spread in our part of the country in 1305 ?

You will well believe that I began at once anxiously to look for the summary of the document in that volume. I found it ; but I grew calmer : there was no sign of the Guild. I went back over the papers and found the document itself : it is dated 1226 *ante Kal. Novembris*, but it is merely a prosy mortgage issued by the priest of the Church itself, drafted by a certain Bellotto Gambarello, public notary in Milan. My disillusionment was complete.[2]

[1] Cf. Giulini, *Memorie*, vol. III, pp. 297, 321, 405.

[2] Cf. Giulini, l. c., vol. IV, p. 830. The copy of the rule and of the diploma mentioned by Giulini is contained in the codex in the Ambrosiana, F.S.IV, 5 (the last of the diplomatic collection of Sormani), folio. 9 ff. Priests also could join the Guild. The second chapter of the rule prescribes confession and communion at least three times a year, at Christmas, Easter and the Feast of the Assumption. The diploma or

Fresh hopes were roused in me by the Guild of the Blessed Sacrament of the parish of *S. Raffaele.* A document labelled ' *Confratern.*' etc., 297, contained a printed copy of a decree of February 6, 1572,[1] by which the Vicar-General Giovanni Battista Castelli, one of the most active helpers of St. Charles and later Bishop of Rimini (see Giussani, Rossi, Oltrocchi, l.c., col. 83), recognised, confirmed and, as far as was necessary, refounded in the said Church the Guild of the Blessed Sacrament, at the request of the Prior and its members, according to whose statement the same Guild had existed ' ab antiquissimo tempore ' with indulgences granted by Paul III (1534–1549) and Julius III (1550–1555). The two Popes gave me more confidence in the promise of the document ; but after what had happened before, I was distrustful rather than comforted. True, another set of papers (*Confratern.* etc., 315, *Registri*) reassured me a little and gave me some satisfaction.

The bundle contained a stout volume bound in leather entitled : ' Index of the Archives of the Guild founded in the Parish Church of S. Raffaele.' On folio 13 I found the summary of a deed of September 3, 1528, drawn up by the notary Agostino Confalonieri concerning the sale of the proprietary rights over a shop by the Procurator of the Cathedral to the Guild. In 1528 the Guild of the Blessed Sacrament in S. Raffaele therefore not only existed but enjoyed already a juridical personality for civil action. We may therefore assume that it had existed for some time.

privilege, in very pious terms, given by the Archbishop Francesco I of Parma, dated June 29, 1505, from Angera, grants an indulgence of 40 days *quibuslibet tum Corpus Christi conficientibus in altari, tum ipsum intuentibus et orantibus* (the words ' fide ' and ' flexis ' are inserted here) *et cum ipsum deferunt, et qui deferentes cum reverentia comitantur.*

[1] An authentic MS. copy is in the folder *Confratern.*, etc., OO VV 312.

In view of these circumstances a little volume of a dozen pages, unnumbered, printed 'in Milan by Francesco Moschenio MDLXI,' in the Archives of the Archiepiscopal Curia (*Miscellanea, A*) has a certain interest. On the first page we find the words, 'In the name of Jesus Christ' and below them in three panels arranged horizontally, on the right the Blessed Virgin on the throne with the Infant on her left knee ; on the left an Angel, holding a lily in his right hand and leading a child with his left ; and in the middle panel an Ambrosian Monstrance flanked by two lighted candelabras.

The invocation of the name of Jesus recalls Blessed Bernardino da Feltre, the paladin of the Divine Name at all times and in every place. To promote its honour and to put a stop to blasphemy was his constant preoccupation during his sojourn in Milan, as the Bollandists (l.c., p. 927) and the 'Documents' of Ghinzoni have pointed out.

Then, after an interminable title, follow the rules which may perhaps be the original rules of the Guild. They lay special stress on the absence of any entrance-fee to the Guild. Then came endless indulgences, amounting to thousands of years, enough to justify the title which states that the indulgences are 'infinite and such as have never before been granted to any other Company, as appears in the Apostolic Bull under the seal of the Rev. Cardinal Trano,[1] Protector of the said Company by order of His Holiness.'

We next encounter a Guild, the foundation of

---

[1] He is Giovanni Bernardino Scoto, one of the most pious and learned prelates of the sixteenth century. He was commonly called Cardinal Trano, or Trani, because before he was created Cardinal, he had been Archbishop of that See. Cf. Ciaconio, *Vitæ et res gestæ Roman. Pont. et S.R.E. Cardinalium*, tom. III, col. 846 ff.

which can be assigned with certainty to the short
space of time between the years 1486 and 1510.
Its origin, its antiquity, its constitution and nature
are fully described by one of its members, Giulio
Cesare Sacco, Advocate and Collegiate Procurator,
in a little volume printed in Milan by Lodovico
Monza in 1652. It bears the title : ' The State of
the Ven. and Distinguished Guild of the Blessed
Sacrament, founded in the Collegiate Church of
S. Georgio in Palazzo of Milan, written and compiled by, etc.' It is quoted and referred to in the
very summary account of the institution of the
Guild added to a list of the members, which was
printed in 1884 (Milan, printing-works of S.
Giuseppe). It is to be found in the Parish Archives
of *S. Giorgio* (Cart. *Confraternite*, 14) and also in the
Ambrosian Library (in two copies) ; but it is, I
believe, hard to find elsewhere. For this reason
among others I quote here textually what seems to
me relevant to the matter under discussion.

There is no doubt in Sacco's mind that the Guild
of S. Giorgio is the oldest in Milan. His argument
is both ingenious and sound, and if it does not
carry him as far as he means it to go, it leaves
at least no doubt that his Guild is among the
oldest of the city. I may add that it is the
best documented of all. But let us hear Sacco
himself :

' There cannot be, I believe, any doubt that the
Company or Society of the Blessed Body of our
Lord founded in Santo Georgio in Palazzo, belongs
to the oldest, or rather is the first that can be found
in this City ; for I find in some old books of this
Society, especially in a large book bound in red
leather and begun in the year 1510, that it had
been founded earlier and before the said time ;
for in the aforesaid book mention is made of entries
of the years 1508 and 1509 in another old book in

Q

white cardboard which I have been unable to find, and of a legacy to the said Chapel of *Corpus Domini*, left in 1508 by one Simone Barzo.[1] How it came to be founded, or by whom, or in what manner I have not been able to ascertain from the documents. I incline to think that from the year 1510 onwards it began to be conducted under a regular constitution, for in that year the complement of officers is given and who and how many they were to be.' Then he gives the names of the Prior, the Vice-Prior, the Consul, the Syndic, the Chancellor (the local Provost, Rev. Alessandro Leuco), the Consul (Andrea de Lovino). 'These,' he continues, 'were elected at the Congregation of Thursday, December 27, 1510, confirmed by a public document drawn up by Bartolomeo Sormano, Notary in Milan.' It was, he said, resolved 'that the aforesaid officers should be changed every year, i.e., in one year the Vice-Prior, the Syndic and the Chancellor, and in the next year the Prior, the Consul and the Treasurer. This change was made, and had to be made all the six officers being present, as I find was the case in the year 1511, and is proved by another document drawn up by the same Sormano on October 12, 1511. . . . This rule, I find, was followed for many years, during which from 1510 onwards certain regulations were adopted for the better government of the Society which can be found in its books and especially in a square book bound in blue leather. These regulations were later re-enacted and amplified in the year 1566,

[1] In the Parish Archives of S. Giorgio, a copy of a ' Libro attinente al Capitolo di S. Giorgio,' on folio 33 mentions under the title *Capella Corporis Christi* : ' Capella dotata per messer Simone Barzo.'

It is not irrelevant but does not absolutely prove the argument of the aforementioned list of 1884 (for the absolute priority of the Guild of S. Giorgio), when we read (cf. Sacco, l.c., p. 5), that notable personalities also of other parishes were urged to become members of the said Guild.

as can be seen from the small printed book of that year which is in the archives of the Guild.'[1]

At this point he mentions and inserts Letters Patent of the Duke Massimiliano Sforza, similar in substance to those granted to the Guild of Sta Maria dei Servi, which I have mentioned elsewhere.[2] The Duke, under date November 22, 1513, grants and extends to the Guild the benefices and privileges (power to own property, to receive gifts by bequest, legacy or donation, etc.), which had been granted to charitable institutions, to the Hospital and to Chapter of the Cathedral, by Privilege dated January 2, 1486.

The parchment original of the Duke's Letter is still preserved in the Parish Archives of S. Giorgio, in the same set of documents as Sacco's book. As the Duke's Letter, mentioning the date 1486, expressly states that *ab inde citra* the Guild of Corpus Domini was founded, it proves that the Guild was established, as I said, between that year and 1508, when it received the legacy of Simone Barzo.

In the same file, a ' Register of the Archives of the Ven. Guild of the Blessed Sacrament founded in the Collegiate Church of S. Giorgio in Palazzo, compiled by the notary Giovanni Federico Ferrari in 1711,' on its folio 25 gives the information that this Barzo left to the Guild the handsome sum of 50 florins, with the obligation to say a daily Mass and to ' pay a pound of wax annually to the Archiepiscopal Household.' The Guild received further favours from a certain Bartolomeo Galiano, who by his will, drawn up by Bartolomeo Sormano, dated June 25, 1524, bequeathed to the Guild a

---

[1] I have not been able to find the little book in the Archives of S. Giorgio, nor have I had any better luck than Sacco over the ' book in white cardboard.'

[2] A. Ratti : *Contribuzione alla storia eucaristica di Milano*, Milano, 1895, p. 5.

gold *scudo* and annually four pounds of wax, on condition of celebrating a Mass on the anniversary of his death or thereabout, and to ' use the said wax for the illumination of the Blessed Sacrament during the whole octave of the Feast of *Corpus Domini*, for the repose of his soul.'

We must admit that the members of the Guild of S. Giorgio made the best possible use of the means thus placed at their disposal. Sacco tells us (l.c., p. 8) that the Guild commissioned Bernardino Luini (perhaps a relation of that same Andrea Lovino whom we found mentioned as Consul of the Guild) in 1516 to paint the pictures which are still an object of our admiration in the Provost's Lodge of S. Giorgio.[1]

It is curious, especially in view of a testamentary disposition like that of Barzo, that the members should claim that they were not subject to the jurisdiction of the Archbishop of Milan. It is curious and deplorable that, when the Vicar-General of the Archbishop communicated to them on May 20, 1623 certain decrees issued by Cardinal Federico Borromeo on the occasion of a visitation to the Collegiate Church and to the Guild, they should have replied by appealing to the Senate, on the ground that the Guild was a purely lay body ; and, complaining of being summoned under censure either to obey or to come up for judgment, they protested that this was a procedure ' wholly contrary to the jurisdiction of His Majesty.' The developments of this controversy can be found in the documents quoted, in the Archives of S. Giorgio.

After the Guild, like so many other things, had become a victim of the Josephine legislation and had been suppressed, it was re-established by Archiepis-

---

[1] Cf. Mongeri, *L'arte in Milano*, Milano, 1872, p. 304 ; also Lattuada, l.c., tom. III, p. 135.

copal Bull in 1831 and continues down to the present day.

Another Guild of the Blessed Sacrament, which claims with justice to be one of the oldest in the city, is that of *S. Lorenzo*.

I have not been able to find any ancient documents concerning it. The best that can be produced from the Archives of the Archiepiscopal Curia (Sect. X., *S. Lorenzo*, vol. I) is the *Visitatio Scolæ SS. Sacramenti erectæ in Ecclesia Collegiata insigni S. Laurentii P(ortæ) T(icinensis) Mediolani*, which is an extract of an authentic copy of the Acts of the visitation[1] carried out by Cardinal Federico Borromeo in 1611 (ibid., l.c., Vol. V), authenticated by the notary Giuseppe Brenna, and all written in a contemporary hand. On folio 2, under the title, ' De erectione, fundatione et antiquitate Sodalitatis' the following passage occurs :

' Quemadmodum Ecclesia Collegiata insignis S. Laurentii Maioris Mediolani est omnium aliarum ecclesiarum antiquissima (ut in libro visitationis eiusdem Basilicæ dictum fuit)[2] ita etiam hæc Sodalitas Sanctissimi Sacramenti ibidem erecta adeo antiqua existit, ut de eius erectione atque fundatione nihil certe habeatur ; hæc enim prima fuit quæ iam de anno 1512 usum baldachini in hac civitate cum SS. Sacramento deferendi introducere coepit, ex qua postea reliquæ parochiæ tum Civitatis tum Diœcesis hanc laudabilem consuetudinem

---

[1] Another MS. copy of the Acts of visitation is preserved in the Parish Archives of S. Lorenzo and was one of the exhibits at the Eucharistic Exhibition, together with a crude picture (of uncertain date and archæological value) representing the Viaticum, being carried under escort from the Church to a sick person.

[2] Cf. Lattuada, l.c., tom. III, p. 296 ; Rotta, *Sulle sette basiliche stazionali. S. Lorenzo*. Milano, 1828, together with the ' Addizionali.'

baldachini eiusdem adhibendi didicerunt. Reperitur autem eadem Sodalitas unita Societati Divæ Mariæ Virginis et Sanctæ Catharinæ virginis et martyris quæ ante Ecclesiæ ruinam subtus organum a parte epistolæ sita erat ut constat ex libris manuscriptis eiusdem Societatis Anno 1496. Nunc vero ad capellam Sanctæ Mariæ miraculorum a latere Evangelii translata cernitur.'

On folio 3 follows the rule of the members of the Guild ' della Madonna et di S. Catarina,' which contains nothing about the Brothers of the Blessed Sacrament. Concerning them, folio 4 states that ' legibus item et regulis ex parte utuntur quibus Sodalitates Corporis Christi in civitate uti consueverunt iisque se quamvis non omnes parere affirmant.' But in the book of the Visitation (l.c., vol. V, p. 502) it is said that they had no rule before and accepted that imposed generally by Antonio Albergato, Vicar-General of Archbishop Federico Borromeo.[1]

Soon afterwards, it is noted that ' non deliguntur singulis mensibus qui umbellam sive baldachinum portent.'

Most interesting is what follows on folio 10, namely the ' Inventory of the furnishings of the Guild of the Blessed Sacrament.' I pick out the following items : No. 1: 'A baldacchino of crimson damask with gold fringes and six poles '; No. 2 : ' Another baldacchino of silk to carry the Blessed Sacrament to the sick '; No. 71 : ' Another old baldacchino '; No. 80 : ' A baldacchino of crimson taffeta to place over the High Altar, with its attachment '; No. 73 : ' Two lanterns to accompany the Blessed Sacrament to the sick '; and

---

[1] Cf. Rivola : *Vita di Federico Borromeo*. Milano, 1656, p. 225.

under Nos. 77 and 78 : 'A large silver pyx' and a 'silver reliquary.'[1]

It is evident that S. Lorenzo justifies its name of the 'Basilica of the Baldacchino.' It may well be that the Basilica of S. Lorenzo was actually the first to introduce among us the use of the baldacchino in the processions of the Blessed Sacrament. I underline 'processions' on purpose, for it is well known that the ritual use of the baldacchino, both ecclesiastical and lay, is very much older.

The information contained in the Acts of the Visitation is confined to the city and the diocese of Milan. Others had in fact anticipated Milan, as is clear from—to confine myself to sources at hand— the 'Cronache Forlivesi' which speak of the 'tabachino' which is simply a baldacchino (*Dei Monumenti istorici pertinenti alle Provincie della Romangna*, serie III, vol. I, p. 350). There one of the headings runs : 'How a procession for the Corpus Domini Feast was instituted.' The chapter is so short, so closely relevant to the Eucharist, and so interesting, incidentally also on account of the information it contains about an ancient Guild of the Blessed Sacrament and of a pious follower and contemporary of Fra Bernardino da Feltre, that I cannot resist the temptation of quoting it here :

'Eodem millesimo (1491) on the last day of March, Maundy Thursday, a Procession of Corpus Domini took place with great devotion. The Procession started from Sta Croce, passed through the Town, turned in the piazza and came back there viâ Sta Maria and ended again at Sta

---

[1] In the same volume, folio 150 at the end of a note of the debts left by a certain 'Giacomo de Albiate' who in 1607 had made a bequest in favour of the Guild, I found the insertion : 'Paid the taxes of the " Casa del Corpus Domini," ' 2 *lire*, 16 *soldi*, 6 *denari*. But possibly it concerns only some property which belonged to the Guild.

Croce. The Lord Octaviano, Lord of Forlì and
Imola, with many shieldbearers and men, all with
candles of white wax, took part in the Procession ;
then all the doctors and citizens and artisans with
small and large candles all of white wax ; and so
also all the men. I did not count the number of
candles, but I am sure there were more than 200
large candles, not including the small ones.'

'The Vicar of the Bishop carried the *Corpus
Domini* and the Canons bore the " tabachino," and
when the Procession was ended, all candles were
left at Sta Croce : and this to honour the Blessed
Sacrament when It is taken to give communion
to sick persons in their houses, and it was decided
that ten candles with many men of the " Compagnia de Corpo Christi " should accompany It.
And this Company was formed by the devotion of
all the people ; and the cause of this was a Fra
Bartolomeo of the Observants of St. Francis who
were preaching in Sta Croce. May God preserve
and prosper this decision and the Company and this
practice. And it was also decided to have a Mass
on the first Sunday of the month in honour of the
Corpus Domini, with many of the candles aforesaid.
And meanwhile I pray to God that the said Devotion may flourish per sæcula sæculorum, Amen.'

Is this not a charming, edifying and instructive
story ? The editor of it, L. Corbelli, completes the
information by telling us in a note (p. 463), that
the excellent Fra Bartolomeo appears as witness to
the last will of Pino Ordelaffi in 1480, and is there
said to be ' de Arimino ' (Rimini) ; Marchesi[1]
states that he came from Bologna. He, as we
saw, introduced both the Procession and the Guild
of the Blessed Sacrament in the Cathedral. The
monks of S. Mercuriale wanted to institute another
Guild, whence discords arose which were settled

[1] Sigism. Marchesi : *Supplemento istorico dell'antica città di
Forlì.* Forlì, 1678, p. 560.

by an edict of Caterina Sforza that the Guild might be set up in any place. Corbelli makes reference to all this and refers to the ' Cronache Forlivesi,' written by Alessandro Padovani (*doc*. No. 190).[1]

Here would be the occasion to mention the Guild of the Blessed Sacrament which had been established in the Church of *Sta Maria dei Servi* : but we must refer the reader to what we have noted elsewhere[2] when speaking of the Chapel and the Charitable Institute of *Corpus Domini*.

Another Guild which can boast of a long and splendid past, is that of *S. Babila*.

A Guild of the Blessed Virgin Mary of All Graces existed in that venerable Basilica as early as 1457. Our State Archives (*F. R. Confraternite. Milano. S. Babila. OO. VV.*) preserve a copy of a decree of Archbishop Charles I in a hand of the sixteenth century, under date December 8, 1457 (missing in Sassi), which approves and confirms the statutes and rules ' of the members of the Guild of the Blessed Virgin established in S. Babila.' The text of the statutes and the rules is inserted in the decree itself. A little later the Guild of the Blessed Sacrament was united with this Guild : up to 1560 both the titles and the accounts were kept separate, but after that the two Guilds were definitely fused. I am unable to say precisely when the Guild of the Blessed Sacrament began, but it seems probable that it goes back to 1520.

On May 18, 1527, the Bishop of Palestrina,[3] in the name and by authority of Clement VII and on

---

[1] Cf. Pasolini : *Caterina Sforza*. Roma, 1893. He mentions neither the procession nor the Company nor the edict of Caterina, although he speaks of Ottaviano, her son (vol. I, p. 195 ff.) and perhaps also of fra Bartolomeo (vol. III, p. 402, *n*. 1088).

[2] A. Ratti ; *Contribuzione*, etc. Part III, p. 42 ff.

[3] Lorenzo Pucci (Puccejus), formerly Bp. of Pistoia, Cf. Ughelli: *Italia Sacra*, tom. III, col. 308

his verbal instructions, confirmed the establishment of the Guild and the main points of its statutes and rules. He did so at the instance of the members themselves who, having established the Guild, were in doubt whether they should have done it without the authority of the Holy See (State Archives, l.c.).

The Guild in the persons of its Priors and members is mentioned as universal legatee of a certain Giovanni Antonio de Marliano in his will, drawn up by Antonio Cisnusculo and completed by Giacomantonio Martignono on June 26, 1524. This is stated in an 'Inventory of the documents and papers, referring to the said Guild and found in a volume at present in possession of our Prior,' on folio 10 of a book[1] which is of the greatest interest to us now, as its title indicates : 'Libro delle Ordinationi e Cose importante si farano per li Signori Priore e Deputati dilla Compagnia overo Scolla del Corpo de nostro Signor Iesu Christo Constructa in la ecclesia di Santo Babilla Porta Orientale e di Madonna Santa Maria delle gratie di Milano.'

The MS. is in various sixteenth century hands. The oldest ordinances in it do not go further back than to the year 1549.

The folios 11 ff. contain the new rules which the Guild adopted in 1557. The introduction runs as follows : 'In the name of our Lord Jesus Christ. And of His Mother Mary. Here follows the text of the Rules and Ordinances made and instituted to be observed by us, the deputy-members and brothers of the Guild of the Body of our Lord established in the Church of S. Babila, Porta Orientale, in Milan. For the information of all our descendants it is hereby made known that since the year 1520 in the said Church of S. Babila a Chapel had been founded by certain devout persons

---

[1] The volume is in the Archives of the Archiep. Curia, Sect. X, *S. Babila*, vol. ix.

and neighbours of this Parish, entitled the Chapel of the Blessed Sacrament of our Lord Jesus Christ, which Chapel in course of time, by alms and legacies left by various persons, has continued down to the present time with some improvements under the administration and rule of the said Deputies and the members. To whom it seeming expedient and needful both in their interest and in that of the Deputies and brothers who will succeed them in the said Guild, that there be a rule and ordinances in writing concerning their procedure, in order that they may know what they have to observe and not to omit, they have decreed, and by common consent signed and accepted, the ordinances written below.' Then follow the ordinances set out in thirteen chapters. The introduction is headed by the number MDLVII.

The suggestion that this is the year when the rules were composed, is obvious ; that it is so, is proved by the minutes in the volume quoted, folio 9, of a Congregation held on October 17, 1557. ' Then the new Ordinances, made to settle the procedure and rules for the brothers of the Guild concerning what should have to be done in the future for the salvation of our souls as well as for the benefit and convenience of the Guild, were read to the said brothers and members. And so the said Ordinances have been accepted by all the said brothers in the form in which they have been set out here.'

Some of these Ordinances deserve special mention. No. 1 lays down that those elected to govern the Guild must not exceed twelve, including the Prior and the officers, but excluding the Chaplain. Chapter 3 rules that a priest should be Assistant to the Guild and should be present at the meetings and that nothing be done without his advice and vote. (The priest was at that time a certain Bernardino Giussano, who was not one of

the parish priests of S. Babila, who in the days of
Lattuada[1] were still three, instead of four, as they
had been before.)   Chapter 9 orders that the
brothers should make a general Communion
' together ' at least on Christmas Day, the Feast
of Corpus Domini and the Feast of the Madonna
in August.   Chapter 10 says that they should
recite every week five *Pater* and five *Ave Maria* to
the Blessed Sacrament to obtain the Indulgences.
It is also noteworthy that on September 19 of the
same year 1557 it had also ' been ordered that all
the brothers come every morning to be shriven and
make their devotions in our Chapel, in order that,
while they are engaged in their devotions, should
it be necessary to carry the Body of our Lord
Jesus Christ to some sick person in the Parish,
such brothers as may be in Church, can provide
the escort as our duty and obligation demands.
And that all consider which persons would be
suitable for such escort so that, when required,
they may be ready for it ' (Vol. cit., fol. 8). Chapter
11 lays it down that ' according to custom a High
Mass ' be caused to be celebrated every third
Sunday of the month.

The arrangements contained in the third Chapter
were modified on June 21, 1569 in the sense that
the priest is no longer to assist at the Meetings
(Vol. cit., fol. 37).

On January 2, 1558 (ibid., fol. 9) it was decided
to enquire of ' some theologian or doctor whether
the Guild is obliged (in order to obtain the indulgences granted to the Guilds of the Blessed
Sacrament) to combine with the Parish for the
expenses of providing the lamp of the Blessed
Sacrament.'

This was by no means the result of stinginess or
lack of zeal, for immediately afterwards it was
' decided to have a purple silk-lined baldacchino

Cf. Lattuada, l.c., tom. I, p. 182.

made, with six tassels and four posts of a suitable size, for the Viaticum' (l.c.). In the same year, 1558, on March 20, it is noted that 'two large lanterns, handsome and of a size to hold two large wax candles' have been provided, as well as 'a cover of waxed linen to put over the baldacchino, when it rains, in order that the Blessed Sacrament and the priest may be under shelter and the baldacchino not be spoilt' (l.c., fol. 140). On June 4 it is 'ordered that in honour of the Octave of the Feast of our Lord, wax and candles be provided in sufficient quantities, and that the Rev. Bernardino and Giovan Antonio Pozzo should pay calls in the Parish and the neighbourhood to beg the people to arrange altars and awnings for the Octave[1] so that the Blessed Sacrament may be carried round the Parish as had been ordered ; and that the same should see to the provision of the escort' (l.c., fol. 15). Soon afterwards I find a note to the effect that it has been ' decided to come to an arrangement with the members of the Guild of St. Roche outside Porta Orientale to receive the Blessed Sacrament with the baldacchino in their Church on rainy and windy days' ; a note is added that this ' seemed to all a sound and excellent thing.'

Equally sound and excellent is the decision of December 5, 1557 (l.c., fol. 9) to cause to be cast and set up on the Church tower a bell to be rung only for the Viaticum and in order to notify the brothers so that, when they hear it, ' they may come to accompany the Blessed Sacrament with due escort.' No less sound and excellent is the instruction given on October 17, 1557 (l.c.) ' to the Rev. Bernardino to confer with the other priests of S.

---

[1] The Guild had already set the example. In the inventory of 1557, Aug. 22 (l.c., fol. 7) is noted : 'A baldacchino of crimson damask with silk and golden fringes, to be carried on eight poles, very suitably made for the Octave of Corpus Domini.'

Babila, to ascertain whether they would agree that
the Blessed Sacrament be kept continuously in our
Chapel as provided for this purpose.'

Whether the reverend clergy agreed I do not know;
but I can add that the excellent brothers of the
Guild had taken care to render their Chapel less
unworthy of its Divine Guest. As early as March
15, 1553 (l.c., fol. 3) 'it was ordered . . . that the
reredos of the altar of our Guild Chapel, set up in
S. Babila, be provided with a painting on wood of
Christ standing, with angels and other embellish-
ments, to fit over the said reredos. And thus *in
usum* of the said order a contract was made in
duplicate with Master John Crespo, painter in
encaustic, of Sta Margarita,[1] to paint the said
picture in accordance with the design submitted
by him.[2] The said Master John be held to deliver
the painting for the sum of ten *scudi*, though estimated when finished at fourteen, like one painted
by myself, Beltramo da Glussiano,[3] the contract
being signed by the said Master John and our Prior
and our Treasurer.'

The work proceeded but slowly. The financial
resources did not come up to the spirit of enterprise,
though the spirit was there both for this and for
other activities. On June 16, 1555 (l.c., fol. 4)
. . . 'many things were discussed and settled ;
and, first, that the reredos of the altar with the
angels be completed and that the brothers should
take courage and have the outer face of the arch

[1] He is not mentioned by Lattuada (l.c.) though he gives
the names of several painters who worked in S. Babila.
Neither does Magenta mention him in the *Appendice alle
Chiese* (l.c., p. 312), where he refers to S. Babila. The Master
John Crespo cannot be Giovanni Battista Crespi called
' Cerano,' b. in 1557. There is no trace or memory of the
pictures.

[2] ' by him ' : ' per lui ' : I cannot guarantee the reading
' per lui.'

[3] Perhaps the Chancellor of the Guild *pro tempore*.

over the Chapel decorated down to the two pilasters.
The task of attending and seeing to the execution
of these resolutions be assigned by the said brothers
to the Prior and Treasurer, namely to enquire
into the costs, obtain the masters and all the things
needed and to report to the Guild. Thirdly it was
decided to provide a suitable silver monstrance,
according to our means, to contain the Blessed
Sacrament.'

It is evident that the admirable Guild of S. Babila
lacked neither piety, nor enterprise, nor courage,
nor prudence.

I must not forget the Blessed Sacrament Guild of
S. Simplicianus. Its establishment had been discussed as early as 1524 in so much detail that in that
same year it was called upon to receive a bequest
left by a certain munificent Antonio Ferrari.[1]

'An account of the conventions concluded
between the Monastery of S. Simplicianus[2] and
the Members of the Guild in the said Church'
states that to the Guild was assigned the altar of
St. Peter set up in the Church of the S. Simplicianus
with authority ' illud removendi . . . et intitulandi
sub vocabulo *Corporis Christi.*'

The deed of these conventions concerning the
Chapel in the Church, drawn up by Gio. Abel
Merone, under date November 25, 1538, was
formerly in the State Archives. Now only the
outer cover with a summary is there.[3] The Guild
disappeared during the suppressions of Joseph II,
when it was fused with the Confraternity of Charity
which was at that time set up at S. Simplicianus as

[1] State Archives : *F. R. Confrat. Milano. S. Simpliciano
Santissimo,* no. 347. A large leather-bound volume : ' Indice
delle carte ed Istrumenti,' etc., fol. 6.

[2] This was a Monastery of Cassinese monks, who in 1672
were also charged with the cure of souls, which formerly had
been in charge of two secular priests. Cf. Lattuada, l.c., p.
66 ff.

[3] l.c., no. 334

elsewhere. An index of the documents of the Guild, compiled in 1719 and going down to 1778, is preserved in the volume quoted above.

Some remarks may be expected here on the Guild founded in *S. Sepolcro* of Milan in 1527 by Mgr. Giovanni Antonio Bellotti, who held the Priorship of St. Anthony of Grenoble. But I am not altogether certain that this was a real Guild of the Blessed Sacrament, although his Guild had objects and adopted practices of a definitely eucharistic kind ; it was also undoubtedly due to him that the ' Quarant'Ore ' were introduced in Milan, though not in all the form and solemnity which were added later. A proper Blessed Sacrament Guild existed in the neighbouring Parish Church of Sta Maria Beltrade (the Church of S. Sepolcro was only a Collegiate Church) in 1568. This is clear from the arrangements made in that year between the members of the Guild and the two Parish Priests (Arch. of the Curia, Sect. X, *S. Sepolcro*, Vol. III). Secondly, Bellotti and his institution have been already the subject of discussion by several writers : I mention only the principal authors who give references to others : Mazzucchelli (*Osservazioni*, etc. *sopra il Rito Ambrosiano*, Milano, 1828, p. 237 ff.), and the unknown Barnabite, author of ' *L'orazione delle XL ore e il B. Antonmaria Zaccaria*, Roma, 1895.[1]

[1] The following are the several points made by the Barnabite author : (i) ' Continuous prayers in some of the Churches, on certain feast days or other special occasions, but without Exposition of the Sacrament and without pomp, had been instituted in Milan before Bl. Zaccaria came there ; (ii) After some lapse of time, the institution having lapsed, it was reestablished by him, with Exposition and candles and hangings ; (iii) The chief helper of Bl. Zaccaria in Milan as elsewhere was Fra Buono ; (iv) P. Giuseppe da Ferno was not only the champion, but one of the most eager promotors of churches taking turns, so that the " Quarant'Ore " should be going on all the year round.' These points seem to me substantially well argued and proved in the above work and in the evidence

A single entry, written in a hand of the sixteenth to seventeenth centuries,[1] suggests that a Blessed Sacrament Guild existed as early as 1539 in the Church of *S. Protaso*, at present a Chapel of ease of the Church of S. Fedele. An appeal by the heirs of Pacifico Ponzio[2] informs us that this well-known Archiepiscopal printer of the time of St. Charles had left to the Guild five thousand *lire* on condition of a daily Mass and the recital of the Office of the Dead.

The Church of *S. Vittore al Teatro* also possessed a Guild perhaps prior to 1554. A permit was issued by the Archbishop Gio. Angelo Arcimboldi in that year on August 2, for the establishment of the Guild in the said Church.[3] But possibly the

appended. I emphasise ' in substance ' because (i) instead of saying ' in some of the churches and on certain feast-days,' documentary evidence justifies the expression : ' in the Church of S. Sepolcro and on the Feasts of Christmas, Easter, Whitsun and the Assumption,' as it is also stated in the work (l.c., n. 5) ; (ii) that the first solemn Exposition occurred in 1534 seems to me not quite certain, nor proved, in contradiction to the assertion (l.c., p. xv, *n.* 28). The best evidence is that of Moriggia, who, if he was born in 1525—not in 1528 (cf. Cesare Morigi, *Discorso sulla vita e sulle opere di P.M.*, Milano, 1602), wrote his *Santuario di Milano* not less than half a century after the event and in great haste (cf. *Discorso*, towards the end) whence he is often inexact, especially in the matter of figures. In this case he lacks the support of Burigozzo, who says that the ' Quarant'Ore ' ' comenzorno al principio de Mazo 1537 in Porta Orientale.' (iii) It does not seem to me proved, despite the assertion of Bugati (cf. l.c., p. 3 ff.), that Burigozzo's ' certain priests ' ' towards S. Ambrogio ' (whom the anonymous author, p. 24, note 7, identifies with the Barnabites) are the same as ' some men ' to whom Burigozzo attributes the turns taken by ' ciascuna gexia ' in the ' Quarant'Ore ' and the first solemn Expositions (l.c., p. 24 ff.). Mazzucchelli identifies them with the Guild of the Cathedral.

[1] State Archives, *S. Protaso ad Monachos, OO. VV.* 295.

[2] l.c., *Legati, M-Z*, 294.

[3] Ibid., l.c. *S. Vittore al Teatro, SS.* 363, fol. 2 : ' Archivio o vero Registro universale delle Scritture della Ven. Scuola del SS. Sacramento eretta nella chiesa parocchiale di S. Vettore

foundation goes back a few years earlier, for an authenticated copy of the permit speaks of a ' confirmation and re-establishment.'[1]

Joseph II, in order to justify the numberless suppressions in which he indulged, had the brazen-ness to write : ' I have abolished the superfluous convents and the even more superfluous Guilds.'[2] His words were taken up by his followers, repeated and put in practice down to the present.

Even the little that we have seen, shows on the evidence of historical fact, continuing, thanks to God, down to our own time, what value to set on these words : to call them a falsehood would be putting it very mildly. We have seen that the Guilds, at the same time as they awakened, disci-plined and inspired the pious activities of the laity, also encouraged the arts and industries in the service of the Eucharistic cult and became centres of charity and of a stable and ordered beneficence.[3] To consider all this as superfluous, argues not only a lack of faith, but of heart and intelligence.

The documents which I have mentioned suggest many other reflections ; but there is no need to expound my own. The eloquence of facts is always at the end the most convincing. This must be my excuse, if my love of them has led me to gather together facts perhaps even too minute and detailed.

I stated at the beginning that this would be only a collection of fragments. The collection is so small

al Teatro di Milano ; ordinato da Alessandro Tassi, 1686.' Tassi compiled registers and indices, but is not very accurate. I have discussed the matter in the *Arch. Storico Lombardo*, June 30, 1895, p. 347.

[1] L.c., OO.VV. 362.

[2] Cf. C. Cantù, *Storia Universale*, ed. 10, tom. X, p. 327, n.

[3] The precious little codex previously mentioned, confirms, at least summarily, what I have set out here on documentary evidence. It notes in connexion with several of the Guilds : ' potrebbe mettersi fra i Luoghi Pii.'

that it has already come to an end. But having reached it, I am happy to think that the beginnings of the Blessed Sacrament Guilds cannot but bring to mind also the solemn and joyful days of the thirteenth Eucharistic Congress of Milan.[1] The future writer of the History of the Eucharist in Milan will be able to add that splendid page to these few and feeble indications of mine, this mass of activities and events to my poor fragments. But if History embraces epochs and I have only indicated moments, I am comforted by the thought that epochs are but composed of moments, and that it would indeed be a remarkable and consoling task, if, by gathering not merely fragments but the whole of the component parts of the Eucharistic History of Milan, the full proof could be furnished that in Milan throughout its history 'thanks and praise have been rendered always to the most Holy and Divine Sacrament.'

[1] See the explanatory paragraph following the title of this Essay. (*Translator's note.*)

IV

THE 'CODEX ATLANTICUS' OF LEONARDO DA VINCI IN THE AMBROSIAN LIBRARY

Published originally in 1907 (Milan, Tip. Allegretti, 8⁰), and dedicated to Fermo and Ernestina Ratti. The illustrations here inserted were included in that first publication.

THE manuscript, world-famous under the title 'Codex Atlanticus,' is one of the most treasured possessions of the Ambrosian Library, rich as it is especially in manuscripts. Figures 1 and 2 show the state and condition in which it came into possession of the Library. The volume itself is displayed in a case in the room called 'Gabinetto Leonardo' under the new rearrangement of the Gallery, attached to the Ambrosian Library (see *Guida sommaria per il visitatore della Biblioteca Ambrosiana e delle collezioni annesse*, Milano, Tip. Allegretti, 1907, pp. 82–91).

I take from this 'Guide' the greater part of the information on this famous volume and its fate. Except for some few variants and additions, the same facts will also be found in that little, but in so many ways precious, work, *La Biblioteca Ambrosiana*, published in 1895 by Senatore Luca Beltrami.

The Codex is a stout volume of 804 pages, measuring 0.67 by 0.45 cm. and contains fully 1750 passages of text and designs of the most varied kind by Leonardo. It was the size of, and the vast range of the material covered in, this volume which gave it the name of 'Codex Atlanticus.'

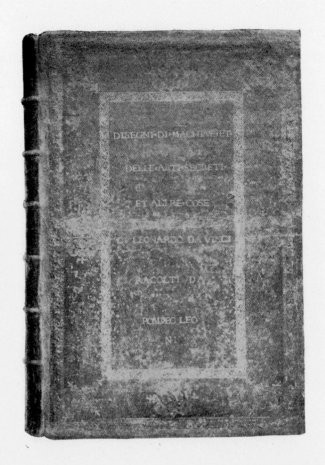

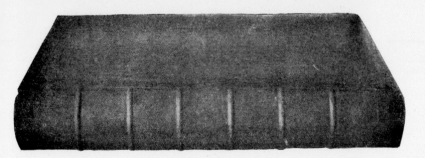

THE 'CODEX ATLANTICUS

The many-sided genius of Leonardo there asserts itself in the most widely different spheres and is represented in all its variety by numerous samples : in military art by designs of artillery anticipating its most modern applications ; by studies of fortifications, men-of-war, even by suggestions of steamships ;   in Astronomy by observations on the movement of the earth ; in Physics and Chemistry by notes on gravity, equilibrium, light, sound, properties and combinations of bodies ; in Hydraulics, by various machines for raising water, and by designs and studies for navigable canals ; in Geometry, by sketches of geometrical figures, prepared for the treatise *De divina proportione* by Luca Paciolo (a magnificent MS., still in the possession of the Ambrosian Library, which its founder, so Bosca says, used to kiss out of sheer admiration) ; in Geodesy, by studies on mensuration ;   in Cartography by sketches and plans of regions and various localities ; in Mechanics, by designs of implements and engines for flying and every other kind of use ; in Industry by suggestions of rational methods for the construction of pavements, locks, handles, textiles and metallurgy ; Architecture is represented by numerous plans of churches, designs of cupolas and monuments ; Painting by studies in perspective and observations on the manner and technique of painting ; Art properly speaking by schemes for landscapes, by sketches for the picture of the Adoration of the Magi, and of St. John, for the equestrian statue of Francesco Sforza, studies for the Leda subject and the famous picture of Beatrice d'Este. Leonardo was left-handed, and his habit of writing from right to left is well-known and is his practice throughout this Codex.

When Leonardo died on May 2, 1519 at Cloux in France, Francesco Melzi who had been his favourite pupil, the faithful companion of his voluntary exile and his heir, brought all the scientific and artistic material he had inherited back to Italy and deposited it in his country house at Vaprio which had already previously sheltered his Master. These precious objects were faithfully cared for by Melzi ; but it was otherwise after his death, for they were then dispersed, largely on account of the very fame of the Master and the eager search for records and relics of his, especially in the matter of designs. Among the most pertinacious and successful collectors of that time was Pompeo Leoni, the son and successor of Leone Leoni, the favourite sculptor of King Philip II of Spain.

Availing himself of various volumes of different size and contents in which Leonardo had, as it were in note-books, set down his thoughts and observations, and by taking these to pieces and rearranging them, Pompeo Leoni composed the great volume which we now possess. He left the order largely to the whim of the binder, which inevitably resulted in confusion and gaps in the series of designs and also in the insertion of a few non-genuine drawings, perhaps the work or copies by his pupils. Nicolas Cochin, who had seen the MSS. of Leonardo in the Ambrosian Library during his travels in Italy, had already pointed out such insertions (*Voyage d'Italie*, etc., 2nd ed., Paris, 1773, p. 48), and the same observation was made by La Lande (*Voyage en Italie fait dans les années* 1765–66, Vol. I, p. 294, 3rd ed., Genève, 1790) in reference to some drawings of bombs. Indeed, on folio No. 9 (*recto, a*) of the ' Codex Atlanticus,' Leonardo had drawn two mortars firing bombs, and the design is repeated on the *verso* of the same folio in a copy (Cochin seems to have seen only this copy), which is evidently later and by a somewhat inexperienced hand. Leoni had the coat of arms of his family stamped on either side of the red-leather volume (see Figs.

1 and 2) with a border and the text : ' Disegni di macchine et delle arti secreti et altre cose di Leonardo da Vinci. Raccolti da Pompeo Leoni.'

The volume, composed, it would seem, during the years 1587-9 in Milan, was taken by Leoni with other records of Leonardo to Spain, where perhaps in 1589 it was bound, and then brought back to Milan in 1604. On the death of Leoni in 1610 the volume passed by inheritance to Cleodoro Calchi who sold it for 300 *scudi* to the Marchese Galeazzo Arconati. He was another of the great Milanese collectors of that time, as the museum in his magnificent country house at Castellazzo shows, and succeeded in gathering several other Leonardo MSS. in his possession. In 1626 Cardinal Federico Borromeo ordered a transcription of the ' Codex ' to be made, urged by his own wish and by the desire of Cardinal Francesco Barberini, who wanted to possess a copy of the ' Codex Atlanticus ' for the precious library in Rome, with which he tried to rival his Eminent Colleague in Milan. In 1637, by a deed drawn up on January 22, the Marchese Arconati presented the ' Codex Atlanticus ' and eleven other Leonardo manuscripts to the Ambrosian Library, after having previously refused an offer of 1000 doubloons made to him by the King of England for the ' Codex ' alone. An inscription put up in the Ambrosian Library in 1637 embellished with a representation of Arconati records the gratitude of the Library and the lasting memory of such munificence.

This handsome gesture of Arconati was not only worthy of the nobility of his lineage and an act of high patriotism, but also a posthumous act of homage to the friendship with which Cardinal Federico had honoured him. We still possess his letters (MS. G. 247 inf.) of the year 1623 from which we can gather that the Cardinal gave him his confidence in important family matters and showed him a trust

and friendship for which Arconati felt as grateful
as he professed himself honoured.

It was also a tribute and expression of Cardinal
Federico's admiration for Leonardo, and of the
eagerness with which he collected his works. It
was this admiration which led the Cardinal, as it
did others, to attribute to Leonardo all the paintings
and designs which displayed any extraordinary
features : for example to confine ourselves to the
Ambrosian collections, the portrait of a young
woman, famous under the name of Beatrice d'Este,
which has a whole literature to itself ; or the
small pictures of Giovanni Galeazzo and of Petrarch
(cf. *Rassegna d'Arte*, Jan. 1907 : ' Un antico ri-
tratto di F. Petrarca all' Ambrosiana,' printed also
separately with a reproduction in natural size of
the little painting), although the latter shows
unmistakable features of the end of the fourteenth
century and has therefore been attributed by many
critics to other painters.

The admiration which the Cardinal felt for
Leonardo, must have been well known at the time,
for a distinguished poet, Benedetto Sossago, one of
the first Doctors of the Ambrosiana, dedicated to
him one of his elegant—and by the Cardinal much
appreciated—Latin epigrams (Benedicti Sociaci
Ambrosiani Collegii doctoris, *Epigrammatum libri
septem*, *Odarum duo*, Mediolani, ex Ambrosiani
Collegii Typographia, MDCXVI, Lib. IV, p. 130).
He took his inspiration from the tradition which
represented Leonardo as dying in the arms of the
King of France, his admirer and Mæcenas. I insert
it here, among other reasons because it is so little
known as to be as good as unpublished :

DE CARDINALI BORROMOEO ET LEONARDO PICTORE

Dum caput expirans, pictor Leonarde, reclinas,
gallorum dominus brachia supposuit.
Ecce tuas tabulas Federicus servat ab ævo :
his mentis custos, corporis ille fuit,

Sossago dedicated not only one but two of his
Latin epigrams to Arconati, praising the new
palace he was building, and even more his person.
But there are no references either to Leonardo, or
to his MSS. ; perhaps Arconati was not then
in possession of them, not even of the 'Codex
Atlanticus.' Another witness to the friendship of
Arconati for Cardinal Federico may be the picture,
bearing the number 88 in the hall of the ' Museo
Settala,' which is an old copy of the Sta Cecilia
of Raphael. It bears in gold lettering on the frame,
dating from the early seventeenth century, the
legend : *Maria Arconati | apellea expressit arte | patre
Galeaz editam | ex ipsa indole agnoscas.*

The Leonardo MSS., and especially the ' Codex
Atlanticus,' were ever afterwards preserved with
the greatest care and honour. The 'Codex' had
first been placed in the great hall of the Library
which Cardinal Federico had simply called ' his
library,' in the case marked ' P,' and then in the
case marked ' O ' under number 248, which can
still be seen on the back of the volume. Later it
was transferred to the Picture Gallery, or ' Sala
Fagnani,' so called after the Marchese Fagnani who
on his death in 1840 left to the Ambrosian Library
the whole contents which fill this hall, quite
23,000 volumes with, in addition, pictures and
engravings to the number of more than 16,000,
as well as funds to continue the collection. In this
Gallery the ' Codex Atlanticus ' was, in the words of
the Prefect, Bonsignori, in 1790, kept ' with great
care in a painted box, with various golden ornaments, shaped like an urn, in walnut, upon a table,
and fastened to the wall was a marble tablet with
an inscription to the lasting memory of Galeazzo
Arconati, the donor of the volume in 1637.'

The inventory of 1661 describes it in the following
terms which recur in that of 1685 : ' A small low
table, gilt, with ancient figures on which rests a

wooden ark decorated with golden floral designs
and containing the famous volume written in Leonardo da Vinci's own hand, consisting of 393 leaves,
10.1 bra. long, 0.9 bra. wide, bound in red leather
gilt, for which 3000 Spanish doubloons were
offered, if we may believe the inscription in marble
attached to the wall of the aforesaid Gallery on
which a medallion in black marble with the likeness
of Galeazzo Arconati, donor of the said volume,
may be seen. A concave mirror is kept in the said
ark, and is used to give the right presentation of
the characters of the writing which has been diligently written in the reverse way. Above the said
ark are placed three small pictures, etc. . . .'
Actually the pictures did not rest on the ' ark,' but
on iron brackets attached to the wall.

The famous volume was seen in this condition
and admired by the Abbé Coyer in 1763 (*Oeuvres
complètes, Voyage en Italie*, Paris, Duchesne, 1783,
Vol. IV, 61) : ' on lit au dessus du coffre qui
renferme ce trésor que Jacques, Roi d'Angleterre,
en offrit en vain 3000 pistoles d'Espagne.' And
even after the volume had been, as we shall see,
removed, another inventory records : ' A small
table painted with floral designs with twisted iron
legs. Upon it an urn of wood also painted ; it
used to contain the great volume of designs by
Leonardo da Vinci which has been transferred to
France, as appears from the requisition order.'

Charles de Brosses, in his famous letters on Italy
(*Lettres historiques et critiques sur l'Italie*, t. l, p. 152,
Paris, an. VII) in which he recorded his impressions
and observations during his journey in 1739,
mentions the ' Codex Atlanticus ', but says nothing
either of the ' ark ' or the table or of the inscription :
' Il faut encore voir dans la galérie de peinture
à l'Ambrosienne un énorme livre *infolio*, dont on
a refusé un tel prix, que je n'ose pas vous le
rapporter. Ce sont des dessins, avec des explica-

tions, de toutes les machines imaginables, soit de
guerre, soit de statique, le tout dessiné et écrit
de la propre main de Léonard da Vinci.' Substantially the same is the record of La Lande
(*Voyage en Italie*, etc., 3rd ed., Genève, 1790, p. 293) :
' une des choses qu'on prise le plus dans ce cabinet
est la collection des manuscrits de *Leonardo da Vinci*
ou *del Vinci*, qui a coûté, dit-on, des sommes con-
sidérables, et qu'on laisse voir à peine, surtout aux
savants ; il y a un grand volume, et onze petits ;
il y en a sur les ombres et les couleurs, mais la plus
part ne contiennent que des croquis ; tantôt une
figure, tantôt une machine, avec une note abrégée ;
cependant on a imprimé que Jacques I, roi d'Angleterre, avait voulu donner 3000 pistoles d'or pour
un seul de ces volumes à Galéas Arconati et que ce
zélé citoyen aima mieux en enrichir la bibliothèque
de Milan ; c'est en conséquence de cette générosité
qu'on lui a élevé un buste de marbre, avec une
inscription à son honneur.   Ce volume contient
plusieurs dessins ; on voit parmi ces machines, des
figures de bombes ; mais M. Cochin assure qu'elles
sont dessinées d'une autre main, et postérieures à
Léonard da Vinci.'

Here several doubts and questions present themselves. The greater number of them have repeatedly
agitated the learned world and have recently been
dealt with in a solid and instructive article by Dr.
Ettore Verga (*Raccolta Vinciana*, fasc. I, January–
June, 1905, pp. 59–66).

In the first place the handsome offer of the King
of England, and by implication the generous
gesture of Arconati have been denied altogether.
The author of this denial, as Dr. Verga tells us on
the information of Professor A. Favaro of the
University of Padua, was an English writer of the
seventeenth century, John Evelyn. Evelyn, recording a visit of his to the Ambrosian Library in the
year 1645, states among other things that the marble

inscription, according to him ' boasting ' rather
than impressive, wrongly ' pretends ' that the King
of England—he calls him Charles—had made an
offer—he says of £1000, certainly pound sterling—
to Arconati ; that the agent of the King had been
a ' Lord Martial ', assisted by the Duke of Feria, then
Governor of Milan ; and that the Lord, having
inspected the designs (according to him they were
' scratches of Indians, etc.'), did not think the
volume worth all that money.[1]

[1] The following are the actual words used by John Evelyn,
the seventeenth-century diarist, in describing his visit to the
Ambrosian Library in 1646 (not 1645, as stated above) :

' Early next morning came the learned Dr. Ferarius to
visite us, and took us in his coach to see the Ambrosian Librarie,
where Cardinal Fred. Borromeo has expended so vast a sum
on this building and in furnishing it with curiosities, especialy
paintings and drawings of inestimable value amongst painters.
It is a schole fit to make the ablest artists. There are many
rare things of Hans Breugill, and amongst them the *Four
Elements*. In this room stands the glorious (boasting) inscription of Cavaliero Galeazzo Arconati, valueing his gift to the
librarie of severall drawings by Da Vinci, but these we could
not see, the keeper of them being out of towne and he always
carrying the keys with him ; but my Lord Martial, who had
seene them, told me all but one booke are small, that an huge
folio contain'd 400 leaves full of scratches of Indians, &c. but
whereas the inscription pretends that our King Charles had
offer'd £1000 for them, the truth is, and my Lord himselfe
told me, that it was he who treated with Galeazzo for himselfe
in the name and by permission of the king, and that the Duke
of Feria, who was then Governour, should make the bargain :
but my Lord having seene them since, did not think them of
so much worth.'

It is obvious that the ' Lord Martial ' here mentioned is none
other than the ' Earl Marshall,' namely the Earl of Arundel, referred to by Annoni in his statement on p. 250 below.

There would consequently appear to be no discrepancy
between the versions of what had happened given by Annoni
and by John Evelyn, except that Evelyn was evidently in
ignorance of the earlier attempts to secure the volume by
Annoni, and knew only of the subsequent efforts initiated by
the ' Conte di Arendel ' according to Annoni's account.—
(*Translator's note.*)

But against Evelyn's contention we have two
unimpeachable documents. The first the deed,
mentioned above, of the gift of 1637. Among
other things it states expressly (I translate from the
Latin of the deed) : 'Great Princes indeed tried
at any cost to tear them (the Leonardo MSS.)
from his (Arconati's) hands ; but they tried
in vain ; more easily might they have wrenched
the club of Hercules from the hero's hands. For
even the King of England, having endeavoured to
arrange the matter by means of that " pan-
chrestum " (we should say that *passe-par-tout*) which
money is, and having offered for a single of the
codices 1000 doubloons, as they say, of Spain,
which represent here a sum of three thousand
scudi, found it of no avail. The magnanimity of
the King was shown no more gloriously in his
offer than that of Arconati in his refusal.'

The second document, inserted in the deed of
gift, concerns the identity of the agent, whom
Evelyn not only passes over in silence, but replaces
by another. Mentioning, moreover, King James,
it has a bearing on another problematic point. It
is the sworn statement, supported by witnessses to its
signature, of the very person who asserts that *he* was
the agent between Arconati and the King, at the
insistent request of the latter.

It is a certain Antonio Annoni, a Milanese as the
name suggests, or certainly a Lombard. It must
be remembered that several business men of our city
kept open house in Brussels, Antwerp and London
and were thus in constant and rapid communications with their home, in the matter both of goods
and money transactions. Private persons also
availed themselves of these facilities, as nowadays
they do of the firms of Gondrand, Mangili and
others. In the correspondence between the famous
Antwerp painter John Brueghel and Cardinal
Federico, his protector, the names of Vergani,

Lavelli, Annoni often occur, for in their bales and boxes the paintings which now adorn the Ambrosiana, came to Milan, and together with their orders and remittances went also the orders and the drafts of the Cardinal to Antwerp. Orders dispatched from Milan in July were in Antwerp as early as August. Antonio Annoni's explicit statement runs :

' In the name of God, I, the undersigned, make the sworn statement that in the year 1630, having been insistently urged by His Majesty the King of England, James, now reigning, to secure from the noble Lord Galeazzo Arconati a large volume in folio on Imperial paper, which contains a very large number of designs of engines and instruments, also for the Secret Arts, all the products of the genius and of the hand of the famous Leonardo da Vinci, collected with the greatest diligence by Pompeo Leoni and put together in that volume, which bears on the front in gold letters the title : " Dissegni di macchine et delle arti secrette, et altre cose di Leonardo da Vinci, raccolti da Pompeo Leoni," I insistently begged the said Lord to cede it to the King, offering him a royal gift of one thousand gold doubloons. To which offer he gave a reply worthy of his noble mind and of that affection and zeal which he has always displayed towards our glorious country, saying that he did not wish to deprive his country of so great a treasure, and if this had not been the case, he would have made a present of it to His Majesty without any recompense. And because later I received fresh requests, both by letter and by word of mouth from an agent of that Crown who had come to these parts to purchase pictures, books and other similar objects, I suggested that it was impossible to obtain the volume from that Lord by any offer of money whatever and that therefore only favours remained to be tried. Thus a letter was sent me

by the noble Count of Arendel (Arundel) through
His Excellency the Duke of Feria, at that time
Governor of this State, in which he begged that all
possible efforts be made to obtain from the said
Lord this book which His Majesty so much desired.
As H.E. the Duke told me afterwards, the Lord
Arconati gave the same reply to these instances
as he had given me earlier, and as he gave me again
at that same time, when I renewed to him the offer
of the Royal gift. And the aforesaid things being
in conformity with the truth, as they happened,
I have signed this present statement with my own
hand in the presence of the undersigned witnesses
and the Notary, on this day 8 December, 1636.

' I, Iacomo Antonio Annone, affirm and swear
as above.

' I, Gio. Giacomo Vadabella, have seen the
said Iacomo Antonio Annone sign with his own
hand, and at his request I sign this statement as
a witness on the aforesaid date, etc.

' I, Luca Fr. Locarni, have seen the above, etc.

' I, Carlo Annone, was present and have seen
the said Iacomo Antonio Annone sign.'

Then follows in Latin a similar certificate for
all four signatures on behalf of the public Notary
Cristoforo Sola, who states that all the above
statements have been made in his presence and
under the authority of Pier Paolo Confalonieri,
Collegiate Advocate and one of the Councillors of
Justice of Milan and Judge in Ordinary of the City
and the Duchy of Milan.

This same Cristoforo Sola was also the executor
of the donation of Arconati, who had appointed
him for that purpose as his Attorney by a special
deed. This deed is inserted in the Notary's act of
the Donation itself, drawn up by the Notary Matteo
Croce. This last-named also inserted in it the
Declaration of Annoni and a statement of the Conservators and Doctors of the Ambrosian Library,

in which they, after an eulogy both of the donor and of the gift, express effusively their gratitude and formally undertake to set up the commemorative tablet and the inscription which we have still to-day. The first of the two documents quoted above is taken from this statement. These documents are so solemn, so explicit, serious and convincing as far as the facts are concerned, that it is surely unreasonable to ask for more proof of the truth asserted in them. Dr. Verga may well be justified in thinking (l.c., p. 61) that the inconsiderate remarks of 'Lord Martial,' having become known in Milan, were the cause of these repeated and solemn, one feels inclined to say, emphatic and protesting declarations of Annoni and of the authorities of the Ambrosian Library.

There is, however, one point on which the second of these documents is open to question : where it states as still reigning in 1636 King James, who had unquestionably died on April 6, 1625. This is the relevance of this document to the second of the aforementioned questions : which of the English kings is the one who made this high offer to Arconati ? The reader will certainly have observed that this question remains open even after this awkward assertion of Annoni's Declaration. He will have noticed that some writers give no name at all, Evelyn mentions Charles, and others, like my Rev. colleague, Dr. Antonio Ceruti (*La Biblioteca Ambrosiana*, in the volume *Istituti scientifici di Milano*, 1880, p. 125), mention King James. One secondary point we can dismiss at once. Dr. Verga (l.c., p. 62) seems somewhat shocked that Dr. Ceruti should speak of James VI instead of James I. But the mistake—if there is a mistake—goes back to Pier Paolo Bosca (*De origine et statu Bibliothecae Ambrosianae*, etc., Mediolani, 1672, p. 153). I say, if there is a mistake ; for it is the same James Stuart who was James VI in Scotland

and James I in England. So there is no cause
for being shocked. But Bosca seems to me really
open to reproach when he quotes the *Commenti
Historici* of Alfonso Loschi (Bologna, 1669) in a
manner which suggests that Loschi confirms the
efforts made by the King in his dealings with
Arconati ; whereas Loschi merely says that King
James was ' interested in the study of every science
and of Moral Philosophy, Mathematics, Politics
and political philosophy more than Princes are
wont to be.' The fact certainly favours the
theory of efforts being made by such a king ;
but the quotation, as made by Bosca, is certainly
ambiguous and made in a way calculated to
exaggerate its value in the eyes of the unwary
reader.

As to the question in itself, viz. whether it was
King James or King Charles, Dr. Verga is quite
right when he says that the intervention of the
Duke of Feria proves nothing. He was Governor
of Milan from 1610 to 1625 during the reign of
James, and again from 1631 to 1633, while Charles
was reigning, and therefore in both cases previously
to 1636 when Annoni made his Declaration. I
should not agree as easily with Dr. Verga when he
asserts that the year 1625 and King James must be
excluded, and that we must assume the negotiations to have been begun in 1630 and taken up
again after the Duke Feria's return to Milan (as,
according to Verga, Annoni is alleged to have said),
but in any case during the reign of Charles, not of
James.

In the first place Annoni makes no reference to
the return of the Duke of Feria ; speaking of him
in 1636, he seems—I say *seems*—rather to refer to
some fairly distant date, when he says that he was
' at that time Governor of this State.' Secondly,
though it is true that Arconati did not come into
possession of the ' Codex Atlanticus ' until 1625, it

s

is also true that King James was still alive for quite
four months of that year, sufficient to allow—as
we have seen—several couriers to pass between
London and Milan viâ Antwerp, all the more as
the very reasons and needs, political and military,
of the Spanish Domination rendered this route both
expeditious and popular.

Lastly, a third observation seems to me to the
point. It is improbable, not to say impossible, that
Annoni, however long ago back in Milan, should
have been mistaken about the name of the king,
who had honoured him with his 'insistent requests';
quite apart from the fact that in 1636 eleven years
had passed since Charles I had begun to reign in
England, and that some rumour of this fact must
have reached Milan, especially after the purchase
of art-objects made by Charles in the early years of
his reign in Upper Italy. If therefore the actuary
wrote ' James ' in the text of Annoni's Declaration,
the name must have been given to him by Annoni
himself. I say, the actuary wrote it, for it is evident
that the text was written by a clerk, only the
signatures of Annoni and witnesses being autograph. There would be nothing strange or even
unusual, if the actuary, having been given the name
of the King by Annoni, should have added on his
own, following his professional custom, the words
' now reigning,' and that, as, alas, happens only
too frequently, neither Annoni nor anyone else
should have paid attention to this point of the long
statement covering eight pages. We must also
not overlook that the name ' James ' issued victoriously from doubts and difficulties, perhaps in the
actuary's own mind, for the first two letters have
been scratched out, but what had first been written
we cannot guess, much less read.

There remains the difficulty of the year 1630,
explicitly given in the Declaration signed by
Annoni. It is a difficulty, I readily admit, which

Fig. 4.

Fig. 5.

Fig. 3.

reopens the whole problem, and might seem definitely to favour Dr. Verga's conclusion, if it were not
generally and on good grounds admitted that
errors, whether of memory or of writing, occur
much more easily in figures than in names. My
final conclusion would accordingly be that—apart
from the substance of the matter—we are not in a
position to reach any certainty on the details of the
year and the person of the king in question.

Another interesting problem might be the actual
amount of the sum offered to Arconati by the King
of England, in terms of our currency. But Dr.
Verga has (l c., p. 63 ff.) clearly settled that matter,
concluding that ' the sum offered by the King was
equal to 20,000 or at most 25,000 of our *lire* '—a
sum, as he rightly observes, which is enormous for
a single manuscript at that time.

I pass to other matters, going with more detail
into the manner how the ' Codex Atlanticus '
fared, once it had entered the precincts and had
been entrusted to the care of the Ambrosian
Library. I say ' with more detail,' for I have
already stated that the ' Codex,' after being placed
for some time (probably the time needed for preparing the tablet) in the main hall of the Library
in the case marked ' P ' and then in that marked
' O ' under the number 248, was transferred to the
Picture Gallery, now called ' Sala Fagnani,' and
that there it was placed into what some call an
' ark,' others an ' urn ' or a ' coffer,' upon a table
(see Fig. 3), underneath a marble medallion
on the north wall of the Gallery, bearing the image
of Arconati, and the inscription recording his
munificence. It was a sort of altar set up in
gratitude and admiration in a real sanctuary of
art and science in homage to the genius of Leonardo
and the generosity of Arconati.

But it is obvious—especially when we consider

Figures 3, 4 and 5—that gratitude had pressed into its service whatever it found at hand and had put together things which did not really harmonise. For it must strike anyone that the style of the table is neither that of 'ark' or rectangular chest, nor that of the 'urn' that rests on it ; nor do the ornamentation, the lines and the proportions of the 'ark' correspond with those of the little 'urn' on the top. Yet, that these three pieces remained together for a time we cannot doubt in face of the documents which mention them. I say, 'for a time' and not ' since the appearance of the " Codex" in the Ambrosiana,' nor even since it was placed into the rectangular 'ark' or upon this table ; for Bosca (l.c., p. 154) mentions merely the small 'ark' (arcula), underneath the tablet. He does not speak of the 'urn' nor of the table ; and yet the latter certainly stood there, since the inventory of 1661, as we saw, makes mention of 'a low table, gilt, with ancient figures on it,' and upon it 'a wooden ark, decorated with floral designs in gold.' On the other hand, the same inventory in another place, but still referring to the Picture Gallery, describes 'a chest lined with red satin, stamped on it " singuli singula," with the following objects in it . . .' (and enumerates a letter of St. Charles Borromeo on the occasion of the shot fired at him by Farina, a letter of St. Philip Neri and one of St. Francis de Sales addressed to Cardinal Federico, some of his hair, and a shirt of his, a piece of the Cardinal's purple of St. Charles, a silver phial with some balm which Cardinal Federico used when he visited the plague-stricken people ; all these objects are now placed elsewhere : the first letter in the Manuscript Room, the other two in the Autograph Hall, the rest among the curios in the case No. 118 of the ' Settala Museum '). Now, the 'little urn' is precisely lined inside with crimson satin and bears the inscription 'singuli singula,' and, however inexact its description may be as a ' chest,' I can find neither in the inventories nor among the objects that have come down to us, any one that answers better to the description than our ' urn.'

But then, as we saw, in 1763 the Abbé Coyer said that he had seen underneath the tablet a ' coffre,' and still more plainly the Prefect, Bonsignori, in 1790 speaks of an ' urn ' ; and the inventory of 1798 mentions ' a wooden urn painted with flowers ' in which the ' Codex ' was placed upon a little table ' with twisted iron feet ' : it is evident that the mention of the metal refers only to the upper parts of the supports.

First the absence and then the addition of the ' little urn ' seem confirmed by a fact which can be checked plainly even now : at first the ' ark ' or rectangular box was opened by lifting the lid which turned by means of two hinges (which are still there) on the side opposite the one represented by Fig. 4. Now, however, by an arrangement introduced later, the lid is fixed, and the box opens by the side swinging out *horizontally* turning on the left angle (of the photograph—the right from the spectator), while near the right angle of the box (on the left of the spectator) the keyhole is plainly visible for the key which locks the box now. It is certain that the ' little urn ' shows no signs, except some faint traces of glue, of having ever been attached to the lid of the box. It is, on the other hand, easily observable that, doubtless in order the better to harmonise the rather narrow base of the ' urn ' with the relatively wide lid of the box, a slip of soft wood had been inserted by way of a narrow plinth between the two. Both the imprint of it and the traces can still be seen, but the piece itself has disappeared, so that it was found necessary to supply a fresh base, designed by Senatore Luca Beltrami who adapted the form from the surviving pieces ; this is the only new, non-original, part that has been introduced in reconstructing this interesting group of objects.

I use the words ' reconstructing the group,' for it had been completely broken up ; but this breaking up was at least intelligible, as we shall see.

We have repeatedly referred to the lines and proportions of the ' urn ' in relation to those of the box. To give the reader an exact notion, supplementing the photographs, we add here the measurements : Height of the ' urn ' : 0.18 m. ; base, 0.34 × 0.18 m. ; cover : 0.405 × 0.255 m. ; height of the box : 0.220 m. ; base : 0.81 × 0.615 m. ; lid : 0.79 × 0.605 m. ; internal capacity : 0.5 × 0.69 × 0.17 m. It is obvious that the internal space of the box corresponds so exactly with the volume of the ' Codex ' as to exclude all doubt that it was specially made to contain it.

This does not apply to the table, which forms the main and certainly the most precious part of the three objects. It certainly was not expressly made. Its very appearance indicates that it is much older than the ' urn ' and the box, and it is mentioned as early as in the inventory of 1661 : ' a low little table, gilt, with ancient figures.'

Its precise proportions are : length, 1.40 m. ; width : 0.97 m. ; height, 0.74 m. ; thickness of the table-top : 0.02 m.

It is an interesting piece of furniture by reason of the elegance of its lines, its general form, and its ornamentation. It reminds one at once of those low tables which not infrequently can be seen in woodcuts and pictures of the late fifteenth and early sixteenth centuries. I mention, for purposes of comparison, the general proportions of the table in the print representing St. Jerome in his cell by Albrecht Dürer (A. Bartsch, *Le peintre graveur*, Vienna, 1808, vol. VII, p. 76, no. 60) ; I refer for the legs, partly of iron and of similar make, to the

table in the picture by Carpaccio of the same
subject in the ' Scuola degli Schiavoni' in Venice
(G. Ludwig, and P. Molmenti, *Vittore Carpaccio*,
Milano, Hoepli, 1906, p. 174), and to the painting
representing St. Thomas, St. Mark and St. Augustine by the same in Stuttgart (op. cit., p. 272) ;
closely resembling our table in the legs and the
general design and in the ornamentation of the
edge, are the legs of the seat of the ' General del
Mare' (P. Molmenti, *La storia di Venezia nella vita
privata*, 4th ed., Vol. II, Bergamo, 1906, p. 48).
These are the only not too distant comparisons I
can give. There is nothing like it in the great
Dictionnaire de l'ameublement et de la décoration of
H. Havard ; and competent connoisseurs who have
seen and admired our table, say that they have
never seen anything of the kind before.

It would certainly be much more admirable and
indeed a splendid piece, if the ornamentation of the
top were as well preserved as that of the supports.
The decoration consists of bright gilding on a background of vividly red lacquer. The design is made
up of roses, floral patterns and masks on the supporting limbs, on the underneath side of the top and
—with great richness—on the edge which frames the
actual table-top. The field thus framed presents a
vast and splendid scene of buildings and persons
of unmistakably Chinese type. An inspection,
especially if assisted by a magnifying-glass, reveals
two walls stretching along the whole length of the
field, each with three gateways in the centre. The
greater width of the central gate is much more
striking in the second wall than in the first, as the
gates of this latter only just emerge with their
arches from the framing of the edge.

Beyond the second wall, on the left of the spectator, two enclosures, walled round in the same
manner, are visible ; and within them, as also
between them and the frame, and between the two

walls, can be seen buildings of various sizes of the peculiar and characteristic form of pagodas. Between the first and the second wall two processions can be made out, consisting of persons on foot and on horseback, converging towards the central gate of the second wall. My mind turned to those descriptions which enrich the account of Marco Polo's travels. It is, in fact, impossible to read the description of the 'Palace of the Great Khan' (*I viaggi in Asia, in Africa, nel mare delle Indie descritti nel secolo xiii da Marco Polo veneziano*, Venezia, Alvisopoli, 1829, p. 119), without being struck by the thought that the decorator, certainly a great artist, had drawn his inspiration from, and meant directly to represent in his own way, this description. I say, ' in his own way,' for he reduces, for instance, the five gates of the text to three, perhaps to give greater freedom and continuity to his lines and to the different planes of this scene, or, as seems to me more probable, indeed almost certain, because he drew upon the text of Ramusio (Gio. Batt. Baldelli Boni, *Il milione di messer Marco Polo Viniziano*, Firenze, 1827, p. II, p. 168, Chapter vi, *Del grande e meraviglioso palazzo del Gran Can appresso la città di Cambalú*) where the gates are three in number. We quote here from the former work the chapter mentioned :

' But you must know that the Great Khan dwells for three months in the year, namely December, January and February in the chief city which is called Comblau, and in this city he has his great palace. I will describe what it is like.

' The Palace (city) is surrounded by a square wall, each side a mile long, and in each of its angles stands a very fine palace, and therein are kept all the equipments of the Great Khan, namely bows, and quivers, and saddles and bridles, and cords and tents, and everything that is needed for an army and

for war.   And within these precincts there are
between these palaces four other palaces, so that
within the wall all round are eight palaces and all
are full of equipment, each containing one kind.
And this wall on its southern face has five gates, and
in the middle is one very large gate which is never
opened or closed except when the Great Khan
passes through, going in or coming out.   And by
the side of this gate there are two small ones, one
on each side, by which all the other people enter.
On the other side there is another large gate by
which other people usually enter, that is to say,
everybody.   And within this outer wall there is
another and all around there are again eight
palaces as on the outer wall and they are made in
the same way : they also contain the equipment of
the Great Khan.   On its side towards the South it
has five gates ; on the other sides only one ; and
in the middle of this enclosure is the palace of the
Great Khan, and I will tell you how it is built.   It
is the largest that has ever been seen ; it has no
ceiling, but the floor-space is quite ten palms
higher than the outer ground.   Its roof is very high ;
the walls of its halls and rooms are all covered with
gold and silver and are sculptured with wonderful
representations of ladies and knights and birds and
beasts and many other things, and the roof is made
in the same way so that nothing is visible except
the gold and silver.   The Hall is so long and wide
that six thousand persons can eat therein com-
fortably, and there are so many rooms that it is
almost incredible.   The roof outside is red and
yellow and green and all the other colours, and is
so highly lacquered that it blazes like gold or crystal,
so that from afar you can see the palace shine ; the
roof is very strong.   Between one enclosure and
another within that of which I have told you,
there are beautiful meadows and trees and all
manner of wild beasts, namely white stags, and deer

and does, the beast that yields the musc, and
squirrels and ermin and other beautiful animals.

' The grounds within that garden are full of these
animals, except the way by which people enter, and
on the side towards the south there are many kinds
of fish. I must tell you that a great river flows
through it and it is so arranged that the fish cannot get out (and many sort of fishes have been put
into this lake) and this is done by means of iron
gratings. I must also tell you that towards the
North, a bowshot from the Palace, he has had a hill
made, quite hundred paces high and quite a mile
in circumference : it is is covered with trees which
never lose their leaves but are always green. And
you must know that whenever the Great Khan is
told about a fine tree, he has it brought with all its
roots and much soil, and has it planted on that hill,
let it be as big as you like ; he has it fetched by
elephants. And he has had the hill covered with
special soil which is quite green, so that on that hill
there is nothing that is not green, wherefore it is
called the " Green Hill." And on the top of the hill
stands a very large palace, in which everything is
also green ; so that to look upon it is a great marvel
and there is no man who does not rejoice when he
sees it, and in order to have that lovely view the
Great Lord has had it built for his pleasure and
enjoyment. And I also tell you that near this
palace there is another in which the grandson of the
Great Khan lives, who is to reign after him, and he
is Temur, son of Cinghis, who was the eldest son of
the Great Khan ; and this Temur is to reign and
follows the manner of his grandfather, and has
already a golden seal and the seal of the Empire,
but does not exercise his functions while the grandfather is alive.'

The fact of the evident connexion of the table
ornamentation with the accounts and descriptions

of the great Venetian traveller, seems to me to
render the references, made above to the pictures of
Carpaccio, all the more convincing, for he too was
a Venetian by birth, as well as by his schooling and
work, as new documents have been able to show
(Ludwig and Molmenti, op. cit., p. 37 ff), and I am
confirmed in my belief that those who consider our
table to be the work of a Venetian artist of the early
sixteenth century, are right. It is certainly noteworthy that the first Venetian editions of the wonderful accounts of Marco Polo fall within the years 1496
and 1508.

The predilection of the Venetian artists for information and *motifs* from the East, as might be
expected, given the continuous relations of Venice
with the Levant, is confirmed by another example
furnished yet again by Carpaccio, which another art-
object in the Ambrosiana has called to my mind. In
the ' Martyrdom of Saint Ursula ' (Accademia di
Venezia, n. 580 ; Ludwig and Molmenti, op. cit.,
p. 146) there stands in the foreground an archer
with a quiver of singular shape, and intentionally, as
it were, so arranged as to be in full view. This also
struck Müntz so much that he reproduced the archer
alone, when he (E. Müntz, *L'arte italiana nel quat-
trocento*, Milano, 1894, p. 304) discussed Italian
costumes of the fifteenth century. Now this very
quiver is to be found in the glass-case containing
weapons in the ' Settala Museum ' of the Ambrosiana, and from its decoration and the characters
with which it is ornamented, is unquestionably
Persian, or at least one of the many imitations of
oriental designs and objects which Venetian art
produced in such abundance.

I might also add that some valuable specimens of
lacquered wood (a cup and four plates), richly
gilt, show a certain relationship with our table.
These too, quite independently of the latter, have
been considered products of Venetian art of the

early sixteenth century. Unfortunately I do not know the work of H. Yule (*The Book of ser Marco Polo, the Venetian,* etc.) except from what I read about it in the *Archivio Veneto* (T. II, par. 1, 1871, pp. 124 ff; par. 11, pp. 259 ff), and therefore cannot say whether there is not perhaps among his excellent illustrations one that resembles our table. At any rate, I believe I have sufficiently shown its artistic importance, which more than justifies the care bestowed on preserving what remains of its interesting decoration, by placing it under glass.

There only remains the answer to the very obvious question, whence and how it ever came into the possession of the Ambrosian Library. Unfortunately I cannot find the answer. Seeing that documents are silent about it, the supposition would appear reasonable on many grounds that it belonged to the ' Settala Museum.' But if it did, it certainly did not come to the Ambrosiana from that collection. We saw that a description of the table occurs in the inventory of 1661, and the Settala collection was presented to the Library only in 1751.

I am able on the other hand to explain how the group formed of the tablet, the table, the urn and the box, and, we must add, of the precious volume came in time to be scattered within the precincts of the Ambrosian Library, so that no two of these objects remained together.

The ' Codex Atlanticus,' after having been for a century and a half the object of admiration and almost religious cult, became in 1796 the object and victim of greed, as little scrupulous as it was brutal and overbearing. In that year the ' Codex ' and the eleven other MSS. presented by Arconati, as well as some other objects of art and printed books, came under a military requisition order imposed by the French Army. It was carried out on May 19, June 10 and 25, as far as the Ambrosian was concerned, by a certain Jacques Tinet, an artist attached to the Legation of Toscana. The tablet, the table, the empty box and urn remained in their place, and must have seemed to the friends and familiars of the Library like a funeral monument recording some domestic misfortune. The cases containing the objects requisitioned were meanwhile wandering over the face of the earth and the bulk of them arrived in Paris only at the end of November.

For some time it was feared that the Leonardo MSS. had been lost. When they too finally arrived, the 'Codex' was assigned to the Bibliothèque Nationale, and the other eleven MSS. to the Library of the Institut de France. Thus the precious collection was broken up and dispersed. In 1815, the Powers, after the occupation of Paris and the Hundred Days, demanded the restitution of art-objects carried off to France during the wars of the Republic and the Empire, and each Power appointed a representative for the recovery of its own property.

But while the representatives of England and of Prussia displayed the utmost energy, Baron von Ottenfels, representing Lombardy after its return under Austrian rule, was most easily satisfied, and having discovered the 'Codex Atlanticus' only, in the Bibliothèque Royale, he failed to trace and recover the other MSS., although he had an exact description of them. He rested content with some other works, certainly by Leonardo, but of very different value, three only and those but copies. So the 'Codex' returned to the Ambrosian Library alone, like a sovereign without his escort, after nineteen years, and it was impossible, despite all the efforts made by Count Giovanni Borromeo, the permanent Conservator of the Library, ever to make good the damage the Ambrosiana had suffered.

Now, it was not very likely that the treasure, thus recovered, would have been placed again in a position in which it had been exposed to such danger and harm. Obviously some safer protective measures would be taken. Therewith probably the group of pieces of the Picture Gallery in combination with the MS. which it had been used to display and guard, lost its *raison d'être*. No wonder it was dispersed. The ' urn ' was applied again to its original use, at least in part : no longer the letters, but the wearing apparel of St. Charles and of Cardinal Federico was kept in it.

Other things happened in the Library itself which could not but have an influence upon the group of objects in question.

In order to find room for the constantly growing Library equipment, the original building was enlarged by the addition of a new courtyard and its surrounding rooms designed by the architects Santagostino and Moraglia between 1829 and 1836, after the Church of Sta Maria della Rosa, built in 1456, had been pulled down. Still later the great bequests of the Marchese Federico Fagnani (died 1840) and of Baron Pietro Custodi (died 1843) came to the Library, as already explained, and the ' Sala Fagnani ' and the ' Sala Custodi ' were added, with a general rearrangement of all that occupied the newly built parts.

The tablet with the medallion of Arconati was placed on the wall at the foot of the great staircase ; the table, the box and the urn were distributed in the upper rooms, whence they were moved again to make room for artistic exhibits which the Ambrosiana housed temporarily for the Municipality.

During the recent rearrangement the best that could be done was to place the table, urn and box together on the upper landing of the great staircase in excellent lighting conditions, half-way between the tablet and the Leonardo material proper, displayed in the ' Gabinetto Leonardo.'

When to our more or less distant posterity our

rearrangement will appear old-fashioned and, perhaps, intolerable, they will, I dare say, apply their minds to recomposing the group which the vicissitudes of time had dispersed. Leaving the ' Gabinetto Leonardo ' where it is (if they will be so kind), or transferring it elsewhere, they can also transfer and set up the tablet to Arconati, and underneath it, in place of the actual glass case, restore the former state of things, which for 150 years made the old Picture Gallery, as it were, into the Leonardo sanctuary of the Ambrosian Library.

If this ever happens, we hope that our dear descendants will remember that we too had thought of this and have even taken some steps in the direction of carrying out the scheme.

I conclude with a summary account of the last turn of fortune, of good fortune this time, which befell the ' Codex Atlanticus ' after its return to the Ambrosiana. The revival of the study of Leonardo's works, both of the MSS. scattered in various collections and of the ' Codex Atlanticus,' during the nineteenth century, suggested the idea of publishing the whole ' Codex.' The project was carried into effect, first by the publication, as an experiment, of the *Saggio del Codice Atlantico* (Milano, Ricordi, 1872) on the occasion of the inauguration of the Leonardo Monument in Milan. The complete publication was undertaken later by the Ministry of Public Instruction and entrusted to the Royal Academy dei Lincei, and appeared in 1904 with a photographic reproduction of the entire ' Codex ' (first by Martelli, Rome, fasc. 1–18 ; then by G. Beltrami, Milan, for the fasc. 19 ff). Two transcriptions were prepared by Giovanni Piumati of Bra (in Piedmont) and published by Hoepli of Milan.

Thus the preservation of the ' Codex,' if not in its material entity, at least from the point of view of accuracy and the perfect integrity of its contents, was provided for in the safest way yet known to man, securing its benefits and making them readily accessible to mankind, present and future. Out of a unique MS. the photographic reproduction has made a printed book issued in a relatively large number of copies.

But a reproduction is not the original, and in many cases the need to consult the original is being and will always be felt. It possesses in some inexpressible manner the power of placing us into almost physical contact with the brow of the genius as he bent over these pages, and with that portentous hand, strong as an athlete's and gentle as an angel's, which, modelling and painting as if touching musical instruments, in writing and designs, lent itself, a docile and marvellously perfect instrument, to the interpretation of every thought and feeling, as it scattered wonders of science and of art over these pages.

The reproduction, however, gains in extension what it loses in intensity, by multiplying the facilities of its use and the guarantee of safe preservation. Divine Providence and human foresight have caused Milan to arise in a part of the world exceptionally safe and sheltered from natural disasters : what in our time has happened in San Francisco or Kingston, seems could never happen here. Undefended and open, in open country, the capital of Lombardy has not even had to fear the fate that befell Paris in the war of 1870 or Strassburg with so much damage to its Library. The Ambrosian Library, built extremely solidly and with the greatest forethought expressly to safeguard and protect the treasures collected by the munificence of its founder, Cardinal Federico Borromeo, and by his fellow-citizens who followed in his footsteps, has also taken advantage of all those forms of protection which the daily fight against fire has taught us to adopt. But even so, it is comforting to think that in the

worst and most unhappy event, as long as one
photographic copy survives, nothing in substance
and very little even of the accidental merits could
be lost of a treasure of art and science, which being,
like the 'Codex Atlanticus,' of surpassing value
and general interest, and in itself a vast monument
of so great and universal a mind, belongs to
humanity even more than to one city or one
country.

And thus, on a scale unthought of by him, a
wish of Cardinal Federico's has been fulfilled, a
wish which testifies once again to the wealth of his
mind. He himself composed a small but solid book
describing the Ambrosian Gallery under the title
Musæum (Mediolani MDCXXV), precisely for the
purpose of providing even better for the preservation of the art-treasures he had collected
there. Therein (p. 2) he expounds in his
learned and grave Latin the idea which had inspired him :

' Memineram enim fuisse apud veteres hanc
curam ut prestantissima quæque Picturæ, vel Statu-
ariæ, vel Architecthonices opera, styli etiam ope
conservarentur, duplicemque ita viverent vitam, et
eam quam artificum ingenia dedissent, et eam quæ
beneficio litterarum veniret. Eventusque postea
monstravit ipse, posteriorem hanc priore illa vita
fuisse diuturniorem. Cum enim urbes totæ, non
palatia tantum, et musea conflagrarint, incendium
clademque vitavere latentia in obscuris ignobili-
busque locis monumenta litterarum, et receptaculis
abditæ vilibus memoriæ triumpharunt arcus, pyra-
midesque excelsas, et portentosa alia ludibria opum
humanarum. Collabuntur in ruinas altæ hædium
moles, dissolvitque substructiones pontium vetustas,
et humi sternit, cominuitque Obeliscos, cum
interim infelicium etiam litteratorum, non illus-
trium tantummodo, et inclytorum scripta vitant

cladem, et in media rerum humanarum tabe sempiterno quodam ævo perfruuntur.'

These words seem to me so well said and so expressive of the intention both of my mind and my heart, I mean of my professional, literary and domestic intentions, which moved me to write these few pages, that it is with them that I would like to end.

NOTE

This device was given to the Ambrosian Library by
Cardinal Federico Borromeo
as the motto of the
Doctors.

It represents the words, mentioned on p. 256 :
SINGULA SINGULI,
indicating that each Doctor
was to devote himself to some one special
branch of learning
and
research

V

THE SETTALA MUSEUM

THE RENASCENCE OF A MILANESE MUSEUM

The paper was published originally in the ' Rendiconti ' of the ' Istituto Lombardo di Scienze e Lettere' (Series II, Vol. XXXIX, 1906, pp. 1011–1020). It must be borne in mind that the arrangement of the objects here mentioned as being in the Museum refers to the place they occupied in the Settala Museum at that time.

THE collections which according to the comprehensive design of Cardinal Federico Borromeo were to form part of his Library, have now been rearranged —I say his ' Library,' for in his modesty he did not call it after himself, but after the great Saint of Milan, her battle-cry and standard, the ' Ambrosiana,' when he founded it in the very days of Spanish Domination. The completion of this reordering is signalised by the fact that I am making use of the *Guide to the Ambrosian Library and its Collections*, which is to be published within the next few days, and forms the record of this rearrangement.

Among the fortunate finds and discoveries to which the rearrangement led, I mention but two. One was that of an interesting ancient portrait of Petrarch. I can do no more than mention it ; a fuller discussion of it is destined for publication elsewhere (see *Rassegna d'Arte*, January 1907). The other concerns the remains of an ancient Milanese Museum. The discovery led to the idea of resuscitating or rather completely reconstituting the collection, a mass of objects of singular value and interest, especially in view of the time when it was made. It forms certainly one of the most interesting and expressive pages of the history of Milanese culture at the beginning of the seventeenth century. The collection is the ' Settala Museum,' so-called after Manfredo Settala, who gathered the bulk of the contents and enjoyed so great a reputation that he was called the ' Milanese Archimedes,' as a tablet records which is set up in the northern portico of the Ambrosian Library to recall his friendship and munificence towards it. The friendship and admiration which linked him with Cardinal Federico Borromeo and the early beginnings of his Library, is also the link which eventually attached the Museum to the Library properly speaking.

' The long study and the great love '[1] which for several years now I have devoted to this ancient Museum, make me feel all the more deeply the satisfaction and real pleasure I have in being able to tell you of its resuscitation and reconstruction.

Ever since I first became a member of the Ambrosiana, the scattered remains of the Settala Museum began to attract my attention. I felt the fascination which is peculiar to old things, and recalled studies pursued once upon a time and always lovingly cherished. The first results of my search were, as usually happens, slow in coming and sparse ; gradually they came more quickly and assumed a larger scope in proportion to the more and more numerous interconnexions, observations, and discoveries in archives and in books. I may say at once that, though a recent publication to which I shall have occasion to refer, gave me a fresh stimulus and added greatly to my information, yet even before I had read it, the revival of this ancient Museum was in my mind an accomplished fact,

[1] Dante : *Divina Commedia*, Inf. I, 83. (*Translator's note.*)

and its reconstitution only a question of the material arrangement and of the display of the contents. But let me deal with the Museum itself and its founder.

Manfredo was born in 1600 of the noble family of the Settalas which numbered two Archbishops of Milan among its ancestors; one, Senatore (472–475), the other Enrico (1213–1230), and two Beati, Blessed Manfredo, from whom our Manfredo perhaps took his name, and Blessed Lanfranc who is believed to have been the founder of the Convent and Church of S. Marco in Milan where the monument to a member of the Settala family can still be seen, a work of the fourteenth century attributed to Balduccio da Pisa, or at least to someone belonging to his school. Manfredo's father was Lodovico Settala, famous, thanks to Manzoni, as ' Protophysicus ' or, as we should say nowadays, Director-General of Public Health at the time of the famous Plague. He was certainly celebrated among the doctors of his time and the object of competitive magnificent offers from Italian and foreign Universities ; but he preferred the distinction and honours conferred on him by his own city and her authorities, who created him Senator. His house became the meeting-place of all the literary, and learned and studious men who lived in Milan or happened to come there, thanks also to the rich library and the gallery of paintings and objects of art which Manfredo's grandfather had begun to collect and Lodovico had much extended. You see that the passion and the genius for collecting had been hereditary in the family of the Settalas.

Of course, this passion and genius was widespread, as elsewhere, so also among us at the end of the sixteenth century and the beginnings of the seventeenth, not only as a sheer fondness of things and a certain sense of display which it had been in the first half of the fifteenth century ; but it was beginning to show method and an orientation towards scientific purposes. Among the collectors the most distinguished were Cardinal Cesare Monti, the Marchese Arconati, Valeri, Flamini ; many others might be added from the ranks of the clergy and the patriciate, naturally, for they alone possessed the means and the time needed for training. At the head of these collectors, leaving all others far behind, stand Cardinal Federico with his Library and Manfredo Settala with his Museum.

They may well be considered as typical of their time, so important in the history of Italian thought in all its expressions, so characteristic in the mixture of tradition and novelty, of scientific and empirical method, of childishness and seriousness, destined to give rise to the specifically scientific achievements of our seventeenth century. It may also be said that in Cardinal Federico the virtues of their time stand out more particularly and in Settala the defects, as far as the intellectual movement is concerned. Manfredo, a precocious and versatile mind, was sent, still very young, to the Universities first of Pavia, then of Siena. He immediately showed a great inclination for Mathematics and Mechanics, for the observation and study of natural phenomena, especially such as were rare or unusual, for Geography, Ethnography and Archæology. Nature had endowed him with very special gifts : a distinction and affability of manner which became famous, a prodigious capacity for work, a most tenacious memory, a remarkable aptitude for languages, insatiable curiosity, a manual dexterity so astonishing, that, still quite young, he came to be regarded as almost a portent in working metals, ivory, wood and crystal ; not only a collector but actually a maker of the strangest curios and of scientific apparatus, still worthy of consideration even to-day.

He knew Latin and Greek and Oriental languages as well as all the languages of civilised Europe. He travelled much in Italy and abroad, in Egypt, the Orient, Constantinople. When old age and infirmities forced him to lead a quieter life, he made up for it by buying and reading, nay devouring, every new book, especially those dealing with curious and generally novel things, more particularly with geographical information and discoveries. The affection he had for Geography kept him in constant relations of friendship and correspondence with missionaries in China, Japan and America, offering them his generous hospitality and help, and receiving in exchange direct information and also original products of the lands and peoples among whom they were working.

He was thus able to gather together a collection which seemed to his contemporaries, and was in fact, amazing, and worthy to be placed in the same rank—in some ways outdistancing them,—as the Museo Cospiano at Bologna (presented to that city by Ferdinando Cospi) or the Museo Kircheriano in Rome (founded by Fr. Anastasius Kircher, S.J., at that same time).

The family house of the Settalas, in the parish of S. Nazaro in the street still to-day called ' del Pantano,' became on account of the museum the goal of continual visits of Milanese and all strangers who came to Milan : business-men and students, magistrates and soldiers, princes, prelates and sovereigns who rivalled each other in bestowing honours and sometimes very precious gifts with which Settala enriched his Museum. A good many of these objects are still in existence : for instance, a clock of wonderful construction, made in Germany, in imitation of the famous clock at Strassburg ; a silver automaton in the form of a Diana, riding on a stag ; a mother-of-pearl shell mounted on chiselled silver with wonderfully modelled figures ; saddle-fittings in gilt iron, with beautifully worked scenes and decorations, one of the most handsome of its kind, also in the opinion of experts ; some beautiful daggers and other objects which on account of their precious nature demand special protection and are therefore, together with some other things particularly decorative, kept in the upper halls. They display in their positions the importance of the Settala Collection and mark its most striking features.

The fame of this Collection spread over the whole of Europe.[1] Even during Settala's lifetime, Paolo Terzaghi published in Latin a description and *catalogue raisonné* of it (*Museum Septalium*, 1664) and Francesco Scarabelli another in Italian (*Museo e Galleria adunata dal sapere e dallo studio del signor Canonico Manfredo Settala*, 1666). Several writers abroad also published descriptions of it and quite recently Manfredo Settala and his Museum were the objects of an article in the *Archivio Storico Lombardo* (Sect. III, vol. xvi, 1900), by G. Fogolari.

A woodcut in the book of Scarabelli enables us to form some rough idea of the Museum. Embalmed animals are hanging from the ceiling ; the walls are covered with pictures ; beneath them stand cupboards and glass-cases ; the lower parts are protected by gratings. It is possible to make out

---

[1] English readers may be interested to hear the impression produced on John Evelyn, the seventeenth-century diarist, by a visit to this famous Museum, while still in the possession of Manfredo Settala, in 1646 :

' There is nothing better worth seeing than the collection of Sig. Septalla, a canon of St. Ambrose (Evelyn is here in error, see the text below), famous over Christendome for his learning and virtues. Amongst other things he shew'd us an Indian wood that has the perfect scent of civet ; a flint or pebble, that has a quantity of water in it, which is plainly to be seen, it being cleare as achat ; divers chrystals that have water moving in them, some of them having plants, leaves, and hog-bristles in them ; much amber full of insects etc. and divers things of woven amianthus.' (*Translator's note.*)

INTERIOR OF THE MUSEUM FROM SCARABELLI'S DESCRIPTIVE CATALOGUE OF 1666

(referred to on page 276)

some of the objects : crocodiles and sharks, rhino-
ceros teeth, the skull and teeth of an hippopotamus ;
weapons, curious vessels, wearing apparel ; the
strangest automaton figures ; clocks and spheres.
The letter-press of the books of Terzaghi and Scarabelli gives us a less direct but fuller notion of the
collection ; and although Settala had not given
to these works the authority of official inventories,
we can rely on them not merely in their general
outline, but also in all the details, as is proved by
the documents drawn up to regulate the hereditary
transmission of the Collection, and by the fact that
Settala himself appended to his will the book of
Scarabelli in place of an inventory. We would
have an even more complete picture of the Museum,
especially of the many objects which have been lost,
if we possessed any of the numerous coloured
drawings which had been made in Manfredo's
lifetime by several Milanese artists and, bound in
quarto volumes, formed a regular illustrated catalogue of the Museum. Two of these volumes were
recently for sale by Hiersemann of Leipzig and
were wisely purchased by the Braida Library. I
cannot sufficiently thank the Librarian of our
National Library, Professor G. Fumagalli, for his
great courtesy in not only placing these volumes at
my disposal, but for his willingness to allow the
Ambrosian Library to acquire them at cost-price,
in view of their greater usefulness there, and for
initiating the necessary negotiations to this end with
the Ministry of Public Instruction.

Needless to say we eagerly await and look forward to their conclusion.[1] These volumes would
not only be one of the finest ornaments of the reconstituted Museum, but an almost necessary complement to it, especially for the lost or fragmentary
objects.

[1] These negotiations have since been brought to a successful
end. (Note of Italian Editor.)

A third volume, containing designs of mathematical and physical apparatus, was in possession of Mr. M. Guggenheim of Venice, who with great generosity and kindness placed this, too, at our disposal for the reconstruction of the Museum.

As I am engaged in correcting the proofs of this paper, a letter from Mr. Guggenheim, dated December 17, brings me the news that he is willing to forgo the ownership of his Settala volume and wishes to present it to the Ambrosian Library. I am happy to be able to announce here this generous and munificent gift, advantageous not only to the Ambrosian Library but to the public at large. I trust the distinguished donor will accept this expression of gratitude on behalf of both the Ambrosian Library and of its friends and members on the occasion of this publication.

Summarising the sixty-eight headings given by Terzaghi and Scarabelli under which they arranged the contents of the collection, it is evident that the Settala Museum was intended to be a sort of material encyclopædia.

Mathematics and Physics and Astronomy are represented by various mathematical instruments : pantometers, compasses, attempts to solve the problem of perpetual motion, clocks, lenses, optical mirrors and burning glasses, flat and cylindrical planes, telescopes, ancient and modern astrolabes, armillaries and globes.—Natural Sciences were represented in their three main departments : zoology by complete embalmed animals or by parts of them, bones, skeletons, rare birds, fishes, shells, crustaceans, coral, amber, starfishes ; botany by exotic woods, strange fruits, perfumes, balms, extracts ; mineralogy by crystals, hard stones, minerals from various mines, fossils.—The Fine Arts were displayed in pictures, wax-models, wood and ivory carvings, plain and coloured, large and small statues, in wax, plaster, ancient and modern marbles, musical instruments. Ethnography is represented by products and implements of various countries ; Archæology by mummies, pottery and lamps : Numismatics and History by numerous medals, coins both ancient (Punic, Greek and Roman) and modern, such as medals struck by Pontiffs and prelates, sovereigns and princes, persons distinguished in war and in peace ; Erudition, Letters and Science in general, by a large and carefully selected library of printed books and MSS. of which Muratori, Montfaucont and other students and research-workers have availed themselves with advantage. Both in former times and even now some other collections as well known as they are important, have boasted and still boast of spoils from this and other departments of the collections of Settala.

It is clear at first glance that the collection in its main lines aspired to be something serious, showing at least the beginnings of a systematic and a really remarkable conception which suggests a mind as versatile as it was curious and eager in the search for truth in all its forms and manifestations. Yet, coming down to details, we find almost constantly that what is looked for is, more than truth, the strange and singular, more than what is useful, the odd and, one might feel tempted to say, the amusing; so that we have the impression that serious study was rather overborne by the play of a whimsical genius, and critical science by an almost childish ingenuity. The whole mind of the epoch is thus mirrored in the Collection and herein lies precisely the chief interest and importance of the Settala Museum. For the Museum still exists, if not complete, at least in its main outlines and in objects representing each principal department. Thus it exists within the precincts of the Ambrosian Library, and now, reconstructed as far as was possible, it is open to the public in a room on the ground floor called for that reason the ' Settala Museum.'

The first transfer of the Museum to the rooms of the Ambrosiana goes back to more than a century and a half.

The Ambrosian Library and the Academy of Fine Arts, attached to it in 1625, with its first collections of art-objects, was in its first flower, when Settala was approaching full manhood. He could not remain an outside spectator, detached and indifferent to this great institution. He was, in fact, a frequent visitor and close friend of the Ambrosiana, and was honoured and loved by Cardinal Federico who employed him perhaps to collect books for him during his long and distant journeys and bestowed on him minor orders and a Canonry at the Collegiate Church of S. Nazaro.

He outlived the Cardinal by quite fifty years, dying at the age of eighty on February 16, 1680. But then, and more at that time than ever, he displayed once again his friendship for Cardinal Federico and his Ambrosian Library. By his will, drawn up by the Milanese notary Carlo Cadolini, Settala arranged that his Museum should be held as a trust by his brother Carlo, Bishop of Tortona, and on the latter's death should pass into the keeping of his nephews and their eldest descendants ; on the failure of descendants it was to pass into the possession of the Ambrosian Library, all the time on the basis of the inventory published by Scarabelli.

When Francesco Settala, also a Canon of S. Nazaro like his uncle Manfredo, died in 1716, the Ambrosian Library held that the time foreseen by the testator had arrived ; but the heirs of the Canon did not share this view. An appeal was made to the Senate as to the highest tribunal, and the Senate by sentence of February 19, 1751, ruled that the Settala Museum or ' Gallery and the objects of which it consists shall be handed over to the College of the Ambrosian Library.'

The transfer was effected in 1751, and thus, eighty years after the drawing up of Manfredo's will, his Museum was re-formed in its new home.

But how precisely was this done ? Up to this time it had remained in its original home in Via Pantano, and several witnesses bear out that Canon Francesco had maintained its high repute, following his uncle's example in the courteous liberality with which he received students and interested visitors from all countries, as well as in continuing to care for and extend it. At the same time, it is certain that even then the Museum had begun to suffer and was to suffer yet more. It is enough to recall the solemn and fantastic exequies of Manfredo (described by Gio. Maria Visconti : *Exequiæ in templo S. Nazari*, etc. Milan, 1680), when a great part of the Museum went to decorate the catafalque and the endless procession, and when various objects and groups were used as symbols and trophies. It suffices to add that the Ambrosian Archives contain remonstrances of the curators of the Museum about the frequent and marked differences between the inventory of Manfredo's will and the inventory of the transfer.

Further vicissitudes awaited it in the Ambrosian Library. In the condition of the building in 1752, the objects of the Museum had to be distributed among various rooms, as there simply was no single hall sufficiently large to house it all together ; and yet in the different rooms the contents of the Library in books and artistic treasures, constantly growing, competed with the Museum for space. People still remember crossbows and large zoological specimens set up in the little courtyard now occupied by marble sculptures and marble pieces and inscriptions leaning against the windows which then existed in the rooms, now reserved for incunabula and MSS. ; vases, lamps, crystals, fossils, shells, magnets, mechanical apparatus, maps, burning glasses, crystal and marble globes, black and of all colours, crammed together in what are now the ' Custodi ' and the ' Fagnani ' Halls. Then came the French invasion and the requisitions following, in 1796 : the Museum, too, suffered under them. A large quartz crystal, a big Etruscan vase, cannons, mortars wandered into forced exile to Paris, partly to the Louvre, partly to the Musée des Invalides, and never returned. As a deposit, by no means voluntary, during the days of Liberty and Equality, an enormous elephant tusk remained for nearly twenty-five years in the University Museum at Pavia and was recovered only with great difficulty. There are still, ever since 1840, in our Museo Civico a large crocodile and a ' big boa,' which had been deposited there by the Ambrosiana at the request of Professor Jan and the Podestà Casati who guaranteed the deposit to be revocable *ad nutum* of the Ambrosian Library. It was not hitherto known, but is now certain and proved by documentary evidence, that the Ambrosiana was threatened by another, larger and more systematic requisition in 1798, and we have found traces of an attempt at saving several of the most curious or precious objects of the Museum by hiding them in inconceivable places, so much so that only fortunate chances led to their rediscovery. Then came the extension towards Piazza della Rosa, and the transfer to the new rooms of the contents of the aforementioned ' Custodi ' and ' Fagnani ' Halls, and the Settala Museum was moved for the greater part to the last room of the upper floor, looking out on S. Sepolcro, while some of the exhibits were distributed in other rooms upstairs. A fresh move was occasioned, when the Ambrosian Library offered hospitality to a number of art-objects deposited there by the Municipality of Milan.

Though the care of the Ambrosian Library is well known and almost proverbial, it was during all these changes too difficult, not to say impossible, to avoid divisions, dispersals, damage and rejections, especially as a very great number of the objects were very small, delicate, extremely fragile, and not infrequently of a kind that, once taken from the context of the whole collection, they might easily appear devoid of any value or meaning. For all that, as said earlier, the Settala Museum is now resuscitated and reconstituted. A tablet has recently been set up under the northern portico of the courtyard, by the side of the inscription which records the friendship of the ' Milanese Archimedes ' for the Ambrosian Library, to recall in outline the vicissitudes through which this, the most ancient Museum of Milan, and one of the most ancient and important of Italy, has passed.

The inscription runs as follows :

MUSEUM
A MANFREDO SEPTALIO CONQUISITUM
ET ANNO MDCLXX BIBLIOTHECÆ AMBROSIANÆ
TESTAMENTO DESTINATUM
HEIC HABES O CIVIS
POST AN. LXXX NEC SPONTE NEC INTEGRE TRADITUM
QUÆ POST FATA SUPERSTES
CURA DOCTORUM COLLEGII AMBROSIANI
AN. MCMVI RESTITUTUM

The new Hall has turned out a fairly faithful copy of the room represented in the woodcut of Scarabelli. On the walls hang the pictures which have been eliminated from the upper Gallery, partly because only by so doing a re-arrangement of the Gallery became possible, partly because they are for the most part paintings of minor value, yet worthy of preservation either from the point of view of a history of the Ambrosian foundation, or from that of the history of Art. Some of the paintings possess some intrinsic worth or belong to the first beginnings of the Library or to the original dona-tion of the founder in 1618 ; some also come from the Settala Collection and complete the reconstruc-tion of its original appearance. Below the pictures stand the glass-cases and in most of them the various collections of the Museum are displayed : Archæ-ology, Ethnography, Mathematics and Physics, Zoology, Botany, Mineralogy, turned woodwork, art-objects, and some specimens at least of the numismatic and book collections of Settala. Under-neath the glass-cases is the mineralogical collection behind wire-netting. In the centre of the Hall in two large and tall glass-cases are the zoological specimens and astrolabes and spheres ; in an appropriate case the weapons. So the ancient Settala Museum has been reconstructed, which was once one of the wonders of Milan and thus Milan is again in the possession and enjoyment of its *Museum Kircherianum.*

The distribution and classification of the various objects is still in a primitive and rudimentary state, and attempts at present no more than a divi-sion into large, obviously homogeneous groups. We have to wait for the opinion and assistance of com-petent specialists, before we can proceed to a more rigorous and more modern scientific re-arrangement. But it seems to us that what has been achieved, so far corresponds best with the original condition of that most curious collection and, even if it should have to be modified, it was the first step towards a picture of the collection as it had been, now that resuscitated, it is again open to inspection by the public, after ' all the time that had passed over it.'

THE HOLY FAMILY
BY LUINI
AMBROSIAN LIBRARY, MILAN

VI

'THE HOLY FAMILY' OF BERNARDINO LUINI IN THE AMBROSIANA

This article was first published in the *Rassegna d'Arte*, XII, No. 3, in March, 1912.

READERS of the *Rassegna d'Arte* will remember in it the fine pages which Guido Cagnola devoted to the famous masterpiece of Luini in the Ambrosian Library. They were occasioned by the re-arrangement of the whole setting of this remarkable painting, as part of the whole re-ordering of the collections in the Ambrosiana. The painting had been placed, thanks to the generosity of Cristoforo B. Crespi, in a handsome new frame worthy of the picture. It is but right that the *Rassegna* should once again return to this masterpiece : the painting itself has been restored and has recovered, after four centuries, the freshness and charm of its distant youth, in part by the skill of him who has justly been called the 'elect among restorers,' Professor Cavenaghi, in part by the enlightened munificence of Prince Luigi Alberico Trivulzio.

The work of restoration by Professor Cavenaghi was brought to the notice of the public by Gustavo Frizzoni in the 'Perseveranza' (of December 10, 1911), who very gracefully recalled the emulation in generosity among the Friends of the Ambrosiana ; but he modestly concealed the fact that he himself has always been among the first in that rivalry of munificence ; for it was to him that the Ambrosian Library owed the first restoration of a work of Luini's, namely that delightful 'St. John,' who has come to life again under the able hands of Professor Cavenaghi, and now, thanks to Frizzoni, set in a suitable frame, smiles down on us again and wins all hearts.

The ' *Rassegna* ' recalled the facts for the benefit of its circle of readers, and did so in a manner worthy of the Journal, by adding a reproduction of Luini's 'Holy Family' as perfect even in the colour as the three-colour process nowadays can achieve.

A further event contributed to focus attention on the Luini picture in the Ambrosiana and will justify this brief note on it. This is the magnificent publication, wholly devoted to Luini, by another generous friend of the Ambrosiana, Senatore Luca Beltrami. His work ' *Luini*, 1512–1537 ' (Milano, 1912) is a gallery in which all or almost all the works of Bernardino are collected, carefully arranged and co-ordinated, and discussed with great learning. The author's modesty added the sub-title : ' Materiale di studio raccolto per cura di Luca Beltrami,' and in his short preface he disclaims any intention of a larger scope or of wider conclusions. But there can be no question that his volume with its 440 illustrations and the solid letterpress, linking them all together, will remain a kind of ' Corpus luinicum,' indispensable to all who henceforth intend to deal with this Lombard Raphael and his work. This does not mean that nothing can or should be added to his work. He himself in his modesty points this out and gives reasons for it ; but among these he has forgotten the main reason, namely that *facile est inventis addere*. Beltrami's book (p. 524 ff.) ends the splendid series of so-called ' Luini Madonnas,' the worthy pendant to what among the works of Sanzio is called the ' Raphael Madonnas,' with the picture in the Ambrosiana. Neither Beltrami, nor Frizzoni, nor Guido Cagnola, nor anyone who has preceded them in treating of the picture, has been able to pass over in silence its connexion with the equally famous cartoon of Leonardo in the Diploma Gallery in Burlington House, London, to which Luini's painting undoubtedly owes its inspiration and general composition.

Neither can we ; all the more as the recent restoration of the picture was bound to give a fresh impulse to the detailed study of its relation to the cartoon, from the moment the restoration was begun. On its completion, it made this relation so much more easily appreciated by the clearer and more distinct presentation both of the colouring and of the general lines of the composition. We shall therefore deal first with the painting and its restoration, and then add a few words on the cartoon and its bearing on the picture.

It is well known that Luini's painting originally belonged to the founder of the Ambrosian Library, Cardinal Federico Borromeo, who formally presented it to the Library by a deed dated April 28, 1618, together with many other pictures and drawings which still form the most noteworthy part of the Ambrosian Gallery. It was certainly one of the pictures most cherished by the gifted and famous Cardinal ; no one has before or after spoken of it with more penetrating insight than he. He mentions it twice : for the first time in the deed of gift, just mentioned, breaking just for once—and for it alone—the pedestrian monotony of the legal jargon, when he adds to the dimensions (' braccia 2 x $1\frac{1}{2}$ ' i.e. 1·5 x 0·91 m.) and to indications intended simply for identification, viz. ' a Madonna with St. Anne, Our Lord, and St. John, both children, and St. Joseph, by the hand of Bernardino Luini,' with a certain emphasis : ' the principal painting.' Indeed, that wonderful picture has remained one of the principal treasures of the Ambrosian Gallery ever since.

Sixteen years after the inauguration of what he modestly called 'his' Library, Cardinal Federico published a description of his Gallery, or, as he preferred to call it, his ' Museum ' : *Federici Cardinalis Borromæi Archiepisc . Mediolan . Musæum.* The learned Cardinal wrote the description in a handsome and graceful Latin, as the times and his dignity demanded, with the grave and elegant courtesy of the *grand seigneur* who receives in his palace.

In 1909, when the Ambrosian Library celebrated the third centenary of its foundation with the cordial support of all the authorities and people of the city, Luca Beltrami published a photographic reproduction of the *Musæum*, with an introduction and notes by himself and an Italian translation by Mgr. Luigi Grasselli. I take from this translation (p. 61) of the *Musæum*, the passage where Cardinal Federico mentions for a second time Luini's picture :

' The room immediately beyond contains an example of the admirable art of the elder Luini. The painting, which we purchased for a large sum, is certainly great and is considered by painters as one of the most perfect works of that artist. But the glory of this picture is not wholly due to Luini; it is shared by him with another supreme artist, Leonardo. The exquisite design is by the latter ; Luini added the best he could give, namely a certain delicacy, the movements, and the expression of the faces, affectionate and modest. It is a clear proof that these illustrious artists lent each to the other his own particular skill ; that Luini recognised the excellence of Leonardo in design, and Leonardo in his turn would have attributed all the glory of the painting to his pupil, if he had seen how much he had improved his work. Such traits of kindness are common to great genius ; Pliny too recalls them among the ancient artists. They knew

well how vast is the range of art and how
narrow that of human genius and skill ; they
therefore gladly helped each other. The most
beautiful figure of the painting is that of the Infant
Jesus ; artists praise his face and especially the sup-
pleness of the little body and the softness of his torso.
Leonardo made a clay model to spread the knowledge of so excellent a work of his. The Virgin,
Mother of God, is all the more admirable in that her
singular charm inspires a sacred respect and
banishes all impure thoughts from the mind : an
effect which might be said even to exceed nature.
Elizabeth displays the vigour of a robust old age,
and the little John the lively pleasure with which he
gazes upon the Saviour. We wish we could bestow
equal praise upon other works of our Museum. . . .'

The extract from this work of the great Cardinal
gives us, apart from the æsthetic appreciation, no
positive information beyond the price of the picture,
and not even this with any accuracy : he merely
states that he has bought it for a considerable sum,
satis magno pondere auri emimus. Our picture, in fact,
belongs to that distinguished group which has been
spared the humiliation of a valuation little in keeping with its worth. When the—shall we say—
' military-artistic ' requisition of the French in 1796
carried it off *manu militari* together with the best of
the Ambrosiana and of all Italy, to be returned only
in 1815, the Administration of the Louvre valued it at
fr. 50,000, a large sum for those days and honourable
to the victim even in comparison with many of its
companions in exile.

Who sold the Cardinal the picture and when and
how the vendor had come into possession of it, is
not stated ; nor is it known for whom or when Luini
had painted it.

Frizzoni observes with justice that the work
shows the artist at the fullness of his powers, and
Beltrami too (l.c., p. 526), by placing the picture at

the end of the series of ' Luini Madonnas,' places
it thereby at a point fairly advanced in Luini's
career.　It was a marvellous career, richly studded
with beauties of all kinds, adorned all the way with
his angelic Madonnas, and graced at the start and at
or near the end by two of his most beautiful : the one
in our painting, the other in the fresco of the
Certosa of Chiaravalle of which we have the good
fortune to be able to prove his authorship, the year
of the execution and the price paid for the work,
from a curious little MS. at Chiaravalle to which
Beltrami also refers (l.c., p. 17).

It is perhaps worthy of note that neither Cardinal
Federico nor, as far as I know, any one else, has ever
mentioned any replica or copy of so perfect a
painting as this.　Some resemblance may be found
in two other Madonnas of Luini's :　the one in the
Ambrosiana (L. Beltrami, l.c., p. 544) which exists
in a copy in Rome in the Colonna Collection (ibid.,
p. 545), and the other in Madrid in the Prado
Museum (ibid., p. 546).　But in the former the
figure of St. Joseph is missing, in the latter that of
St. Anne.　But we shall speak of the composition of
the picture further on in dealing with the Leonardo
cartoon from which it is derived.

The reference of Cardinal Federico to the existence of a clay model of the Infant Jesus seems to me
interesting.　That it is the model of the Infant alone,
would appear from the manner in which the text
of the Cardinal passes in review the various parts of
his favourite picture.　Perhaps a connexion may be
pointed out between the reference of Cardinal
Federico and a mention made by Lomazzo (*Trattato dell' arte della pittura*, Milano, 1584, p. 127) :

' I have before me a small clay head of Christ,
when he was a child, by the hand of Leonardo
Avinci.　It shows the simplicity and purity of a
child together with an air of wisdom, intelligence
and majesty, an expression which, while that of a

child of tender years, yet seems to have something of wise old age : indeed an excellent piece of work.'

Possibly, speaking here of Christ as a 'child,' Lomazzo may mean less a 'baby' than our picture and the Leonardo cartoon represent, for referring precisely to the cartoon (almost certainly that of 'St. Anne' of Leonardo's in the Louvre) which —'now,' as he says, 'is in the hands of the painter Aurelio Lovino,'—he notes (l.c., p. 171) among other things that Leonardo there 'expressed in the Blessed Virgin the joy and delight which she felt over having given birth to so beautiful a child as Christ was.'

But what in the Cardinal's description is after all most noteworthy and its most attractive feature, is his joyful, and—I was about to say—naive enthusiasm and the pure delight with which he exalts the beauties and attractions of his picture. It is an enthusiasm and delight which not even the philosophical and classical reflexions can damp, when he speaks of the inborn generosity of really great artists and the vastness of Nature in comparison with the narrow limits of human ingenuity. It is one of the most telling expressions of a sense for Art deeply rooted and highly trained, in Cardinal Federico, a sense which has recently been dealt with in a special article by L. Beltrami (*Miscellanea Ceriani*, pp. 279 ff, Milano, 1910). It is a pleasure to see the Cardinal considering himself fortunate as the owner of so much beauty, appreciating the exquisite grace of colouring and design, feeling the softness of the forms, following the bodily movement, grasping the inner significance of expression and life, and breathing in with joy the perfume of superhuman purity which emanates from it all.

But time and the hand of man had cast a veil over all this beauty and gracefulness. At some period which it is difficult to determine accurately, the whole painting had been covered with a coat of

varnish, perhaps to conceal some slight damage or
retouching, or to protect it against future harm
which rightly or wrongly it was feared might affect
it. Perhaps the varnish had been at first or had
appeared perfectly transparent and colourless, so as
not to affect the appearance of the picture ; perhaps
it was believed and hoped that it was unchangeable.
But in course of years, exposed to the elements and
dust, the varnish had assumed a colour of its own : a
warmish tint not by any means unpleasant, for it
seemed to give the picture a certain patina of age.
There were even people who argued from it in
support of what they chose to call the ' fair manner '
of Luini. Others, on the contrary, maintained that
a good many refinements and just the most delicate
features of the design had been obscured and over-
laid ; that the harmonious vividness and that transparency and the delicate nuances which Luini had
been able to give to his colouring, had been im-
paired ; that a purely accidental monochrome
effect had altered the fundamental tones of all his
colours ; that a rather hard and almost horny
surface damaged the original softness of the forms ;
that—in short—it was not a question of any
' manner ' of Luini's, but is of something purely
external and sufficiently harmful to justify the wish
to see it removed.

In many this desire gained in strength and confidence, after the very successful restoration, mentioned earlier and due to the generosity of Frizzoni
and the skill of Cavenaghi, had given back to
Luini's ' St. John ' its freshness and life and made
it into one of the most charming paintings in the
Ambrosiana. Frizzoni himself, as said at the beginning of this article, has already told the story how
eventually the restoration also of this great painting
of Luini's was finally accomplished.

I shall never forget the deep and delightful
impression, as I watched with my own eyes the

lifting, here and there, as an experiment, of this veil, which covered the painting, and saw, as if by magic, the whole riot of colours and forms, movements and life, burst through. The hand of Cavenaghi seemed to me like that of a kindly fairy, lovingly stroking the canvas and calling forth life and beauty wherever it passed. Never before had I understood and felt, as I did then, the genuine delight and enthusiasm of Cardinal Federico. The painting proved at once to be in an excellent state of preservation, and when it had been brought back from Cavenaghi's studio to its place in the Ambrosian Gallery, it might have come straight from the workshop of Luini.

A mere photograph cannot do full justice to the restoration and will hardly show the great differences between the former and the present state of the picture. For the photograph the fair veil had acted merely as a thin yellow screen. But what a difference for the careful onlooker who also remembered what it had been like ! How much stronger are now the modelling and the relief, where before everything had been more or less flattened out and reduced to a single plane ! How numerous and how true are now the subtle gradations of the colour of the skin, from the delicate complexion of the Infant to the more robust and solid colouring of St. John the Baptist ! And, above, that of the Blessed Virgin, radiant in her spotless beauty, and by her side, in skilful contrast, the colouring of St. Anne as of a hale, elderly woman, and in the upper corner, the manly figure of the ageing of St. Joseph, painted in warm yet dry tones, suggestive of the weight and responsibilities of his toilsome life.

And all the gracefulness and expression of gestures and movements, of charming glances and smiles which before, you only caught and barely guessed rather than saw ! Who could see, as he can now see in relief, the diaphanous and downy

gold of the children's curls ? Who could see the
folds of the veil round the neck of the Virgin, a
marvel of transparency and softness ? Who ever
saw the little flowers peeping out and smiling from
the background ? The mantle of the Blessed Virgin
has recovered its traditional and pure blue, whereas
before under the yellow varnish it had greenish
glints, and all the colours have regained their precise values and vibrate with their true note and
specific tone, without having lost anything of what
I should like to call their warm breath and their
harmonious fusion which time had imparted to
them. Unless I am much mistaken, this is one of
the most exquisite and perfect examples of the art
of restoration of Cavenaghi.

The accompanying reproduction places the work
before the reader's eye and dispenses me from
further comment, except to say : ' Messo t'ho
innanzi ; ormai per te ti ciba.'[1]

––––––

It remains now to add something about the
Leonardo cartoon in the Diploma Gallery of the
Royal Academy, Burlington House, London. As I
said at the beginning, the relation between the
picture and the cartoon is too close and too obvious
and suggestive to make it possible to pass over the
one in speaking of the other ; at the same time the
restoration of the painting could not fail in some
particular ways, as we shall see, to bear on this
relation to the cartoon.

For some time I had entertained the idea of
writing the history and vicissitudes of the cartoon,
but I had to put it aside. I did so, in the first place,
because the history of the cartoon was bound to
develop into a history of the cartoons, or at least of

––––––

[1] *Dante :* Divina Commedia, *Parad.* X, 25 : ' I've set
before thee ; henceforth feed thyself.' (*Translator's note.*)

CARTOON OF THE HOLY FAMILY
BY LEONARDO DA VINCI
BURLINGTON HOUSE, LONDON

three cartoons, and this was too large an undertaking. Secondly, because this history, as far as the
actual state of documentary evidence allowed, had
already been written or almost so, and readers of
the *Rassegna* know where to find it.

Beltrami had shortly summarised it, as far as our
picture is concerned in his book on *Luini* (pp. 555 ff.).
Herbert F. Cook had discussed it at length in the
Gazette des Beaux-Arts, 39, 1897, pp. 371–389, stating
also the sources ; iconographic and other useful
information had been added by Edward McCurdy
(*Leonardo da Vinci*, London, 1904, p. 116 ff. illustr.
35–37). The cartoon has been reproduced again
recently by C. Lewis Hind (*Drawings of Leonardo da
Vinci*, London and New York), omitting, however,
all reference to our painting either in the illustrations
or in the introduction, an omission which, given the
nature of the book, is perhaps more intelligible in
the former than in the latter. Any one interested
in the subject, might consult with advantage the
article in *L'Arte*, ' I disegni di Leonardo da Vinci
a Windsor ' (an. XIV, 1911, pp. 269 ff.) and ' New
Facts and Fancies about Leonardo da Vinci ' in *The
Art Journal* (1912, Jan., pp. 6 ff.).

Finally, I put the idea aside for a third reason,
namely, that, even gathering and co-ordinating all
the data and documents known so far, the history
of the cartoon or cartoons, dealing with St. Anne,
by Leonardo, is still far from clear ; there are gaps
in the documents and some undisclosed information
which cannot be inferred with any certainty, and
one of the chief witnesses, namely Vasari, has all
the appearance of being inaccurate.

Fortunately no document contests or calls in
doubt the fact of Leonardo's authorship of the
London cartoon, which is the one connected with
our picture. If even for a moment as much as a
shadow of doubt could have arisen about this
authorship, it happened, not as a consequence of

the restoration of the painting, but merely incidentally. It is very intelligible that the present restoration could not help producing some result bearing
on the cartoon : indeed, the result was twofold.
One presented itself as a duty, not to say necessity ;
the other was bound to come of itself as a mere
consequence.

This second result, to take that first, was to
render the dependence of the picture on the cartoon
more clearly visible and more exactly appreciable.

The first—in order of time as was but natural—
was to concentrate afresh attention and study upon
the cartoon on the part both of those who were
generally aware of the situation and took an interest in it with knowledge and competence, and,
especially, of the restorer, before embarking upon
his work and in the course of it.

It is the conscientiously observed habit of Professor Cavenaghi to make a careful study of the
works entrusted to him and of the painters and the
schools to which they belong—a habit that accounts
not a little for the success of his restorations. His
wide artistic training and an unrivalled experience
contribute to render these studies all the more easy
and valuable.

I remember the sense of surprise and the impression produced on me when, having gone one
day to pay him a short visit (I dare not say, for no
one would believe me, that the painting played no
part in the visit), I found him absorbed in thought,
bending over a large photograph of the London
cartoon, and after shortly but cordially greeting
me, he asked me point-blank, as if he were continuing a sentence which had been interrupted by
my entry : ' And what, if this were also by Luini ? '
I must add that Professor Cavenaghi was by no
means insistent, and neither then nor later gave
way to forming any settled opinion or to spin-
ning theories : everyone knows that he is prudence

and moderation personified. But after all, the idea
was very suggestive and we spoke of it and discussed it at some length, even though hesitatingly
and with the greatest reserve and caution. Beltrami has recorded an echo of these discussions in
his *Luini* (p. 556), when he writes : ' We might
certainly come to the conclusion that, just as the
art of Leonardo has given many of its pictorial
qualities to Luini, so also the painting in the
Ambrosiana might suggest to us to see the hand of
Luini in the cartoon in the Academy in London.
We are face to face with a direct witness to the ideal
relations which existed between the two artists. It
would be rash to push conclusions any further.'

It would be difficult to express better the sense
of hesitation and of pure hypothesis with which the
idea had presented itself for a moment. But such
an idea, like any hypothesis, is able to render some
service in the search of truth ; it does not, moreover, in the least pretend to upset the common
opinion as recently expressed by C. Lewis Hind
(l.c. p. 14) : ' In the cartoon of the *Virgin and Child
with St. Anne* which hangs in the Diploma Gallery
at Burlington House, one of the nation's greatest
treasures, which so few Londoners ever visit, this
country possesses a characteristic and unapproach-
able Leonardo.' The writer touches here, though
only summarily, on a very strong and perhaps unimpeachable argument for Leonardo's authorship
of the London cartoon. For, on the one side, as
Beltrami says (l.c.) : ' We do not possess a sufficient
number of drawings by Luini which we can be
certain are his, to be able to deduce from them
some such characteristic personal technique as
might help us to identify his hand in the London
cartoon.'

On the other hand, we have drawings of Leonardo
in sufficient quantity, and the characteristic notes
of his manner of feeling, of drawing and expressing

things, are well enough known, and all who have seen and examined the London cartoon with care, find in it these notes.

It must also be remembered that there are great differences between photographs. The characteristics of Leonardo often almost disappear in modern photographs, so-called 'artistic' photographs which are, however, in reality altered and spoilt by shading and retouching ; they are, as Professor Cavenaghi also observed, very much more evident in an older photograph like the one which Frizzoni very kindly gave us.

It is almost needless to add that the aforementioned second result has been to bring out much more clearly that Luini was, in the words of Beltrami, a great admirer and a spiritual pupil of Leonardo's and that Leonardo's art has given many of its pictorial qualities to Luini. Luini, in fact, has obviously seen Leonardo's hand in the cartoon and felt his mind.

He felt it and penetrated its secret with marvellous fidelity and even more wonderful success, all the more wonderful as Leonardo's work in the London cartoon is, and clearly appears to be, far from finished. It was certainly an act of great daring on the part of Luini to complete it. It is no less certain that, when put to the test, his powers were equal to his daring. ' All those considerations truly worthy of Leonardo's intellect and genius,' to quote the words of Vasari, ' which caused the whole population of Florence to come in streams to admire Leonardo's cartoon of " St. Anne," like people stream to a great feast,' have passed over into the mind of Luini. ' All the simplicity and beauty which can embellish with simplicity and beauty a Mother of Christ, displaying the modesty and humility of a Virgin happy in her joy to see the beauty of her child whom she holds in her lap, and watching with tenderness the little St. John at her

feet '—all this has passed into the picture of Luini ;
so has ' the smile of St. Anne, at the height of joy
in seeing her earthly off-spring raised to heavenly
honours.' And if Lomazzo ever saw the painting
of the great Bernardino, as he saw the Leonardo
cartoon when it was in Milan, ' in the hands of the
painter Aurelio Lovino,' he must have seen ' in the
Virgin Mary, the joy and delight which she felt
over having given birth to so beautiful a child as
Christ was, and in realising that she had been
found worthy to be His mother, and in St. Anne
similarly the happiness and contentment, seeing
her daughter the Mother of God, raised to
beatitude.'

How high above and far removed is this from the
—to put it mildly—curious way of looking at it of
one who (cf. Cook, l.c., p. 380) considered the
Leonardo composition as profane, odd and even
irreverent, who could find in it neither St. Anne, nor
the Virgin, nor the biblical austerity of the wife of
St. Joachim, nor the divine humility symbolised by
the Mother of God, but merely two youthful figures,
of the same youthfulness, beautiful with the same
beauty, charming in their smiles, but enigmatical
and mysterious, full of sensibility and even sen-
suality. . . .

We may well ask whether he who thus described
the Leonardo cartoon, had really seen it or with
what strange prejudices and preoccupations of eye
and mind he had considered it.

The same questions occur to me, though with
different meaning, when I read in the same article
the bald statement that Luini did not care to go
beneath the surface of things and that his work bears
the same relation to that of Leonardo as a work of
pure and simple virtuosity bears to one of inspiration,
all the more as the writer is not speaking of the
works of the two masters in general, but in particular
of the Leonardo cartoon in London and of our Luini

picture in Milan. Cardinal Federico, no mean judge, has already told us that in his opinion 'Leonardo would have attributed all the glory of the painting to his pupil, if he could have seen how much he had improved his work.' There are indeed not many pictures in existence in which there is more expression, more vivacity and harmony than in this Luini painting, and rarely has that supreme art of Leonardo been more successfully rivalled which, without seeking expression, obtains it to a marvellous degree, because it penetrates with depth and intimacy and integrity of feeling and thought to the very nature of things and facts, and reaches the very springs of life. All this could be discerned even before the restoration, but it is all the more certain now that we can get a more direct and clearer view and a more immediate and deeper impression of it. For Luini has above all seen and grasped the beauty and depth of Leonardo's fundamental conception and the thought and soul of his composition. Luini did not see anything strange, much less irreverent in the combination of the Blessed Virgin and St. Anne, in setting the Virgin with the Infant on St. Anne's lap, but rather what Leonardo with wonderful and so-called 'realistic' clearness meant to represent and express : a Divine Childhood and Motherhood, grafted on the stock of an old Humanity ; both Childhood and Motherhood at the same time essentially human, arousing the joy of life and salvation in Humanity, a salvation announced by the boy Precursor, presented there in the act of rendering homage to the Saviour and his child-Lord, who receives him sitting on the throne of his Mother's lap, blesses him and as it were dispatches him on his great mission, setting him on his way with a smile and the gesture of affection ; the austere herald seems later to recall and, recalling, to rejoice in this tenderness, when he who had preached penitence in the wilderness, with sudden sweetness called himself ' the bridegroom's friend.'

' Considerations indeed worthy of the mind and genius of Leonardo,' Vasari has said, especially the brilliant introduction of St. Anne who, represented with exquisite womanliness, recalls in her way to our minds the words of St. Paul (Rom. ix. 5) : ' *quorum patres et ex quibus Christus.*' It is all the more to the credit of Leonardo that he created out of the sheer depth of his genius, without a vision or remembrance of the Virgin with the Infant on her lap, the Virgin herself in the lap of St. Anne (Florence, Galleria antica e moderna).

Ferrigni (*Madonne Fiorentine*, Milano, Hoepli, 1912, p. 76) has done well to call attention to, and to stress the novelty of this imposing composition which does great honour to Masaccio. It is a pity— if I may say so *sine ira et studio*—that the book should be disfigured by truly disastrous theological divagations and by profanities in text and illustrations which seem to us neither necessary nor helpful to the development of his theme.

Luini, the admirer and disciple of Leonardo, as the whole of his work attests, has yet been able in all his work to maintain his own artistic personality, even in face and under the fascination of the cartoon. He has added to Leonardo's composition the figure of St. Joseph. Has he done well or ill ? Cagnola (*Rassegna d'Arte*, l.c., p. 19), is of opinion that the figure of the Saint adds nothing in the way of attractiveness to the picture and alters the happy triangular composition of the cartoon. The observation is excellent and worthy of an expert and acute observer. Indeed, comparing the various cartoons and sketches of St. Anne by Leonardo, it is clear that he started from a ' triangular conception ' of the subject. But it is also clear, that he was not satisfied with this conception, and here and there divides

x

the apex of the triangle by more or less detaching the head of the Virgin from that of St. Anne.

Others again have opportunely observed that by introducing the figure of St. Joseph, Luini has filled a void which, coming above the little St. John, might have seemed too large. We may also add that the robust and manly handsomeness and the more suppressed and almost pensive happiness of the Saint do add something to the rich variety of æsthetic elements of the picture and complete the historical elements of the representation.

All considered, it seems to us that if Leonardo himself should have been fated never to complete and paint his cartoon, he could hardly have found a more worthy and faithful interpreter of his thought. It is but just that our gratitude be divided between the two great masters for having prepared for us, the one by his design, the other by his painting, so pure and beautiful and inexhaustible a fount of spiritual delight. It is only fair that our gratitude should be extended also to those who by their generosity and their skill have helped to restore to this fount all its original freshness and attraction.

INDEX

A

Abbondio, Don, 155, 157

Adalbert, King, 54, 61

Adelchis, 30

Adelman, Archbishop of Milan, 59, 60, 61

Adericus, Abbot, 52, 53

Adorno, Fr., S.J., 166, 172

Agathon, Pope, 23

Agilulf, 22, 30, 46

Aicardo, 100

Alaric, King of the Goths, 18

Alaric II, King of the Visigoths, 26

Albergato, Antonio, 226

Alberico, Count, 54

Alboin, 18, 29

Alciati, Andrea and Francesco, 115 ff., 201

Alciato, 77

Alcuin, 42

Aleric of Asti, 64

Alexander II, Pope (Anselm of Baggio), 79, 80, 81

Alexander III, Pope, 59, 89, 97

Alexander V, Pope, 101

Amalasuinta, 27, 28

Ambrose, St., 1, 2, 3, 6, 8, 10 ff. ; elected Bishop of Milan, 12, 13 ff. ; Ambrosian Rite 16 ff., 40, 44, 54, 55, 60, 67, 71, 81, 91, 93, 94

Amidano, Niccolò, Archbishop of Milan, 102

Anacletus II, anti-Pope, 96

Anastasius, Pope, 19

Anatalon, Bishop of Milan, 5, 6

Andreas, Archbishop of Milan, 56

Angilbert I, Archbishop of Milan, 43

Angilbert II, Archbishop of Milan, 44, 45

Annone, Carlo, 251

Annoni, Antonio, 248, 249, 250, 251, 252

Anselm I, Archbishop of Milan, 43

Anselm II, Archbishop of Milan, 55

Anselm III, Archbishop of Milan, 83

Anselm IV, of Bovisio, Archbishop of Milan, 83, 84, 85

Anselm V, Archbishop of Milan, 86, 96, 97

Anspert, Archbishop of Milan 47 ff., 92

Archinti, Giuseppe, Archbishop of Milan, 106

Archinti, Filippo, Bishop of Saluzzo, 104

Arcimboldi, Giovannangelo, Archbishop of Milan, 103, 104, 237

Arcimboldi, Giovanni V, Archbishop of Milan, 102

Arcimboldi, Guidantonio, Archbishop of Milan, 102

Arcimboldi, Ottaviano, Archbishop of Milan, 102

The Mayflower Press, Plymouth. William Brendon & Son, Ltd.